Industrial ARCHITECTURE in Britain

1750-1939

RICHARD WILSON,
STACK, FURNACE,
AND
CHIMNEY BUILDER,
BOILER SETTER &c.
Ternbrook
CHESTER ROAD
MANCHESTER,
DEALER IN FIRE BRICKS &c.

Industrial ARCHITECTURE in Britain

1750-1939

EDGAR JONES

Facts On File Publications
New York, New York • Oxford, England

Industrial Architecture in Britain 1750–1939
Copyright © Edgar Jones 1985

First published in the United Kingdom in 1985 by
B.T. Batsford Ltd., 4 Fitzhardinge Street, London
W1H 0AH.

First published in the United States in 1985 by
Facts On File Inc., 460 Park Avenue South, New
York, New York 10016.

Library of Congress Cataloging in Publication Data
Jones, Edgar, 1953–
     Industrial architecture in Britain.

     Bibliography: p.
     Includes index.
          1. Architecture, Industrial——Great Britain.
2. Architecture, Modern——19th century——Great Britain.
3. Architecture, Modern——20th century——Great Britain.
I. Title.
NA6403.G7J66   1986   725′.4′0941   85-15919
ISBN 0-8160-1295-4

Printed in Great Britain
10 9 8 7 6 5 4 3 2 1

Contents

Illustrations

Preface

This is a general history of British industrial architecture; one that should serve as an introduction to those who wish to study specific types of building, particular regions or industries and individual architects in greater detail. The specialist literature is quoted in the notes to each chapter and in the Bibliography, for there are now several journals concerned with the subject, an increasing number of research projects, mostly at a local level, and societies formed for the preservation of industrial monuments. It is to be hoped that they will flourish and that the wanton destruction of such architecture will be resisted.

There are many people to thank. The entire work was carefully read and commented upon by both Dr R.L. Hills of the North Western Museum of Science and Industry, Manchester, and Dr Stefan Muthesius of the University of East Anglia; the book would have contained many more errors of fact and judgement but for their corrections and advice. Mr R.S. Fitzgerald of the Leeds Industrial Museum, Armley, also read those parts of the text dealing with questions of structure and made an equally valuable contribution. Dr Nigel Bowles of Edinburgh University, who saw an earlier draft, has offered constant encouragement and made many helpful comments.

Special mentions of thanks are due to Mr Frank Smith of Bradshaw Gass & Hope, Bolton, who devoted much time to discussing with me the history of his firm and the practical construction and design of Lancashire mills. Mr Ken Powell, Secretary of SAVE, and Mr Julian Hunt of the Oldham Local Interest Centre, each with specialized knowledge of Britain's manufacturing regions, have contributed both facilities and information. For his unfailing interest and the provision of so many sources, Dr David J. Jeremy, editor of the *Dictionary of Business Biography*, is owed a considerable debt of gratitude. Mr John Griffiths, who has accompanied me on visits to some of the less accessible sites, deserves my thanks for his perseverance and enthusiasm. I am grateful to Mr Edward Sargent for permitting me to consult his RIBA dissertation on the West India Docks and for allowing access to his research material.

Countless others have helped and I can mention only a few: Mr W. Bonwitt, Mr M.F. Bywater, Professor D.C. Coleman, Dr Chris Cook, Mr P.N. Petchey, Dr Richard Roberts, Dr John Stevenson, Mr Robert Thorne and Mr Oliver Westall. The libraries, museums and archive repositories that have offered facilities are listed in the Sources. I am indebted to them for the assistance that they have generously provided. In addition, many companies and institutions have produced material or allowed me to consult their records. Without their co-operation this study of industry could not have been written. They include AEG-Telefunken, Frankfurt; Bird's Eye Walls plc; Mr John Owen, BSC Dowlais Works; Cadbury Schweppes plc, Bournville; Mr Stanley Johnson, Northern Spinning Division, Courtaulds plc; Dublin Port & Docks

Board; Mr Colin Webster, East Midlands Gas; Ford of Europe Incorporated; Guest Keen & Nettlefolds plc; Ironbridge Gorge Museum Trust; Mather & Platt Ltd; Mersey Docks & Harbour Board; North Thames Gas; Pilkington Brothers plc; Port of London Authority; Mr M. McLaren and Dr K.N. Bascombe, Propellants, Explosives and Rocket Motor Establishment (Waltham Abbey); Rheemco Ltd; Mr J.D. Edwards, Quality Assurance Directorate (Ordnance), Royal Arsenal; Sela Fasteners Ltd; Warwick Wright Ltd and Watney, Combe Reid & Co.

The author acknowledges the great assistance given by the publishers, B.T. Batsford. Mr Sam Carr, who commissioned the history, has showed much patience, understanding and

consideration; on his retirement, the role of editor passed to Mr Timothy Auger whose interest and wisdom has resulted in material improvements. For her conscientious work on the text, Rachel Wright deserves my gratitude. Christine Alexander, who typed the manuscript, is owed considerable thanks and admiration for her scrupulous care and skill. Many of the photographs were processed by the staff of A.J. Knowler and I am indebted to them for their expertise.

Many have contributed, but the final text is mine and I take full responsibility for it.

EDGAR JONES
Kensington,
September 1984

ONE

Introduction

In contrast to other types of building, the architecture of industry has received scant or superficial attention. Factories and warehouses have been examined principally in terms of the products they made and the profits they earned, and dismissed as places of work where utilitarian objects have been manufactured and stored, often dirty, occasionally dangerous and the scene of repetitive or strenuous tasks. Though some factories and warehouses may indeed have been unsightly or poorly designed, this history seeks to demonstrate that many were not of this class. Some ranked among the finest architecture of their period. For these outstanding industrial buildings no less care was vested in their appearance and structure than in any mansion, cathedral or public institution, while the experience and vision of the architect and the expenditure on materials and craftsmanship was in certain cases comparable. Secondly, it has not always been fully appreciated that the building itself could play an important part in the success of an industrial enterprise. An effective design (for the smooth running of the various processes and the safety of the workforce) was an integral part of a plant's manufacturing efficiency. In this respect, the factory deserves as much attention as is afforded to new machinery in assessments of productivity, and few would attempt to deny the significance of technological innovations for a business's fortunes. Thus, from both an architectural standpoint and on grounds of economic pragmatism, industrial buildings may be considered worthy of serious study.

Some definitions

Attention has been focused in this book on buildings which lay at the very core of the Industrial Revolution in Britain; principally, therefore, those concerned with its textile, metal and chemical industries. As a result, the structures which most frequently recur in the text are mills (whether for cotton, wool or silk), iron and steel works, engineering works, chemical plants and gasworks. In addition, the warehouses in which raw materials and final output were stored or finished have been discussed.

Yet this classification is not without its drawbacks, for the Industrial Revolution was accompanied by corresponding improvements in agriculture (to feed the multiplying industrial workforce) and transport (to convey the growing volume of manufactured goods around the country and to the ports for export), together with finance and commerce (to fund new enterprises and arrange markets for their products). In this respect, buildings which were closely related to factories (and without which they could not have functioned properly) should be mentioned, or at least the connections indicated. Accordingly reference has been made to canal and railway architecture, pumping stations, farm buildings and 'city' warehouses. But this is not a history of commercial architecture – valuable as such a work would be – which would presumably concentrate on banks, exchanges, markethalls, shops, offices, department stores and financial institutions. Such buildings represent the limits of this study and though, for example, structural and architectural similarities existed between warehouses and arcades, or factories and barracks, considerations of length have precluded the detailed discussion of these links.

General themes

Two main lines of inquiry are to be followed – one architectural, and one that falls within the realm of industrial practicalities. First, the buildings of industry have been placed within their architectural setting in relation both to other types of structure and to the prevailing architectural theories and beliefs. Did they form a class apart, or were factories and warehouses admitted within the circle of architectural respectability? Of course, attitudes altered over the three centuries covered by this survey and the factors responsible for change must be related to fluctuations in popular taste. It has been a question of placing warehouses, ironworks and so forth in the context of their period to discover in what ways they reflected or contradicted generally held notions of style and composition. Did textile mills, for example, break with architectural tradition when they, as a novel form of manufacturing enterprise, started to be erected during the 1780s and 1790s, or did they borrow the clothes of comparable buildings in tune with the accepted tenets of the day? Once established, could the textile mill, or the integrated ironworks, promote original architectural ideas or even generate a style all of its own?

In this respect the authorship of industrial buildings is a question of special importance, for the mill and the warehouse, no less than the church or the country mansion, produced specialist designers. In the early days of the Industrial Revolution these tended to be millwrights or engineers, men of no great academic training but much accumulated practical experience. As the demand for factories grew and became refined, so firms of qualified architects and civil engineers arose. In Lancashire's spinning towns a number of practices prospered from mill contracts – George Woodhouse and later Bradshaw Gass & Hope in Bolton, whilst in Oldham, Potts, Son & Hennings, together with Stott & Sons, attracted a national clientele from industry. In Manchester itself the need for warehouse accommodation provided employment for, among others, Edward Walters, J.E. Gregan and Harry S. Fairhurst.

The buildings of industry have to be examined not only with reference to their designers and the prevailing theories, but also in relation to local architectural traditions. North Staffordshire's building techniques exercised an important influence over the construction of its potteries, while the cottage architecture of the Yorkshire Pennines conditioned the construction of early millstone grit factories in the region of Huddersfield and Halifax. The remote nature of so many pioneering industrial sites made for continuity in building styles, just as the migration of business toward the populous towns in the early nineteenth century encouraged the purchase of expensive materials from distant sources for erection in a fashionable manner.

In the early days entrepreneurs experimented as much as manufactured, but were bedevilled with problems of technology, labour organization and finance, so that architectural considerations tended to occupy a comparatively low priority. Simple structures, and often rectangular in plan for reasons of economy, early factories owed their appearance to watermills and cottage workshops; indeed, some were terraced housing converted for use as business premises. When steam engines replaced waterwheels, manufacturers were able to drive larger numbers of machines and hence increase the size of buildings. As the machines themselves were improved and grew in capacity, so mills were erected of greater widths and lengths. Such an investment in buildings and fixtures increased the pressures on owners to ensure that their premises were fire resistant. Throughout the nineteenth century, efforts were made to design factories that were at the same time structurally sound, would resist the attack of flames and remain cost effective.

As the scale of manufacturing enterprise continued to expand, efficient production came to rely not simply on the introduction of new machines, but also on the logical arrangement of the various processes. In addition, greater latitude could be allowed in overheads, initially for the employment of an architect and the use of good-quality materials, and latterly for the provision of better facilities for health, education and recreation. The value of a building as a source of status and a means of advertising became increasingly apparent throughout a society in which shareholding grew more common. Thus the shape of industrial architecture in Britain was determined by aesthetic considerations and, at root, the evolving needs of manufacturing enterprise.

To summarize, this history seeks to explain how it was, for example, that in a period of not much more than a hundred years the British industrial landscape was changed out of all recognition. During the pioneer period three- and four-storey stone mills, water-powered and fortress-like, were erected in the picturesque valley of the River Derwent. In just over a hundred years a panorama of seemingly endless smoke-blackened red-brick factories had spread in all directions from Oldham. Resembling line upon line of dreadnoughts at Spithead, these multi-storey mills boasted ornate towers and elegant engine houses, their tall chimneys standing like so many monumental masts to industrialization. Within a century stone blast furnaces, raised by streams at the heads of the valleys in South Wales, had been overwhelmed by vast sheds covering rolling mills, banks of open-hearth furnaces and substantial brick blowing engine houses. The workshops and forges of the Black Country now vied with engineering shops as big as the aircraft hangars of today, fitted with powerful overhead cranes and a variety of machine tools, whilst at the docks, the rudimentary storehouses of the early eighteenth century had been replaced by enclosed non-tidal basins surrounded by ranges of fireproof warehouses. The transformation wrought by these buildings exercised a powerful influence on the lives of countless workers and on the economic fortunes of the nation, but also deserves a place in the architectural annals of the era.

The pioneering phase
1750–1800

When trade with America was restored in 1783, following the end of the war for independence, the British economy accelerated and the Industrial Revolution may truly be said to have begun. Yet, just as this growth in output was crucially preceded by transitional developments in transport, agriculture and commerce, so too important factory precedents occurred in pre-industrial Britain. Not all watermills ground corn. Others operated simple machinery to prepare cloth or work metal, and together with ironworks, foundries and silk mills, these provided reference points when the quickening pace of economic growth demanded new structures for its continuing momentum. This transformation, from a country where buildings accommodated an agrarian and commercial community to one in which they were required to house advancing techniques of founding and manufacture, may be fully illustrated by reference to the British experience. The design of these industrial buildings, their authorship and form, is the central theme of this chapter. In addition, the ways in which the prevailing classical, or more strictly Palladian, principles were applied to these factories, warehouses and ironworks are discussed in an attempt to discover why a particular style was felt appropriate and whether, indeed, the development of these types of building contributed anything to architectural theory.

The transitional stage, mills

Naturally the mill, as a structure, could offer no novelty during the early phase of the Industrial Revolution; mills had existed, powered by wind or water, throughout the Middle Ages to grind corn, to bore or saw timber, for fulling wool and mashing rags for paper. In addition, others had been built to rotate lathes, operate bellows and tilt hammers in ironworks, and to prepare gunpowder and chemicals. After the 1770s increasing numbers were built to drive carding and spinning machinery, while many of those designed for agricultural purposes were diverted to industrial tasks. Such a transition occurred, for instance, at Fromebridge Mill, Gloucestershire; it had been a fulling and corn mill from Tudor times, but during the latter part of the eighteenth century became a tilting and rolling mill with wire-drawing facilities.[1] These water-powered mills, adapted from their grain ancestors, will be considered first.

Regional building styles, combined with the use of local materials, had in the past produced any number of pleasing structures. Examples were the weatherboarded and gabled corn mill of 1789 that stood at Horstead, Norfolk;[2] Halstead Old Mill, Essex, a similar structure converted by Samuel Courtauld in 1825 to spin silk;[3] or the stone-built Albert Mill, Keynsham, designed to chip and grind timber, which featured mullioned windows and drip moulds.[4] However, corn mills had not in general attracted the work of architects, nor had their owners often felt the need to embellish their exteriors with obvious symbols of status. They were practical buildings with a charm and distinctiveness that owed to the accumulated abilities of local craftsmen and the fortunate provision of appropriate materials. Such professional expertise as was employed in their creation fell in the field of engineering, with the engagement of mill-wrights (in some senses forerunners of the civil engineer), who travelled from river to river advising on the gearing, types of waterwheel and the arrangement of the stones. James Brindley (1716-72), for example, who rose to fame as Britain's founding canal builder, had started life as a millwright (responsible in 1752 for the design of Leek Mill),[5] as had George Sorocold (d.1720) and William Murdock (1754-1839).[6] 'A good millwright', argued [Sir] William Fairbairn (1789-1874) recalling his own early experiences:

> was a man of large resources; he was generally well educated, and could draw out his own designs and work at the lathe; he had much knowledge of mill machinery, pumps and cranes, and could turn his hand to the bench or the forge with equal adroitness and facility.[7]

Yet the one area which these men's broad skills did not touch was architectural theory. Without the means to undertake a grand tour, their interests, training and the demands of their clients could scarcely have led them along this particular path of classical learning.

To illustrate the watermill in transition, two examples may be quoted, and though they dated from the second half of the eighteenth century, the tasks that they undertook and their external design were, in fact, representative of an earlier era. Higher Mill, Helmshore (1789) was a relatively small-scale fulling mill constructed in a traditional style for the Turner family.[8] The solid stone walls of the oldest block, which contained the waterwheel and fulling stocks, offered only minimal architectural embellishment and were pierced by small-paned mullioned windows. Designed presumably by a local millwright, to the unsuspecting eye this gabled exterior might pass for a large but rather restrained residence. Three Mills, situated on

1 Higher Mill (1789) at Helmshore, south of Haslingden, a water-powered fulling mill.

2 At Bromley-by-Bow astride the River Lea, House Mill (1776), which was used for malt distilling until 1893 when J. & W. Nicholson, distillers of maize, acquired the building.

the River Lea at Bromley-by-Bow, provided a second example. Although water-powered corn mills had existed on this site from the sixteenth century,[9] the present House Mill (1776), once fed by four undershot waterwheels, was erected as a distilling mill. The three-storey elevation, brick at the front, and weatherboarded behind, was timber-framed with a slate roof, forming a pleasant domestic structure.[10] In terms of practical operation and external appearance, early factory designers called upon such buildings as these to provide them with a basic vocabulary of engineering and architectural terms.

What, then, were the early water-powered industrial mills like? The most famous, regarded as a seminal design for the textile industry, was Thomas Lombe's (1685–1739) silk-spinning mill at Derby. Situated on an island in the River Derwent, driven by a 23-ft diameter undershot waterwheel and costing about £30,000, early prints revealed it to have been a five-storey brick structure, 110ft long and 39ft wide, pierced by regular-sized rectangular windows arranged in

15 bays, beneath which 13 semicircular stone arches channelled the water.[11] The only decoration occurred at the parapet, which was raised at the corners and featured two oblong pediments placed symmetrically towards the centre.[12] In outward form and treatment, therefore, Lombe's Mill (1718–21), thought to have been the design of George Sorocold, set the pattern for many of the textile mills planned later in the century. Regular and multi-storey (with an internal framework of timber columns and beams), almost completely devoid of architectural embellishment, it typified a great number of factories that followed.[13] Barlow's description of the works in 1836, which may not apply to the era of its construction, showed how it accommodated the internal workings:

> The extensive mill stands upon a huge pile of oak, doubled planked and covered with stonework, on which are turned thirteen stone arches which sustain the walls. Its length is 110ft, its breadth 39 and its height 55ft; it contains five storeys: in the three upper ones are the Italian winding engines ... In the lower two rooms are the spinning and twisting mills.[14]

This was not, in fact, Britain's first water-

3 Thomas Lombe's water-powered silk mill (1718–21) situated on the River Derwent at Derby.

powered silk mill; that had belonged to Thomas Crotchett, a neighbouring mill-owner, who had established his enterprise on the Derwent in 1702.[15] Also designed by Sorocold, it contained Dutch silk-throwing machinery and was driven by a 13½-ft waterwheel.[16] When Crotchett became bankrupt in 1713, the mill was re-leased by his friend John Lombe (1693–1722), half-brother of Thomas (1685–1739), then a wealthy silk merchant.[17] With the latter's capital they extended Crotchett's works, installing modern Italian machinery. Being a smaller structure, with less advanced technology than Lombe's Mill, it illustrated the gradual transition from the corn mill to the mechanized textile factory; yet no description of its outward appearance seems to have survived. The buildings and organization devised at Derby were copied in six mills at Stockport between 1732 and 1768, and in others at Congleton (1754), Macclesfield (1756), Sheffield (1768) and Watford (1769).[18]

The other important reference for early factories was, of course, the small workshop, often part of the artisan's home. An advertisement in the *Nottingham Journal* for 11 March 1769 indicated the domestic origins of industrialization:

A new-rebuilt house, well situated on the Back-Side consisting of a cellar, pantry, kitchen and large house; first floor three entire chambers on the second floor one large work room (perhaps the best in town) which will hold 13 frames completed; the tiled floor and two large garrets over it will hold four or five beds.[19]

Nottingham Mill (1769), Richard Arkwright's (1732–92) first factory, was in fact a converted house, its roller spinning machines being powered by a horse capstan.[20] Blackner, suggesting that its location was between Woolpack Lane and Hockley, claimed that this 'was the first cotton mill erected in the world', but it was burnt down shortly afterwards and the conversion replaced by a purpose-built structure.[21] This was erected by Stretton (d.1811), whose father had dissipated the family's estate at Longdon, Staffordshire, and forced him to seek work as a builder at Lenton, near Nottingham. His sons, Samuel (c.1732–1811) and William (1755–1828), duly entered the business, becoming the town's leading architects. The firm, though developing as a general practice, won the following industrial commissions: Mrs Melville's Warehouse (1791), Butt Dykes; Dawson's Lace Manufactory, later Fellows' Silk Mill (1791) and Alderman Green's Cotton Mill (1792–3), Broad Marsh.[22]

A shortage of capital could compel partners to acquire a house, making their homes in the lower floors, while the upper half became workshops. Samuel Crompton, for instance, went to Tweat's King Street Mill, Bolton, in 1791 and took over the top storeys of several houses for the installation of spinning machinery.[23] Although the first enterprise of James Hargreaves and Thomas James went under the name Hockley Mill, it could more accurately be termed a workshop, only earning its title in 1777 when converted to warp spinning.[24] By virtue of its size, containing some 50 machines individually worked by about 100 spinners, and with a horse capstan to drive the carding machines, it occupied a transitional stage between domestic and factory production. For, as Edward Baines observed:

> the factory system in England takes its rise from this period [the 1770s and 1780s]. Hitherto cotton manufacture had been carried on almost entirely in the houses of workmen: the hand or stock cards, the spinning wheel, and the loom, required no larger apartment than that of the cottage ... But the water-frame, the carding engine, and the other machines which Arkwright brought out in a

finished state, required both more space than could be found in a cottage and more power than could be applied by the human arm. Their weight also rendered it necessary to place them in strongly built mills, and they could not be advantageously turned by any power known but that of water.[25]

The connection with domestic architecture may be further reinforced by an examination of the weaving trade. Contracted out, the work was undertaken by hand-loom weavers who used their own terraced houses or cottages, devoting the first or second storey to the business while their living quarters were situated below.[26] The millstone grit cottages, built in Lumb Lane, Almondbury, near Huddersfield, during the early eighteenth century, needed long mullioned windows to provide ample daylight for the weavers.[27] Wherever possible these windows faced north, the direction of the light being a key factor in the orientation of the building. The attic or fourth storey of silk weavers' houses in Spitalfields – such as Nos 25–35 Fournier Street (1722–8) and parts of Wilkes Street (1723) and Elder Street (1717–23)[28] – similarly incorporated wide groups of dormer windows to light the workrooms.[29] The looms were placed in the garrets, where, in view of the narrow streets, the light fell uniformly well; these were also the rooms that servants might be expected to occupy. In this fashion some small Georgian factories were erected with their windows in threes between brick piers and mullions of wood or iron, a pattern that later found expression in the workshops of William and Edward Snell at the Grosvenor Basin, designed in 1829–35 by J.B. Papworth (1775–1847).[30] The attachment to established work practices seems to have been so strong in the ribbon-weaving districts of Coventry (Hillfields, Paynes Lane and Foleshill) that the introduction of steam power in the 1840s did not disturb this form of cottage industry. They continued to plan squares of terraces, powered by an engine sited in the enclosure, rather than build single mills. The second floor of each dwelling contained the workshop, and the shafting ran the length of the street, each weaver paying a weekly rent for its use.[31] Thus

4 Weavers' cottages in Lumb Lane, Almondbury, built of local stone; the workshops are apparent from the closely grouped windows.

in both spinning and weaving (not to mention engineering, where much forging and manufacturing was undertaken in small workshops attached to dwellings),[32] house building provided an important architectural precedent for the factory designer.

The use of small-paned timber sash windows in Quarry Bank Mill, Styal (1783–4),[33] and Frost's Mill, Macclesfield (1785)[34] offers an example of the importation of domestic features into industrial structures. In the case of the latter mill, these reflected the vernacular tradition represented by the many silk hand-loom weavers' houses that crowded the town. The former, which was owned by Samuel Greg (1758–1834), also featured a doorway enlivened by an angled pediment and recessed frame that could have graced the entrance to a modest country house. Greg, the son of a Belfast merchant, had inherited sufficient capital to build and equip a mill, but lacked the technical knowledge to effect his

plans. This explains why he took John Massey into partnership as he organized the construction at Styal. Similarly, the retention of stone-mullioned windows in the five-storey brick weaving block of Carlton Mill, Sowerby Bridge (*c*.1780)[35] bore witness to the strength of this tradition. Such domestic features so clearly reproduced in these factories revealed much of the architectural debt owed to local building traditions. The fact that so many entrepreneurs subsequently also had to provide accommodation for their large workforces, often situated in remote areas (such as Ackroydon, Saltaire and Port Sunlight)[36] suggested that this relationship operated in both directions, with architects adapting their house designs to accord with the neighbouring plant; neither was it confined to the early phase of the Industrial Revolution.

The strength of the domestic tradition also revealed itself in America later in the eighteenth century when the earliest spinning mills were erected in New England and Rhode Island.[37] Slater Mill (1793), Pawtucket, was typical of this pioneering phase. A weatherboarded building, it could have been taken for a large farmhouse but for the trap-door monitor in the roof

5 Mullioned windows lit the weaving rooms at Carlton Mill, revealing a link with earlier domestic architecture.

The transitional stage, foundries and warehouses

Of course, foundries and forges had flourished in Britain long before the Industrial Revolution and in certain cases had grown to considerable sizes. However, in general (and this is one reason for arguing that the pre-1780 economy was not industrialized) they remained scattered and limited in output. The lead-smelting mills of the Yorkshire Dales show an important, though embryonic, adoption of Palladian architecture. One of the earliest and also the grandest was the Great Smelting Mill (*c.*1700) near Langthwaite, Arkengarthdale, which used water power to drive its bellows; octagonal in plan (with two opposing sides shorter than the rest) and executed in local stone, this sturdy composition consisted of a regular arrangement of round-arched windows and entrances in a pleasing rhythm. Like the nearby Old Powder House (*c.*1725), a hexagonal stone structure entered by a gabled porch and covered by a corbled roof,[39] the Smelting Mill owed its impact to careful proportions and skilful local building techniques. More obvious attempts at architectural embellishment tended to concentrate on the furnace arch – the focus of manufacturing operations. The Blakethwaite lead-smelting mill (*c.*1775) had two groups of three arches; in each the central one was elliptical, the outer ones being narrower and round-arched, supported by cast-iron Doric columns – a balanced pattern to be repeated at Cockhill Mill, Greenhow Hill (*c.*1785).[40]

Some of the country's largest manufacturing enterprises in the mid-eighteenth century resulted from government contracts or needs. Such a demand resulted in the purchase of the Royal Gunpowder Factory at Waltham Abbey in 1787 (where water-powered mills ground and mixed the vital ingredients), whilst the requirements of the armed forces for cannons and shells prompted the erection of a large foundry at Woolwich, the Royal Arsenal. One of the earliest and most striking of the Royal Arsenal buildings was the Royal Brass Foundry (1715-17). This was an ornate brick structure dominated by a rusticated entrance surmounted by

and the small bell cupola.[38] The influence of British immigrants may be detected from the import of Palladian details – Lippitt Mill (1809) in the Pawtuxet valley had a clerestory roof and belfry – though the essential design and use of materials was inherited from vernacular tradition. Reliant upon water power and so situated in comparatively isolated valleys, it was not surprising that they lacked the finery and splendour of their late nineteenth-century counterparts. When mills became larger, were constructed of masonry rather than timber and were sited in populous towns, they began to exhibit a range of architectural styles and assumed an individuality of their own.

6 The Royal Brass Foundry (1715–17), Woolwich, apparently designed by Sir John Vanbrugh.

7 The entrance to Dial Square (1716–17) now missing the decorative piles of stone cannonballs which stood on top of the flanking pilasters.

a decorative coat-of-arms and topped with an ornate leaded cupola (though this might have been added in 1720 to accommodate a horizontal boring machine) designed for the casting of cannon. While the Dial Square Buildings and the Royal Military Academy were undoubtedly by Sir John Vanbrugh (1664–1726),[41] it can only be supposed that he too was the author of the Brass Foundry.[42] For the plans were unsigned and no corroborative record existed.[43] Furthermore, the formal and slightly fussy decorative treatment applied to the foundry stands in sharp contrast to the highly individual and confident manner seen in the other two buildings.

Nearby, Dial Square, known also as 'The Great Pile of Buildings', designed by Vanbrugh in 1716–17, served originally as an engraving, turning and washing house,[44] but later became a gun factory. The solid brick entrance with its

skilfully constructed voussoirs, now lacking the decorative piles of stone cannonballs from the flanking pilasters, echoed the imposing street gateway in Beresford Square. The Dial's sublime entrance of unrelieved stock brick bore comparison, in view of its proportions and treatment, with the many portals erected to front railway tunnels during the mid-nineteenth century.[45] The military importance of the foundry and its royal ownership were presumably the considerations that prompted special attention (as in the case of the Royal Mint, p. 74) and the employment of a leading architect, while Vanbrugh's particular involvement was governed by his friendship with the Duke of Marlborough, then Master of the Ordnance, and his position as Comptroller of the King's Works. Vanbrugh's own army service made this an appropriate choice and may have filtered through to the actual designs, which possess a toughness and resilience that could be expected from a former soldier. Any other foundry of this period, particularly if situated in a remote part of the country, as the Yorkshire examples have demonstrated, could not expect such elevated architectural treatment.

Whilst no accurate description of the pottery appears to have survived, Thomas Craft, an artist employed there, recorded that the Bow Porcelain Works – founded in 1744 and around 1749 occupying a site in High Street, Stratford – had been constructed in Cantonese style.[46] Because they produced porcelain of quality and character equal to that imported from China itself, the owners, George Arnold, Edward Heylyn and Thomas Fryre, presumably felt that an oriental interpretation was appropriate.[47] For a time in the 1750s the works were known as 'New Canton'. Further, the construction of the Bow Works corresponded with a rising interest in Chinese architecture, publicized by William Halfpenny's *Rural Architecture in the Chinese Taste* and more accurately in 1757 by William Chambers' *Designs of Chinese Buildings*. However, this imitative style of building did not subsequently find favour when pottery manufacture expanded and became concentrated in the Six Towns of North Staffordshire (p. 37), the Bow Works

remaining, as they were in function, an isolated and untypical example of industrial architecture. In fact, the Chinese style remained for all building types something of a rarity, and one of the few examples of its adoption was the façade of Messrs F. & R. Sparrow's Warehouse, Ludgate Hill, by Papworth in 1822–3.[48] That they were tea importers in part explained this preference.

Just as the water-powered corn mill provided a precedent for textile factories, so the tithe barn, with its buttressed walls and timber roof construction (25–30 ft in span) may have offered a model for some warehouses.[49] Government buildings occurred amongst the earliest examples. Defoe, describing the Royal Navy's arsenal at Chatham, speculated in 1724 that they

> are indeed like ships themselves, surprisingly large, and in their several kinds beautiful. The warehouses, or rather streets of ware-houses, and storehouses for laying up the naval treasure are the largest in dimension, and the most in number that are anywhere to be seen in the world ... all like the whole, monstrously great and extensive, and are not easily described.[50]

The decorative gable end of No. 27 Stores, Devonport Naval Dockyard (1769), enlivened by finials and blind lunettes, may be quoted as a further case of architectural embellishment creeping into warehouse design.[51]

The hierarchy of decorum and Palladianism

What, then, was the architectural background into which industrial buildings were born during the mid-eighteenth century? What views did contemporaries hold about their existence and position in relation to established types of building? This period coincided with the 'Age of Reason'; a time when men sought through rational argument to create a symmetrical, consistent and ordered society where everything possessed a designated place. Architecture, like society itself, could not be excluded from such thought. Buildings were ranked in degrees of importance (reflecting the status of those who occupied them), with royal palaces, cathedrals and places of government at the apex, qualifying them for the most dignified designs and elevated ornament by the most distinguished architects. Within the hierarchy of decorum, industrial structures – warehouses, mills or foundries – rated low. In effect they were the Third Estate of the architectural world; not for them the finery of the parliament house or the regal residence. As Fairbairn recollected, in this pioneering phase:

> mill architecture was out of the question ... and the architecture of the country was confined to churches, public buildings and the mansions of the barons or lords of the soil.[52]

The writings of Vitruvius, the Roman architect, which found much popularity in the Palladian period, could be consulted for similar sentiments:

> Those who do business in country produce must have stalls and shops in their entrance courts, with crypts, granaries, storerooms and so forth in their houses, constructed more for the purpose of keeping the product in good condition than for ornamental beauty. For capitalists and farmers of the revenue somewhat comfortable and showy apartments must be constructed, secure against robbery; for advocates and public speakers, handsomer and more roomy to accommodate meetings; for men of rank who, from holding offices and magistrates, have social obligations to their fellow citizens, lofty entrance courts in regal style ... appropriate to their dignity.[53]

Sir William Chambers (1723–96) in his treatise *Civil Architecture* (1759) argued that the ancient orders 'collected from the temples and public structures of Antiquity' might suitably be 'employed in churches, palaces and other buildings of magnificence, where majesty and grandeur may be extended to their utmost ...'[54] Under the dictates of the age, a building's social position, rather than any consideration of its economic importance, critically influenced its architectural execution.

The predominant architectural style was Palladian and, being an ordered, rational system, was particularly suited to this philosophy. Based largely on Roman remains, as well as the buildings of Andrea Palladio (1508–80) in sixteenth-

century Italy and those of Inigo Jones (1573–1652) in seventeenth-century England,[55] the movement produced a significant number of disciples who took to print. While these publications failed to encourage rich theoretical debate, the literature of the Palladian movement did generate a considerable number of illustrative works which clearly showed the orders, their proportions and the many architectural forms that could be adopted. William Halfpenny's *Practical Architecture* (1730),[56] for example, contained no text but comprised engravings of door and window frames, columns and decorative elements. *Vitruvius Britannicus*, Vol. I (1715) and Vol. II (1717), simply consisted of folio engravings depicting classical buildings in Britain. Thus, although the hierarchy of decorum relegated industrial buildings to a low position within the architectural world, the Palladian movement created ample material for its subtle adoption or modified selection through pattern books. No wonder, therefore, that adventurous entrepreneurs should consider the adoption of Palladian details or plans when considering the construction of a new factory or warehouse. Based in remote areas, and often men of little formal education far from genteel society, they might not have felt particularly bound by the hierarchy's dictates, nor as innovators would they have necessarily agreed with all its rules. In time, as industrial buildings became larger and increasingly prominent in the British landscape, and as their value to society became more widely appreciated, they slowly achieved a measure of acceptance in the circle of architectural distinction following the social rise of their ambitious owners; factories, ironworks and the like formed the *nouveaux riches* of the building world.

Mill architecture

Although transitional in terms of its function, Albion Mill (1783–6), designed and managed by Samuel Wyatt (1737–1807), offered an early illustration of how Palladian principles could be effectively applied to a working building.[57] Situated on the Thames at the south-east end of

8 Albion Mill (1783-6) by Samuel Wyatt as depicted in the *New London Magazine* for June 1790. Note the barge about to enter the central shipping hole from the Thames.

Blackfriars Bridge, this steam-powered corn mill, as an illustration in the *New London Magazine* for July 1790 revealed, was a well-proportioned structure of some architectural distinction.[58] The rusticated stone basement was marked at the centre by a watergate for the delivery of grain and coal by barge, above which five ordered storeys featured a variety of symmetrical window forms.[59] Albion Mill's exterior (particularly the western elevation to the street) might have passed for a substantial town house, betraying nothing of the purpose for which it had been constructed. Though concealed beneath a conventional Georgian façade, the mill was then a particularly large example of an internal-framed timber building and foreshadowed the concept of the load-bearing skeleton framework for which walls were little more than protective cladding.[60] Indeed, after it had been gutted by fire in 1791 when the engine overheated, Wyatt planned to re-erect the mill with an internal

structure of cast iron, which would have made the second Albion Mill an early example of a building with an independent load-bearing framework.[61]

By contrast, one of the first textile mills proper, Cromford Mill (1771) exhibited little in the way of architectural embellishment. Built by Richard Arkwright, Samuel Need and Jedediah Strutt (1726-97) – the last a silk manufacturer familiar from his youth with Lombe's Derby Mill[62] – it consisted of a simple five-storey structure of local stone with gabled end walls and lit by many regular-sized windows, of smaller size in the two topmost floors.[63] This spartan design offered few concessions to decoration or appearance.[64] Visitors appear to have been impressed by the size and nature of this mill and its fellows; the Hon. John Byng was reminded in 1794 of 'a first-rate man of war; and when they are lighted up, on a dark night look most luminously beautiful'. However, Masson Mill (1783), nearby on the River Derwent and also built for Arkwright,[65] revealed a greater concern for appearances though this manifested itself in little more than the surface application of Palladian details: simplified Venetian and semicircular

9 Cromford Mill (1771), undergoing restoration by the Arkwright Society, but lacking its upper two storeys.

10 Masson Mill (1783) situated in the picturesque valley of the Derwent south of Matlock.

SIR RICHARD ARKWRIGHT & CO.

ESTABLISHED 1769·

1769-1969
200 YEARS OF
SERVICE TO INDUSTRY

windows arranged in a regular pattern beneath a bell cupola. It has been suggested that the borrowing of these features reflected Arkwright's 'desire to live like and behave like a country gentleman'.[66] By this time Arkwright, who was to be knighted in 1786, had attained a certain status in Derbyshire and was later, c.1791, to commission a Gothic country house, Willersley Castle.

That Carlton Mill (c. 1780), at Sowerby Bridge, a rising woollen centre in the Calder Valley, incorporated classical details was further evidence of the growing appeal of the Palladian style. The four-storey stone block was distinguished by a central three-bay pediment with lunette and a regular arrangement of windows.[67] Larger in size but not significantly different in terms of their stylistic execution were both Darley Abbey Mills (1789–92) and Bean Ing Mill, Leeds (1792–3). The former, constructed for

11 Carlton Mill (c. 1780) by the River Calder at Sowerby Bridge, showing some Palladian details.

Thomas Evans (1723–1814) a mile north of Derby on the River Derwent for cotton spinning, exhibited few architectural features, excepting the semi-circular window beneath the gable and limited use of stone for string courses, sills and drip moulds for the ground floor.[68] Wooden sash windows of regular size lit the top four storeys. Darley Abbey Mills earned distinction by their ordered scale, and the quality of the local building tradition rather than by the pursuance of classical excellence. It is possible that their design was influenced by Cromford and Belper as the Evans family had intermarried with the Strutts, and William Strutt appears once to have been a partner in the concern.

Although only four storeys high, Bean Ing or Park Mills, built for Benjamin Gott, drew attention because of its great length – some 54 bays. John Sutcliffe, a Halifax millwright, had been employed in 1791 to produce plans, corresponding with Gott over their details, but resigned in 1792 over disputed fees.[69] Accordingly the first section of the mill was erected in 1792–3 with

12 An aerial view of Bean Ing Mill (1792–1802), at Leeds, photographed in 1965. The River Aire is in the foreground while the entrance to Wellington Street was marked by a cupola.

the assistance of John Moxson (probably the son of John Moxson who designed the Mixed Cloth Hall, Leeds) as the surveyor. Being timber-framed internally, it was not fireproof and burned down in 1799 when insured for £6,000, only to be rebuilt on a larger scale in 1801–2, but to a similar pattern. The main mill, 203 ft by 34 ft, was four storeys and L-shaped in plan, with an attached engine house, the shorter arm being used as spinning rooms.[70] Moreover, the hand-weaving shops which formed the frontage to Wellington Street (1793–4), some 350 ft long, consisted of a simple repetitious brick façade relieved only by two symmetrically placed gables (each four bays wide), typifying much mill architecture at the turn of the eighteenth century. Humphry Repton, writing of Bean Ing in c.1820, echoed Byng's impression of Cromford Mill when he suggested that the former could 'never fail to be an interesting object by daylight, and at night presents a most splendid illumination of gas light.' He complimented Gott on his 'good taste ... on the unaffected simplicity of this large building which looks like what it is – a Mill and Manufactory and is not disguised by Gothic windows, or other architectural pretensions, too often misapplied by way of ornament.'[71] In plan the mill was arranged around a courtyard; 'the main body of the manufactory forming one side of the square, and the weaving rooms for hand-looms, stove-rooms, dye-houses &c. forming the other sides. One great gateway serves the entrance for all the workmen ... and also for that of the raw materials.'[72] In this way 'the whole process of the manufacture of cloth from the first breaking of the wool to the finishing of the piece ready for the consumer is carried on'.[73] Significantly, when an extension was ordered in 1824, for which Fairbairn performed the engineering work, it was cast-iron framed, and featured a large entrance archway topped by an ornate bell cupola.

Examples from the far north of England and Scotland reveal that the subtle importation of Palladian architectural features was not confined to limited areas of Britain. Netherwitton Mill, Northumberland, a late eighteenth-century stone three-storey structure, had a regular arrangement of windows with a central projecting bay capped by an angled pediment,[74] in the character of those buildings cited in Derbyshire and Yorkshire. That the situation differed little in Scotland, where no obvious attempt occurred to introduce local architectural features into mill design, was partly a reflection of their English ownership and management. At New Lanark, where a cotton-spinning community had its origins in a partnership between Richard Arkwright and David Dale (1739–1806),[75] a Glaswegian merchant and banker, the mills and associated housing outwardly resembled their southern counterparts. No. 1 Mill (1788–9), for example, though characterized by a severe fenestration, was enlivened by semicircular windows similar to those in Arkwright's Masson Mill, while New Buildings (1789), built to house the workforce, mirrored this diluted Palladian treatment, and its bell cupola, which marked shifts, was originally situated on No. 1 Mill. Arriving as manager in 1799, Robert Owen (1771–1858) maintained an allegiance to the distilled Palladian style, for the many subsequent extensions – No. 2 Mill and No. 3 Mill, the Institute and School, together with additional housing – were all executed in this manner. No. 3 Mill, for instance, constructed as late as 1826, and specifically for Owen, followed this pattern with a central pedimented bay, symmetrical arrangement of windows and restrained use of quoins and dressings. Costing £3,000, the 'Institute for the Formation of Character', planned in 1809 but not fully operational until 1816, contained a library, and reading and recreation rooms. A three-storey building of dignified appearance, it was entered through a porch supported by classical columns. The school (1817) was a simpler, ordered block enlivened by ashlar quoins and a central pediment. Although performing quite different roles, they remained in keeping with the architecture of the mills and housing, if in a slightly more elevated fashion.

It was said that Woodside Mills, Aberdeen, had been modelled on New Lanark.[76] The symmetrical fenestration and arrangement of the twin staircase towers (each lit by five Venetian windows and capped by a cupola), together with the comparative restraint shown in this six-storey stone mill, reflected those examples at Cromford and Matlock.

Further north, Stanley Mills, Kinclaven, founded in 1785, also involved Arkwright, who entered into a partnership there with George Dempster and Graham of Fintry.[77] In connection with the proposed venture Graham visited Cromford, and by 1790 Bell or West Mill was complete. The influence of the Derbyshire prototypes may be detected from its appearance. For this five-storey brick mill, built upon stone foundations, rose as a rectangular block with gabled ends and a regular fenestration, and was decorated with a central angled pediment and bellcote. The subsequent additions – East Mill (c.1840) and Mid Mill (c.1850) – followed in a similar architectural tradition such that they formed an integrated whole, though advances had been made in their internal structure.

Returning to England, in the degree to which they borrowed ornament and ideas from Palladian country houses, both Mellor Mill (1790) and Cressbrook Mill were exceptions. The former's E-plan, flanked on each side by lower gabled pavilions and the adoption of classical motifs such as the cupola, Venetian window, cornice and lunette,[78] all pointed to a deliberate attempt to fit the traditional square-box mill design into well-cut architectural clothes. The repetition of large numbers of regular-sized windows (six storeys in the central block), needed for adequate daylight, marked the building as a factory rather than a country house. Samuel

13 No. 3 Mill (1826) at New Lanark, erected for Robert Owen. It had a fireproof interior (the original No. 3 having been destroyed by fire in November 1819) and at 45 ft was half as wide again as the building it replaced.

Oldknow (1756–1828), who constructed the mill with financial assistance from the Arkwrights, was reputed to have employed Derbyshire lead miners for its erection because of their skill in working with stone. Robert Owen's description confirmed that Oldknow had paid particular attention to its appearance:

> He built a large, handsome and very imposing cotton mill, amidst grounds well laid out, and the mill was beautifully situated, for he possessed general good taste in these matters ... He had, however, expended his capital so freely in building this mill, fitting it with machinery and purchasing land around it, in addition to splendid buildings and arrangements in and near Stockport for carrying on his extensive muslin manufacture and for its sale that when the trying time of 1792 arrived, he was too wide of his plans to sustain their expenditure without making great sacrifices.[79]

The central projecting bay contained the offices, store and making-up room, and the smaller bays housed the staircases, while the

wings were used for miscellaneous tasks.[80] Unfortunately this mill was burnt down in 1892.

Smaller in size than Mellor, Wye Mill (1814–16), part of the Cressbrook complex, exhibited marked Palladian features.[81] The site, at Miller's Dale, had been originally developed by Arkwright in 1783 when the first Cressbrook Mill was erected.[82] This structure was destroyed by fire two years later but was not rebuilt until 1787, making use of the same foundations. Wye Mill, a much bigger version, was begun in 1814 and when completed represented the skilful incorporation of Palladian principles into factory design.

Although Edale Mill (1795), built probably at the instigation of Nicholas Cresswell, was smaller than either Wye or Mellor Mills and was situated in a remote part of the Peak District, it too exhibited a number of Palladian details: a semicircular window beneath the gable, a rounded staircase bay and regular fenestration.[83] The example of Broadclough Mill at Bacup, designed in 1791 for Messrs Ormrod & Whitaker by John Sutcliffe of Halifax revealed that Palladianism had percolated through to quite limited structures.[84] For this three-storey, seven-bay stone mill had ordered and symmetrical fenestration, a central pediment, and wings to

14 Wye Mill (1814–16) at Cressbrook in Miller's Dale, one of the most attractive water-powered factories.

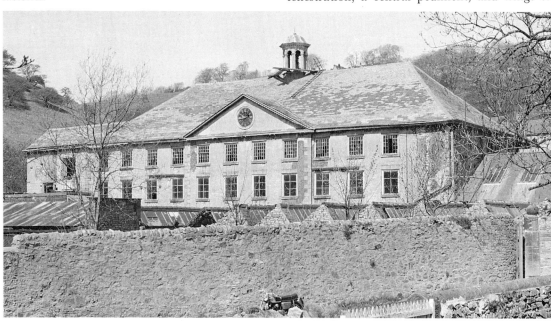

15 Broadclough Mill (1791); although small-scale it showed a concern for appearance and reflected Palladian principles.

16 The east elevation of Smithies Mill, Birstall, dated 1796–7, as supplied by Messrs Nussey to Boulton & Watt, who were to provide them with a 'sun-and-planet' rotative engine.

accommodate the joiners' and blacksmiths' shops and the cottage and turning room. Similar in size and appearance was Smithies Mill (1796–7), Birstall, erected for Nussey & Co., which demonstrated that even when constrained by capital requirements entrepreneurs felt compelled to add a few architectural features, albeit in a diluted form. These, added to the eastern elevation of this steam-powered scribbling and fulling mill, faced down the valley and would have been seen by travellers coming from Batley and Dewsbury. Nevertheless, practical considerations overruled, and the boilers and chimney were placed beside the two right-hand bays, thereby obscuring part of the design.[85] The symmetry and incorporation of a pediment and lunette in the London starch mill constructed for Stonard & Curtis (1784) meant that this building fell into the same category.[86]

In a society still in the throes of industrialization, breweries, and especially those in centres of great population, were among the largest businesses and demanded plant of considerable size and cost. The Griffin Brewery, Liquorpond Street, Clerkenwell, may serve as a fine example. Originally built in 1763, its new owners, Andrew Reid and Richard Meux, decided in 1793 to spend some £15,400 on rebuilding and by 1795 over £50,000 had been devoted to the brewery. The order and detailing of the street façade revealed Palladian influence, whilst its overall plan was determined by the practical requirements of the trade.[87] The malt and liquor were commonly hoisted to the top of the building so that their movement through subsequent processes might be left to gravity. Ideally the three sides of the upper storey of the brewhouse itself were of open battens, slatted against sunlight yet open to the air; the solid wall was best placed facing south-west. Other large breweries in London included the Black Eagle Brewery, enlarged by Sir Benjamin Truman in 1774–5; the Hour-Glass Brewery belonging to the Calverts (c. 1780); and the Lion Brewery at Lambeth, whose classical storehouse was designed by Francis Edwards in 1836, followed in the early nineteenth century.

17 The front and end elevations of the starch mill erected in London for Stonard & Curtis, dated September 1784.

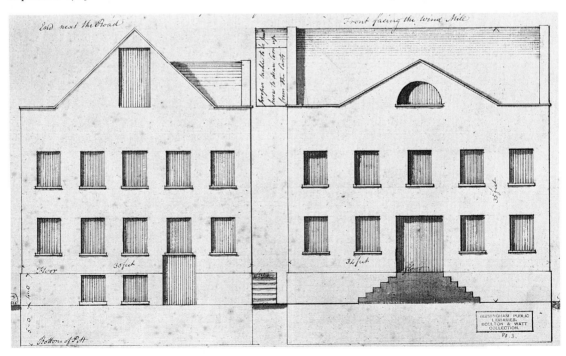

18 Sir William and Felix Calvert's Hour-Glass Brewery and dwelling house in Upper Thames Street. Revealing the appeal of Palladian details, it also helps to explain the connection between domestic and industrial architecture. Shown here in 1820 and dating back to at least the sixteenth century, the brewery had been substantially rebuilt around 1780.

The general conclusion remains, as Fairbairn suggested in his *Treatise on Mills and Millwork*, that:

the large profits arising from cotton manufacture at that time [the 1780s] enabled proprietors to build mills some of them considered of colossal dimensions. At first, these mills were square brick buildings, without any pretensions to architectural form

... This description of building with bare walls was for many years the distinguishing feature of a cotton mill, and for a long period they continued to be of the same form and character throughout all parts of the country.[88]

Better than this was Frost's Mill, Macclesfield (1785), originally a water-powered silk-throwing mill, whose elevations of regular fenestration were relieved by a projecting bay topped with a clock pediment.[89] Yet Robert Peel's Mill, Burton-on-Trent (1791),[90] a mean four-storey brick structure devoid of any ornament, typified much of this phase of industrial building. This, in part, reflected the economic and social background into which these factories were born. Because they were in many senses pioneering ventures, the owner, often a man of broad practical skills,[91] usually played a significant part in the building's execution – Arkwright at Cromford, the Strutts at Belper and Gott at Bean Ing – so that architects or surveyors, when actually employed, occupied a subsidiary role, commissioned merely to design a suitable façade or advise on the decorative details that might be applied. So far architects were not in general given instructions to execute important industrial projects, nor, indeed, did they feel that they should be associated with such work.

To generalize, early mill buildings, those of the 1770–90 period, were rectangular in plan, seldom more than 30 ft in width, and rose several storeys in height, though not often more than four. The foundations had to be sufficiently solid to withstand possible undermining by the millstream or the vibrations of a beam engine, and support the weight of the building above. The maximum dimensions of mills were imposed not by architectural or even structural considerations but by questions of operation.[92] The need for adequate daylight limited the breadth. There were two distinct types of textile machinery: the mule, and the throstle and fly frame,

19 Frost's Mill (1785), Park Green, Macclesfield, originally a water-powered factory but from 1811 driven by steam and after 1914 by electricity.

each having different characteristics and producing different floor plans. For the former a multiple of 20–21 ft (being the space required to house a pair of mules) often determined actual measurements, buildings of the 1780s rarely exceeding 30 ft in width. Those mills with throstles assumed a linear plan axially aligned around a single or double line of columns, such as Low Mill (1780), at Keighley. The overall size of a mill (its length and height) was ultimately determined by the strength of the waterwheel or engine. To add another storey in fact demanded a disproportionate increase in the power required because of the need for a greater number of mitre gears and heavier vertical shaft.

Ceilings tended to be low; in the West Riding they were commonly 8 or 9 ft and elsewhere probably not much over 10 ft.[93] Early machinery did not demand great headroom and given the desire not to waste space or spend excessively on building materials, smaller rooms were economically advantageous and could be heated cheaply. It was only later in the nineteenth century, with the need for wider mills to house greater numbers of improved mules, that ceilings were raised to provide bigger windows (p. 185). With the exception of the few mills which attempted to embody fireproof principles, floors, doors, beams and window frames were all of wood. The small size of windows was in part an inheritance from their domestic counterparts, but may also have resulted from a fear of weakening the building's structure. The cellar was often used to store raw materials and finished goods and occasionally served as a stable. The garret or attic rooms were used for storage and hand processes, while ancillary functions took place nearby: workshops, drying houses, warehouses and offices.

Foundries and forges

Matthew Boulton, who was particularly concerned to raise the standard of workmanship and design in the Birmingham area, cultivated the new classical taste and aimed at satisfying the fashionable market with his ormolu and silver. It was not surprising, therefore, that he should want his factory to express these cultural preferences.[94] He asked the firm of Benj. Wyatt & Sons to design the works when the original architect, T. Lightoler, proved unsatisfactory. The task fell to William Wyatt II (1734–80), helped by his younger brother, Benjamin Wyatt II (1744–1818), who assisted with the drawings.[95] When finished, at a cost of £9,000, the Soho Manufactory (1764–6) was the largest of its kind in Europe. The architects had modified their plans in accordance with Matthew Boulton's wishes, the final version, based upon a Palladian villa, being a symmetrical, ordered three-storey block with gabled wings and a central entrance. Located at the foot of a hill with a garden, it was described by the Revd Stebbing Shaw as a 'scene of picturesque beauty',[96] following the Palladian notion that a house should be considered within its landscape.[97] The transformation of this barren heath into a populous town where 600 people were employed greatly struck contemporaries.[98] Although mimicking a mansion in outward appearance, the Soho Manufactory had a practical rationale; the workers lived in the upper floors of the wings (as domestic servants might have done in a rural counterpart), while the forges and furnaces, with the huge waterwheel that gave them life, were located at the back. Soho was unusual not only for its size at such a comparatively early date, but also for the extent to which architects had been involved.

Whilst the Soho Manufactory represented one of the finer Palladian industrial buildings, the Abbeydale Works, Sheffield corresponded with the so-called 'primitive' Palladianism reflected in Masson Mill. Its owners, the Goddard family, who doubtless conceived it as a practical structure for the production of tools and cutting instruments, nevertheless felt constrained to include certain architectural features, and the tilt forge (1785)[99] was lit by Venetian windows of dressed stone. Similarly, Cannon Mill, Dock Walk, Chesterfield (1816), a small-scale, water-powered foundry – originally part of John and Ebenezer Smith's Griffin Foundry – was constructed of local red brick with coped gable ends.

20 The Soho Manufactory (1764–6) by William
Wyatt II assisted by Benjamin Wyatt II.

Although ornament remained sparse, the side
wall visible from the road was enlivened by three
blind Gothic arches.[100] The Birmingham Gun-
Barrel Proof House, Banbury Street (1813), designed by John Horton, 'architect and builder of
Deritend',[101] had its once-symmetrical façade
decorated by an ornate and colourful group of
trophies (by William Hollins) placed above the
entrance and beneath a central curved gable.

Unfortunately, most ironworks of this period
have survived only as partially ruined sites.
Their most important architectural feature, the
blast furnace, a tapered tower of brick and rubble covered with dressed stone, was commonly
stripped of its valuable outer skin for building
elsewhere. However, early photographs and
prints – of Neath Abbey, Blaenavon and
Brymbo, all with blast furnaces dating from the
1790s[102] – showed that although practical and

technical considerations were uppermost in the
minds of their builders, they also achieved a
massive dignity in their design through the use
of quality materials and simple, effective forms.

Glass manufacturers also demanded buildings
in which materials could be heated, with uninterrupted space available for their treatment.
Accordingly, one of Britain's largest industrial
structures was then the casting hall (340 ft by
150 ft) at Ravenhead, near St Helens. Erected
in 1773–6 by the British Plate Glass Co., 'this
establishment occupies nearly 30 acres of land,
and is enclosed by a wall, round which are
placed the houses of the workmen, which renders it a sort of distinct colony; the buildings
cost at the time £40,000'.[103] The casting hall
stood like a cathedral of brick: the nave was
formed by a succession of Gothic arches, flanked
by lower aisles. Yet it was entered through a
Palladian porch surmounted by a pediment and
cupola. Glassworks resulted in the construction
of some particularly spacious halls in the era
before railways and exhibitions produced even
bigger structures. (A casting hall nearly twice as

big as that at Ravenhead, with two foundry- and two firing-kilns, was built at St Helens by the Union Plate Glass Works in 1836-7.)

The Potteries

An aspect of industrial Britain that called for regional treatment, by virtue of its independent spirit and consistent adoption of one architectural theme, was the Potteries. Almost from the outset, when manufacturers felt that the scale of their operations required buildings of greater dimensions with finer adornment than the existing small-scale workshops, the Palladian schema, suitably muted and modified, became an enduring basis for their factory designs. Earlier, kilns and rooms for finishing processes had been arranged in an *ad hoc* fashion around a small courtyard incorporating the owner's home.[104] In his efforts to improve output and efficiency Josiah Wedgwood (1730-95) found that two major elements of the domestic pottery could be employed in a larger purpose-built

factory: the courtyard, and living quarters for the master.[105] He also demonstrated that if a regular plan with separate places for distinct processes were adopted, there should be no reason why certain features of Palladian architecture could not be incorporated in the overall design. The courtyard arrangement often meant that potteries such as Etruria (1767-73), designed by Wedgwood and Joseph Pickford (a Derby architect and builder),[106] that became a model for the Six Towns, had an entrance situated in an office and warehouse block which fronted the main road or canal.[107] This elevation generally received the greatest architectural attention. The courtyard behind, containing the ovens and various workshops, screened from public view, remained unadorned, the dictates of practical operation ruling there. Thus Etruria's frontage facing the Trent and Mersey Canal featured an

21 Etruria (1767-73), by Wedgwood and Pickford, facing the Trent and Mersey Canal.

angled pediment surmounted by a cupola in a restrained, ordered composition, though a circular tower pierced by lunettes is all that survives of this once mighty pottery. Like Boulton at Soho, Wedgwood presumably selected the Palladian style as an outward expression of the classical theme that his artists had adopted as the source for plates, vases and so forth.[108] Pickford was also employed by Wedgwood to design his country house, Etruria Hall (1767–9), and a showroom at the corner of Newport Street and St Martin's Lane, London in 1768.

One of the first to follow the Etruria example was William Adams, who built the Greengate Works, Tunstall (1784–6).[109] Enlivened by a three-bay pediment surmounted by an ornate cupola, the Palladian three-storey entrance building shielded the courtyard, works and kilns behind.[110] Other potteries that typified this treatment included, in Longton, the Boundary Works (1818) built by Jacob Marsh,[111] whose ordered brick warehouse block fronted King Street. The warehouse was entered through a typical basket arch, and the semicircular and Venetian windows above were topped by an angled pediment. The Palladian design could also be successfully applied to factories occupying a corner site, as in the case of Enoch Wood's Fountain Place Works (1789), Burslem, where the entrance, surmounted by Venetian and three-light windows beneath a cupola, was placed at the angle between the office and warehouse blocks forming two sides of the courtyard behind[112] – a similar arrangement being adopted for the nearby Wade Heath Pottery (1814).[113] In effect, the Fountain Place Works were divided into two halves by Packhorse Lane, and the bridge which crossed it resembled a medieval gateway, though the Gothic detailing extended no further than battlements, and Wood's house, situated within the pottery, conformed to classical models.[114]

That this style, which found such favour with North Staffordshire's master potters and so suited the design of their works, continued to be executed long after the rest of Britain had passed over Palladianism, was demonstrated by the following examples: the Hill Pottery, Burslem,

22 The Boundary Works (1818), King Street, Longton, whose entrance building typified much of the pottery architecture of North Staffordshire.

which when extended in 1839 by Samuel Alcock featured a Greek Ionic portico with decorative urns surmounted by a rusticated Venetian window, John Aynsley's Longton Works, completed in 1861 and designed by Yorath,[115] and the nearby St Mary's Works (1862). Daisey Bank Pottery, Longton, when rebuilt by Hulse, Nixon and Adderley between 1854–78, maintained the traditional plan and form in its pedimented main entrance to the three-storey frontage,[116] though the polychromy introduced through contrasting bands of brickwork was an innovation.

One feature that further served to unite these potteries was the distinctive shape of their kilns. Kohl, recounting his tour of England, wrote in 1844 that the view of Burslem and Hanley if approached from Newcastle-under-Lyme was unique of its kind, as:

a stranger might be tempted to believe that he saw a vast line of fortifications rising before him. The surrounding hills are crowned with the lofty columns and the huge pyramids of the chimneys, and with the great rounded furnaces, of which dozens are often seen together looking like colossal bomb-mortars.[117]

While the chimneys were on occasion decorated with a simple dentil cap, the differences between individual bottle ovens owed more to the skills of the local bricklayer than to any preconceived notions of proportion.

The conclusion to be drawn from this survey of the Six Towns is that Palladian architecture, adopted at the peak of its popularity, held a particular fascination for pottery owners, who found it an appealing image as well as a practical solution to their manufacturing needs. The restraint and order, together with a reliance upon a few features (the basket arch, Venetian window and angled pediment), suited local building materials: brick walls, tiled roofs and a limited use of stone. As a result, architects, if

employed, appear to have occupied a subordinate position. They were not given their head, nor generally trusted with the pottery's overall design; Wedgwood, for example, provided the basic plans and operational details for Etruria, undertaking his own surveying,[118] and presumably left Pickford to devise the ornamental additions. When George Coxon was commissioned in 1845 to redesign the frontage of the Phoenix Pottery in Broad Street, Hanley, it was simply to improve the works' poor public image, the operational areas remaining untouched by his efforts.[119] A concern with surface finery was observed by Arnold Bennett, who wrote of one fictional pottery that:

> the arched entrance for carts into the yard was at the top of the steepest rise in the street, when it might as well have been at the bottom; and this was but one example of the architect's fine disregard for the principle of economy in working – that principle to which in the scheming of manufactories everything else is now so strictly subordinated.[120]

Warehouses

Whilst warehouses, like water-powered mills, have a long ancestry pre-dating the Industrial Revolution, it was in this period that demands for their use stimulated their construction on a much wider scale, and ultimately (p. 45) produced the materials and techniques necessary for their advanced design. The Grocers' Company Warehouse (c.1770–80) at the Castlefield Basin of the Bridgewater Canal, Manchester, may serve as a superior, yet in many ways representative, example of an industrial warehouse.[121] The symmetrical arrangement of regular-sized windows around an internal dock was not untypical, though the adoption of simple stone window facings (not repeated elsewhere in the district) was novel, and the warehouse may have been the first to be constructed with a shipping hole to enable barges to be unloaded under cover. Alternatively, however, this distinction may have been earned by its neighbour, the Duke's Warehouse, erected at much the same time on the head of the navigation in Alport

Lane. (The Duke's Warehouse was destroyed by fire in 1789,[122] to be rebuilt in the two succeeding years, but was burnt down in 1914, while the Grocers' Warehouse was demolished in 1960, so today only the Merchant's and the Middle Warehouses remain at Castlefield.) When the Grocers' Warehouse (so named c.1811) was extended at some time between 1794 and 1807, it involved the cutting of a second shipping hole; similar materials were employed in a similar manner. The Middle Warehouse, off Chester Road, Manchester, was of comparable size, while the earlier Merchant's Warehouse (c.1800) probably occupied an intermediate position in design terms, as this smaller structure had two purpose-built shipping holes placed side by side and supported by stone piers. Like its predecessors, this example was not fireproof, having an internal timber framework.

That these warehouses formed architectural models not only for Manchester but elsewhere may be demonstrated by reference to the Clock Warehouse (1780) at Shardlow on the Grand Trunk Canal. The Trent section of this waterway had been completed under the superintendence of James Brindley's brother-in-law, Hugh Henshall, who in 1777 from a base at Castle Quay had been one of the first carriers on the Bridgewater Navigation – in fact, after 1793 he also occupied the Grocer's Warehouse under the style Henshall, Gilbert & Co.[123] As clerk of the works to the Grand Trunk Canal and a pioneering carrier to Shardlow, Henshall presumably was responsible for the transmission of this architectural feature, for the Clock Warehouse also had a central shipping hole, and incorporated Palladian details (clock pediment, louvred ventilator) with restraint in a way that did not interfere with the building's practical operation.[124] That a waterway could be responsible for conveying such ideas seems to have been confirmed in 1811, when a similar-looking design was erected at the Duke's Dock, Liverpool, the western terminal of much merchandise being conveyed on the Bridgewater Canal. Much larger than the Shardlow version, this six-storey brick building was characterized by two centrally situated shipping holes framed by an embracing blind

23 The Duke's grain warehouse (1811), Liverpool, which served narrow boats from the Bridgewater Canal – a building similar in plan and appearance to those at Castlefield, Manchester, but unlike them it possessed elements of an internal iron frame.

arch.[125] Unlike the earlier Manchester examples, the Duke's Grain Warehouse incorporated cast-iron columns and 'elephant beams' (cast-iron arches of 'I'-section) that helped to spread the load over each of the shipping holes. Although the rectangular windows were simpler, the rusticated stone ground floor and dressings and the angled pediment represented stylistic flourishes.

The use of Palladian semicircular windows at Shardlow was not uncommon, as the Navigation Warehouses, Quay Lane, Sudbury (dated 1791) showed.[126] The stone two-storey warehouse at Todmorden on the Rochdale Canal was entered by a shipping hole, but also exhibited a Venetian window in the gable. The Dale Street Warehouse, at the Manchester basin of the Rochdale Canal (although traced to that site only in the 1820s and believed to have been moved from Yorkshire),[127] exhibited the limited adoption of 'primitive' Palladian details such as a Venetian window in one of its gables, which suggested, along with its structure, a date in the latter part of the eighteenth century. A warehouse of similar appearance and treatment is that off Water Lane, Leeds, situated at the beginning of the Leeds and Liverpool Canal.

Although the meanest brick shed attached to an ironworks or spinning mill could, of course, serve as an efficient warehouse, some of the finest and most lasting examples from this pioneering phase resulted from the prestigious commissions granted by the various London dock companies. Situated in or on the fringes of the City, their owners felt compelled to employ an architect and to spend that little extra on materials to ensure a building fitting their status in the commercial world of the capital. In this sense, therefore, they differ from so many warehouses erected by mill-owners, ironmasters or canal companies, whose sites in remote or industrial districts did not catch the attention of a fashionable mercantile community.

At Cutler Street the East India Company's solid six-storey brick warehouses of 1792 were designed by Richard Jupp. Forming the northern end of the western courtyard, these austere buildings with their ordered pattern of segment-headed windows had a sublime power and dignity offset by sparse stone dressings. When Jupp, a founder member of the Architects' Club, died in 1799,[128] his post as surveyor passed to Henry Holland (1745–1806) who, it is believed, was responsible for the design of the Middlesex range. Above a monumental wall of fine brickwork (prison-like to prevent goods from escaping), the three L-shaped blocks formed a spectacular zigzag; their asymmetrical pediments were so arranged that the apex lay

slightly to the left of centre in an unexpected and inventive manner.

Outside the City, situated on the Thames in The Highway, Ratcliff, the East India Company built their saltpetre warehouses at the Free Trade Wharf (1795). It is thought that Richard Jupp was also responsible for their design and construction.[129] Although executed in stock brick with limited stone dressings and treated in a restrained but ordered fashion, the two warehouse blocks and the rusticated entrance possessed a classical dignity and style that would not normally be associated with such a store.[130] Because of the inflammable nature of saltpetre, brick piers and vaulting were introduced in an attempt to fireproof the building.

More substantial were the London Docks, whose warehouses fell to Daniel Asher Alexander (c.1768–1846), who later constructed Dartmoor and Maidstone gaols. Assisted by John Rennie (1761–1821), the Scottish civil engineer, he designed the five stacks (1802–5) that stood along the northern quay of the Western Dock.[131] In each, the vault, ground floor and rusticated plinth below a stone string course

24 A Victorian photograph of the North Quay, London Docks (1802–5). John Rennie was the engineer and Alexander the architect.

25 An impressive range of warehouses (1802–3) at West India Docks with elevations of deceptive simplicity.

formed a solid base, while the eye's upward movement was arrested by shorter segment-headed windows for the third storey. A simple stone cornice concealed part of the hipped slate roof. Horizontal emphasis, and practical access, was provided by four bands of shuttered entrances arranged in a symmetrical rhythm.

The West India Docks, engineered by William Jessop (1745–1814) and Ralph Walker, produced a larger and more complicated arrangement of warehouses.[132] Designed by George Gwilt (1746–1807), a former mason and surveyor to the Company, and assisted by his son, George (1775–1856),[133] the six linked blocks that formed the northern half of the dock were completed in 1802–3.[134] Using a greater range

of architectural motifs and adopting a plan of greater complexity than had been employed for the London Docks, the Gwilts produced an original and varied composition. Stone string courses divided the basement and ground-floor windows and the semicircular third-storey lights, whilst columns of loopholes balanced the ranges of doors in an ordered classical design.[135]

Related structural developments

Improved ironmaking methods and a growing understanding of civil engineering, albeit of a practical rather than a rigorously scientific nature, resulted in major innovations in the structural design of industrial buildings. In a later period these developments were also to dictate their exterior form. While the outer load-bearing walls of the earliest factories were solidly constructed from local stone or brick, the internal arrangement of floors owed its strength to substantial timber posts and beams, which, of course, made these buildings a fire hazard. In textile mills oil from machines dripped on floorboards; lighting was by candle or lamps; cotton dust created a flammable mixture and fire-fighting methods were inefficient. Arkwright's Nottingham Mill burnt down in 1781, but despite this and other conflagrations, factories continued to be erected in this fashion. Although it possessed immensely strong stone walls and high windows to make it impenetrable to rioting hand-loom weavers, the five-storey mill at Cromford, erected in 1785, did not have a fireproof internal structure.[136] Some attempt to

minimize risks had been made at Belper Round Mill (*c*.1803–13) where division of this massive stone mill into eight segments with a central overseer was possibly influenced by the mill's use for scutching, a process much prone to fire, as it would allow any outbreak to be quickly sealed off. Another prison-like building, the mill was said to have owed much to Jeremy Bentham's

26 An Arkwright mill at Cromford; erected in 1785, it was designed to resist the attacks of hand-loom weavers angered by the loss of employment.

Panopticon (a six-storey circular penitentiary with a central observation post, publicized in 1791), designed on principles which, he argued, could be applied to factories, asylums, hospitals or schools.

However, the continued destruction of mills by fire encouraged the search for a safer method of construction. It was Jedediah Strutt (1726–97), a former partner of Arkwright and with him responsible for the construction of mills at Cromford, who inspired the building of factories from non-combustible materials. Erected in 1792–3 at Derby,[137] and actually designed by his son William Strutt (1756–1830), this six-storey calico mill was made fire-resistant by the use of cruciform cast-iron columns supporting plaster-covered timber beams and brick arches overlaid with sand and tiles.[138] The Milford Warehouse (1792–3), also by William Strutt, a four-storey building constructed at the same time, followed an identical structural system.[139] Success there encouraged him to erect Belper West Mill (1793–5), a six-storey and larger version of the Derby prototype. This was presumably the 'principal' mill (200 ft long and 30 ft wide) described by the Revd Davies in 1811,[140] which was powered by three waterwheels.

Nevertheless, the first iron-framed building was not, as the eminent engineer William Fairbairn believed, Philips and Lee's Salford Twist Mill (1799–1801),[141] a claim reiterated in *The Builder*,[142] nor at Belper, but had been the work of Charles Bage (1752–1822), a wine merchant with a passion for engineering who had been in regular contact with William Strutt. In 1796 he had designed a flax-spinning mill for Thomas and Benjamin Benyon at Shrewsbury.[143] Completed in the following year, its cast-iron columns and beams supported brick arches made for a comparatively strong, fireproof structure, which, in turn, encouraged a second version in Meadow Lane, Leeds (for Marshall, Benyon and Bage) in c.1804.[144] Charles Bage may also have assisted George A. Lee (1761–1826) in the design of the cast-iron beams used in the third example, the Salford Twist Mill.[145] There the adoption of hollow cast-iron columns, in place of the earlier cruciform section, allowed Lee to

steam-heat his factories, though the first recorded case of this innovation was Dale & McIntosh's Speyside Cotton Works of 1799.[146] The Twist Mill probably influenced the design of the seven-storey Houldsworth Mill, Glasgow, completed in 1803, which employed both inverted T-section beams and cylindrical cast-iron columns.[147] It played a substantial role in the planning of Armley Mill, Leeds, which was rebuilt in 1805 following a fire that destroyed its eighteenth-century predecessor.[148] The new building, erected by Benjamin Gott, a close friend of Lee, had cylindrical columns that could be used for steam heating. North Mill, Belper (1803–4), also by William Strutt, erected to replace the 1786 original burnt down in 1803, incorporated cast-iron beams on Bage's advice, its cast-iron roof truss being one of the earliest examples of its type.[149] Architecturally highly restrained, this brick five-storey mill was enlivened by a small semicircular window in its gable and the limited use of stone for the ground floor, string courses, sills and cornice.

Although these mills have rightly attracted much comment in view of their seminal structural advances, their external appearance would not justify such attention in an architectural study. Of critical importance in the development of construction techniques, and designed by men who would be categorized primarily as engineers, it was understandable that these buildings did not pioneer innovations in style. Belper West Mill, for instance, though marked by its size and the regularity of its many windows, was enlivened merely by the provision of a simple bell cupola (the bell being used to mark periods of work), which could scarcely be regarded as a major architectural feature. Externally, Bage's Shrewsbury Mill of 1796–7 seems to have been a simple brick box pierced at regular intervals by identical windows, while his Leeds Mill principally owed its distinction to the novel structural framework, as was only to be expected from a man whose genius and enthusiasm focused on engineering problems. The Milford Warehouse appears not to have possessed any decoration, and the absence of windows in its lower floors, for security reasons, gave it a gaol-like appearance.[150] Although these iron-framed buildings failed to produce fundamental change in the outward appearance of factories, they stood at the head of a structural revolution that in the 1850s was to be exploited by the Crystal Palace and in the era of steel and concrete was to permit the skyscraper. Further, despite the examples produced by Bage, and later advanced by Fairbairn with Hodgkinson, many mills and warehouses continued to be erected using timber without any attempt to make them fireproof. A ferrous structure was invariably more expensive, more complex in building and had a higher dead-load on the floor beams. It was employed where particularly inflammable atmospheres prevailed, such as those produced by cotton and flax. In Yorkshire, iron frameworks never attained the popularity achieved in Lancashire and mills continued to be built in the wool and worsted districts with cast-iron columns and timber floors.

Summary

These fifty or so years saw the beginnings of a fundamental transformation which was to affect many people's places of employment. For the Industrial Revolution, as it unfolded in Britain, resulted in the progressive replacement of small workshops, water-powered textile mills, forges and primitive foundries by substantial factories and ironworks. Yet the speed of this change should not be exaggerated, nor the continuity ignored. 'The use of water for motive power by means of water-wheels', argued Thwaite:

> was very general at this epoch ... and the choice of a site for a manufactory was greatly influenced by the presence of a good stream of water. The manufacturers had their homes and weaving appliances under one roof ... As the products of the looms were generally destined for local requirements, the buildings, at once workshops and dwellings, were scattered over farming districts, their number proportionate to the agricultural population. The buildings were ordinarily constructed of uncoursed rubble loosely walled ... the windows and doors being mostly of the rudest description.[151]

Initially entrepreneurs employed builders or millwrights, rather than architects, to design their new plant. Using local materials and tending to follow vernacular tradition, they introduced Palladian features (a Venetian window or cupola) when these could be afforded or might perform a useful role. It was only in the case of a particular site (close to the City of London) or elevated role (the Royal Arsenal) that industrial buildings received special attention. As mill-owners, who commonly started life in a humble way with little formal education, achieved wealth, social standing and came themselves to inhabit country houses, so in time they began to consider the architecture of their factories. Hence, a few mills and foundries were constructed towards the end of the eighteenth century either directly by an architect or with his assistance: Etruria, Bean Ing Mill and Soho Manufactory. For most, therefore, the entrepreneur had supervised, or at least assisted with, the construction, hiring craftsmen to satisfy the specific demands of his building. Neighbours learned from each other, and accordingly the smaller mills within regions of common materials often possessed a marked similarity in appearance and structural techniques.

In a period when entrepreneurs and mill designers were largely preoccupied by structural questions and organizing a building's practical operation (the ways in which new technology could be fitted into compact boxes and powered by waterwheels or beam engines), it was scarcely surprising that architecture occupied a low priority. The width of these early factories was often determined not by any calculations of proportion to satisfy the eye but by the dimensions of the machines and the desirability of keeping them as close to the drive shafting as possible, whilst the insertion of so many windows of similar size resulted from the need to have plentiful natural light rather than from notions of Palladian order and symmetry.[152] A further reason why architectural questions remained secondary during this pioneering phase was the reluctance on the part of many entrepreneurs to build large-scale mills. The finite power of waterwheels to work machinery, even when supplemented by beam engines, in part determined these decisions. But they also reflected capital constraints and considerable delays between the decision to build and the realization of investments,[153] which meant that entrepreneurs could not afford to spend extravagantly on an architect's fee or for the extra materials and craftsmen that his plans might require. The Peels, for instance, who owned the biggest cotton-spinning firm of the 1790s, spread their output among 23 mills centred on Blackburn, Bury, Bolton, Burton-upon-Trent and Tamworth, rather than concentrate production in a few mammoth factories.[154] Belper, Milford and Cromford all grew in a similar manner, with rising demand being satisfied by the duplication of plant.

Finally, the factory was an unusual expression of industrialization during this pioneering phase. Even in the middle of the nineteenth century the majority of English industrial workers were employed in manufacturing enterprises of less than fifty. Artists, such as Joseph Wright of Derby (1734-97), whose patrons included Arkwright and Strutt, depicted large mills like Cromford,[155] not because they considered them architecturally distinguished subjects, but for their rarity. The size, awesome aspect and novelty of these buildings were the qualities that attracted notice. Thus the second half of the eighteenth century laid the foundations for industrial architecture when it fostered the growth of new building types and witnessed their hesitant entry into the world of classical design.

Notes

1 Jennifer Tann, *Industrial Archaeology, Gloucestershire Woollen Mills*, Newton Abbot (1967), pp. 141-2.

2 John Winter, *Industrial Architecture, A Survey of Factory Building*, London (1970), pp. 12-14.

3 D.C. Coleman, *Courtaulds, an Economic and Social History*, Vol. 1, Oxford (1969), pp. 70-1; J.M. Richards, *The Functional Tradition in Early Industrial Buildings*, London (1958), p. 110.

4 Brian Bracegirdle, *The Archaeology of the Industrial Revolution*, London (1973), plate 26(a), p. 93.

5 C.T.G. Boucher, *James Brindley, Engineer 1716-1772*, Norwich (1968), p. 4.

6 F.D. Klingender, *Art and the Industrial Revolution*, London (1968), p. 9.

7 Sir William Fairbairn, *Useful Information for Engineers*, London (1860), p. 212; Samuel Smiles, *Industrial Biography*, London (1863), pp. 313-14.

8 Owen Ashmore, *The Industrial Archaeology of Lancashire*, Newton Abbot (1969), p. 39; *Higher Mill, Helmshore, An 18th-Century Woollen Fulling Mill* (Museum Publication).

9 *VCHE*, Vol. 6, London (1973), p. 93; E.M. Gardner, *The Three Mills, Bromley by Bow*, London (1957), pp. 7-8.

10 *East London Papers*, Vol. 12, No. 2 (1969), Denis Smith, 'Industrial Archaeology of the Lower Lea Valley', pp. 104-5; Keith Falconer, *Guide to England's Industrial Heritage*, London (1980), p. 145.

11 Daniel Defoe, *A Tour through the Whole Island of Great Britain*, London (1724-26), Harmondsworth (1971), p. 458; Winter, *op. cit.*, pp. 24-5.

12 Jennifer Tann, *The Development of the Factory*, London (1970), pp. 4, 7; W. English, *The Textile Industry*, London (1969), pp. 22, 25.

13 It remained a silk mill until *c.*1890 when part collapsed and in 1910 it was further damaged after a fire; only the foundations and part of the tower now survive, incorporated within Derby's Industrial Museum.

14 P. Barlow, *Treatise of Manufactures*, London (1836), p. 709; Richard L. Hills, *Power in the Industrial Revolution*, Manchester (1970), p. 29.

15 W. Hutton, *The History of Derby*, London (1817), p. 161; S.D. Chapman, *The Cotton Industry in the Industrial Revolution*, London (1972), pp. 14-15.

16 David M. Smith, *The Industrial Archaeology of the East Midlands*, Newton Abbot (1965), pp. 54-5.

17 William Bray, *Sketch of a Tour into Derbyshire and Yorkshire*, London (1783), p. 107.

18 Chapman, *Cotton Industry, op. cit.*, p. 15.

19 Stanley D. Chapman, *The Early Factory Masters*, Newton Abbot (1967), p. 35.

20 Chapman, *Cotton Industry, op. cit.*, p. 17; William Felkin, *A History of the Machine-Wrought Hosiery and Lace Manufactures*, London (1867), p. 95.

21 John Blackner, *The History of Nottingham, Embracing its Antiquities, Trade and Manufactures*, Nottingham (1815), p. 247.

22 H.M. Colvin, *A Biographical Dictionary of English Architects 1660–1840*, London (1954), pp. 575–6.

23 Bolton Library ref. B725.4[B], John F. Bradley, 'The Evolution of the Cotton Mill in Bolton' (typescript, n.d.), p. 3.

24 Chapman, *Early Factory Masters, op. cit.*, pp. 48, 51.

25 Edward Baines Junior, *History of the Cotton Manufacture in Great Britain*, London (1835), p. 184.

26 Chapman, *Early Factory Masters, op. cit.*, pp. 35–6.

27 W.B. Crump and Gertrude Ghorbal, *History of the Huddersfield Woollen Industry*, Huddersfield (1935), pp. 50–3, 63.

28 John Summerson, *Georgian London*, Harmondsworth (1962), pp. 324–5.

29 Henry-Russell Hitchcock, *Early Victorian Architecture in Britain*, Vol. I, Yale (1954), p. 404.

30 Colvin, *op. cit.*, pp. 436–43.

31 John Prest, *The Industrial Revolution in Coventry*, Oxford (1960), pp. 96, 99, 101; *VCHL*, Vol. IV, London (1958), pp. 306–8.

32 See p. 100.

33 Mary Rose, *The Gregs of Styal*, Quarry Bank (1978), p. 8.

34 Bracegirdle, *op. cit.*, J. Tann, 'Building for Industry', pp. 168, 177.

35 Ken Powell, *Pennine Mill Trail* (Save Britain's Heritage), p. 8.

36 See pp. 95, 97, 195, respectively.

37 John Coolidge, *Mill and Mansion, A Study of Architecture and Society in Lowell, Massachusetts 1820–1865*, New York (1942), p. 99.

38 Henry-Russell Hitchcock, *Rhode Island Architecture*, Providence (1939), p. 39.

39 Robert T. Clough, *The Lead Smelting Mills of the Yorkshire Dales*, Leeds (1962).

40 *Ibid.*, pp. 143, 136–7, 126, 63–4.

41 O.F.G. Hogg, *The Royal Arsenal, Its Background, Origin and Subsequent History*, Vol. I, Oxford (1963), pp. 254, 257–8.

42 N. Pevsner, *BoE, London, Volume One*, Harmondsworth (1952), p. 453.

43 Hogg, *op. cit.*, p. 255.

44 *Ibid.*, p. 260.

45 H.J. Dyos and M. Wolff, *The Victorian City*, Vol. 2, London (1973), Nicholas Taylor, 'The Awful Sublimity of the Victorian City', p. 436.

46 *VCHE*, Vol. 2, London (1907), pp. 407, 417.

47 *Essex Review*, Vol. XX (1911), H.W. Lever, 'Thomas Fryre and Bow China', pp. 2–4; F. Hurlbutt, *Bow Porcelain*, London (1926), pp. 1–3; *Bow Porcelain 1744–1776*, British Museum (1959), p. 13.

48 Colvin, *op. cit.*, p. 442.

49 A later example of an architect-designed barn was at Solihull (1798), by Sir John Soane, see p. 69.

50 Defoe, *op. cit.*, p. 123.

51 Richards, *Functional Tradition, op. cit.*, p. 58.

52 William Fairbairn, *Treatise on Mills and Millwork*, Vol. II, London (1865), p. 110.

53 Vitruvius, *The Ten Books on Architecture*, translated by M.H. Morgan, New York (1960), p. 182.

54 William Chambers, *A Treatise on Civil Architecture*, London (1759), p. 14.

55 John Summerson, *Architecture in Britain 1530–1830*, Harmondsworth (1977), pp. 318–19, 363–4.

56 William Halfpenny, *Practical Architecture, or a sure guide to the true working according to the rules of that science: representing the five orders*, London (1730).

57 John Martin Robinson, *The Wyatts, An Architectural Dynasty*, Oxford (1979), pp. 44–6; A.W. Skempton, *Architectural History*, Vol. 14 (1971), 'Samuel Wyatt and the Albion Mill', pp. 53–73.

58 *The New London Magazine*, Vol. VI, July 1790, p. 329.

59 BRL, Boulton & Watt Collection, Portfolio 152, Plans of the various storeys, 1786.

60 Erich Roll, *An Early Experiment in Industrial Organization, being a history of the firm of Boulton & Watt, 1755–1805*, London (1930), p. 110.

61 Robinson, *op. cit.*, p. 52.

62 R.S. Fitton and A.P. Wadsworth, *The Strutts and the Arkwrights 1758–1830, A Study of the Early Factory System*, Manchester (1958), pp. 64–5.

63 Chapman, *Early Factory Masters, op. cit.*, p. 64.

64 Klingender, *op. cit.*, p. 49, plate 28.

65 Bray, *Sketch of a Tour, op. cit.*, p. 119.

66 Tann, *Development of the Factory, op. cit.*, p. 153.

67 *Pennine Mill Trail, op. cit.*, p. 17.

68 Chapman, *Early Factory Masters, op. cit.*, pp. 94–5; Frank Nixon, *The Industrial Archaeology of Derbyshire*, Newton Abbot (1969), p. 243.

69 Derek Linstrum, *West Yorkshire, Architects and Architecture*, London (1978), pp. 290–1.

70 D.T. Jenkins, *The West Riding Wool Textile Industry 1770–1835, A Study of Fixed Capital Formation*, Edington (1975), pp. 56–8.

71 Repton's *Red Book*, quoted from *ibid.*, p. 292.

72 Zachariah Allen, *The Practical Tourist, or Sketches of the State of the Useful Arts, and of Society*, Vol. I, Providence (1832), p. 195.

73 Edward Baines, *History, Directory & Gazetteer of the County of York*, Vol. I, Leeds (1822), p. 30.

74 Bruce Allsopp and Ursula Clark, *Historic Architecture of Northumberland and Newcastle upon Tyne*, London (1977), p. 70.

75 John Butt, *The Industrial Archaeology of Scotland*, Newton Abbot (1967), pp. 69–70; J. Butt, I. Donnachie and J.R. Hume, *Robert Owen and New Lanark*, Scotland (1978) p. 5.

76 J. Donnachie, J. Hume and M. Moss, *Historic Industrial Scenes, Scotland*, Hartington, Buxton (1977), plate 30.

77 Butt, *op. cit.*, pp. 67–8; John R. Hume, *The Industrial Archaeology of Scotland, 2, The Highlands and Islands*, London (1977), pp. 270–1.

78 GMRO, DX, *Plan of an Estate in the Townships of Mellor and Marple in the Counties of Derby and Chester Allotted for Sale, 1867, Lot 1*; Tann, *Development of the Factory, op. cit.*, pp. 154–5; Nixon, *Derbyshire, op. cit.*, pp. 194–5, 268.

79 *Life of Robert Owen*, p. 55; quoted from George Unwin, *Samuel Oldknow and the Arkwrights, The Industrial Revolution at Stockport and Marple*, Manchester (1924), p. 124.

80 *Ibid., Enlarged Plan of Mellor Mill.*

81 *Derbyshire Archaeological Journal*, Vol. XC (1970), M.H. Mackenzie, 'Cressbrook Mill 1810–1835', pp. 60–1.

82 *Derbyshire Archaeological Journal*, Vol. LXXXVIII (1968), M.H. Mackenzie, 'Cressbrook and Litton Mills 1779–1835', p. 4.

83 Chapman, *Early Factory Masters, op. cit.*, p. 59.

84 LRO, DDX 1350 Whittaker Family Records, Broadclough Mill, Plan 1791.

85 BRL, Boulton & Watt Collection, Portfolio 138, Elevations and Plans, 1796; John Nussey, *Smithies Mill, Birstall*, Chester (1984), pp. 6–9.

86 BRL, Boulton & Watt Collection, Portfolio 3, Elevations and Plans, 1784.

87 Hurford Janes, *The Red Barrel, A History of Watney Mann*, London (1963), pp. 50–4; P. Mathias, *The Brewing Industry in England 1700–1830*, Cambridge (1959), pp. 38–40.

88 Fairbairn, *Treatise on Mills, op. cit.*, Vol. II (1865), p. 113–14.

89 Bracegirdle, *op. cit.*, p. 177.

90 Chapman, *Early Factory Masters, op. cit.*, p. 87, plates 5 and 6.

91 John Banks, *A Treatise on Mills*, London (1795), pp. xv–xxiv, for example, concentrated on the mechanical and scientific knowledge relevant to their operation, the list of subscribers mostly coming from the textile districts of Northern England.

92 Jenkins, *West Riding Wool Textile Industry, op. cit.*, p. 49.

93 *Ibid.*, pp. 49–50; W.D. Shepherd, 'Early Industrial Buildings 1700–1850', RIBA Thesis (1950).

94 Revd Stebbing Shaw, *The History and Antiquities of Staffordshire*, Vol. II, London (1801), pp. 117–18; Tann, *Development of the Factory, op. cit.*, pp. 77, 153–4; Robinson, *op. cit.*, p. 19, plate 9.

95 BRL, Tew MSS, William Wyatt II to Mathew Boulton, 16 September 1763; 22 January 1766.

96 Shaw, *History of Staffordshire, op. cit.*

97 Summerson, *op. cit.*, p. 346.

98 Samuel Timmins (Editor), *Birmingham and the Midland Hardware District*, London (1866), p. 218; Robinson, *op. cit.*, pp. 19–21.

99 *Abbeydale Industrial Hamlet*, Sheffield (1981).

100 N. Pevsner, *BoE, Derbyshire*, Harmondsworth (1978), p. 147.

101 N. Pevsner and Alexandra Wedgwood, *BoE, Warwickshire*, Harmondsworth (1966), pp. 132–3.

102 W.K.V. Gale, *Historic Industrial Scenes, Iron and Steel*, Hartington (1977), pp. 19–20.

103 Edward Baines, *History, Directory ... of the County of Lancaster*, Vol. 2, Liverpool (1825), p. 547.

104 Malcolm I. Nixon, 'The Emergence of the Factory System in the Staffordshire Pottery Industry' (Ph.D., Aston, 1976), p. 20.

105 *Ibid.*, p. 27.

106 E. Saunders, *Country Life*, 9 November 1892, 'An Eighteenth Century Provincial Architect, Joseph Pickford of Derby'; he was also involved in the design of Etruria Hall, p. 1209.

107 *Building News*, Vol. XIII, 2 November 1866, p. 728; Tann, *Development of the Factory, op. cit.*, p. 11; Fred Brook, *The Industrial Archaeology of the British Isles, 1, The West Midlands*, London (1977), p. 127.

108 G.W. Rhead and F.A. Rhead, *Staffordshire Pots and Potteries*, London (1906), pp. 208-9.

109 *VCHS*, Vol. 8, London (1963), p. 100.

110 John Thomas, *The Rise of the Staffordshire Potteries* [n.d.], p. 68.

111 Nixon, *op. cit.*, pp. 162, 163.

112 Tann, *Development of the Factory, op. cit.*, p. 154.

113 Brook, *op. cit.*, p. 125; *VCHS*, Vol. 8, p. 239.

114 *VCHS*, Vol. 8, pp. 135-6.

115 Brook, *op. cit.*, p. 131; *VCHS*, Vol. 8, p. 239.

116 Nixon, *op cit.*, p. 192.

117 J.G. Kohl, *Ireland, Scotland and England*, London (1844), p. 21.

118 Nixon, *op. cit.*, pp. 194-5.

119 *VCHS*, Vol. 8, p. 168; *Staffordshire Advertiser*, No. 55, 2 June 1849.

120 Arnold Bennett, *Anna of the Five Towns*, London (1902), Harmondsworth (1936), p. 48.

121 *TLCAS*, Vol. 71 for 1961, Manchester (1963), V.I. Tomlinson, 'Early Warehouses on Manchester Waterways', pp. 136, 149.

122 *TLCAS*, Vol. LXV for 1955, Manchester (1956), Herbert Clegg, 'The Third Duke of Bridgewater's Canal Works in Manchester', p. 99.

123 Clegg, *op. cit.*, p. 100; Tomlinson, *op. cit.*, p. 150.

124 *AR*, Vol. CXXII, No. 726, July 1957, J.M. Richards, 'The Functional Tradition', p. 57.

125 W.H. Pyne, *Lancashire Illustrated*, London

(1831), p. 87; N. Ritchie-Noakes, *Liverpool's Historic Waterfront*, London HMSO (1984), pp. 31, 140-5.

126 David Alderton and John Booker, *The Batsford Guide to the Industrial Archaeology of East Anglia*, London (1980), p. 178.

127 R.S. Fitzgerald, *Liverpool Road Station, Manchester*, Manchester (1980), pp. 33, 60.

128 *Cutler Street Warehouses, Save Pamphlet*, Clive Aslet, 'The Architecture'; W. Papworth, *Dictionary of Architecture*, Vol. IV, 'J', p. 30; GLC, 2031/11 02 and 04 Blocks; 2031/10 01, 02, 04 Buildings; 2031/5 'N' Warehouse, Elevation, 1792.

129 GLC, Tower Hamlets Box, No. 5.

130 GLC, 2885/3 Drawing of Free Trade Wharf warehouses.

131 GLC, Tower Hamlets Box, No. 3; John Pudney, *London's Docks*, London (1975), pp. 38-40; Summerson, *Georgian London, op. cit.*, p. 260.

132 Charles Hadfield and A.W. Skempton, *William Jessop, Engineer*, Newton Abbot (1979), pp. 205-7.

133 *B*, Vol. XXI, No. 1078, 3 October 1863, p. 701; *AR*, Vol. 118, September 1955, S.H. Kessels, 'A Great Georgian Warehouse', p. 191; *B*, Vol. XIV, No. 701, 12 July 1856, Obituary, p. 386; Papworth, *Dictionary, op. cit.*, Vol. III, 'G', p. 110.

134 Edward Sargent's RIBA dissertation; Colvin, *op. cit.*, pp. 251-2.

135 GLC, 2185/1 Drawing of No. 1 Warehouse, West India Dock.

136 Fitton and Wadsworth, *op. cit.*, p. 221.

137 *AR*, Vol. CXXXI, March 1962, A.W. Skempton and H.R. Johnson, 'The First Iron Frames', p. 176; Felkin, *op. cit.*, pp. 96-7; see also ICOMOS, *Eisen Architektur, The Role of Iron in the Historic Architecture of the First Half of the Nineteenth Century*, Mainz (1979), R.S. Fitzgerald, 'Technological Aspects of Early English Iron Architecture', pp. 270 ff.

138 Fitton and Wadsworth, *op. cit.*, pp. 200-201; *AR*, Vol. CVII, April 1950, Turpin Bannister, 'The First Iron-Framed Buildings', p. 236.

139 Skempton and Johnson, *op. cit.*, pp. 177-8.

140 Revd D.P. Davies, *A New Historical and Descriptive View of Derbyshire*, Belper (1811), p. 346.

141 William Fairbairn, *On the Application of Cast and Wrought Iron to Building Purposes*, London (1854), pp. 3, 5.

142 *B*, Vol. 3, No. CII, 18 January 1845 p. 35.

143 Bannister, *op. cit.* pp. 178–9; W.G. Rimmer, *Marshalls of Leeds Flax Spinners 1788–1886*, Cambridge (1960), p. 54; Rimmer, *Transactions of the Shropshire Archaeological Society*, Vol. LVI (1959), 'The Castle Foregate Flax Mill'.

144 Skempton and Johnson, *op. cit.*, p. 243.

145 *AR*, Vol. CXLV, February 1969, A.J. Pacey, 'Earliest Cast-Iron Beams', p. 140; BRL, Boulton & Watt Collection, Portfolio 242.

146 Robertson Buchanan, *An Essay on the Warming of Mills and Other Buildings by Steam*, Glasgow (1807), p. 8.

147 *Satanic Mills*, R.S. Fitzgerald, 'Structural Development', p. 61.

148 *Ibid.; Eisen Architektur, op. cit.*, pp. 273–4.

149 Bannister, *op. cit.*, p. 186.

150 Fitton and Wadsworth, *op cit.*, Fig. 3.

151 B.H. Thwaite, *Our Factories, Workshops, and Warehouses, Their Sanitary and Fire-Resisting Arrangements*, London (1882), pp. 4–5.

152 Tann, *Development of the Factory, op. cit.*, p. 149.

153 S.D. Chapman, *The Cotton Industry in the Industrial Revolution*, London (1972), p. 37.

154 *Ibid.*, p. 29.

155 Benedict Nicolson, *Joseph Wright of Derby, Painter of Light*, Vol. 1, London (1968), p. 265; Vol. 11, pp. 155, 203–4, 209; Klingender, *op. cit.*, plate 28, p. 179.

THREE

Consolidation and growth
1800–1835

The Macclesfield Bridge, erected in 1815–16 to carry a park road over the Regent's Canal, then a major waterway linking Paddington and the Grand Junction Canal with the rapidly rising docklands of East London, exhibited a number of features typical of industrial architecture during this period. Its ten Greek Doric columns cast in iron at Coalbrookdale, one of England's seminal ironworks, supported a restrained but elegant brick arch enlivened by symmetrical circular openings. Although James Elmes (1782–1862) has been suggested as the architect,[1] it seems to have been designed by the canal company's engineer James Morgan, who was also responsible for the eastern portal of the Islington Tunnel.[2] The naming of the bridge was a tribute to the Earl of Macclesfield, and his coat-of-arms, cast in iron, were to decorate the railings on each side.[3] Using the vital elements of the Industrial Revolution, the Macclesfield Bridge[4] illustrated the popularity of the Greek Revival and the degree to which companies were prepared to satisfy the demands of fashion, while the canal which it spanned functioned as one of the transport improvements that continued economic growth demanded.

Mills

This period saw builders, engineers and, more rarely, architects constructing mills according to the structural and architectural traditions that had developed in the latter part of the eighteenth century. What did change was the mills' size and situation. The application of increasingly reliable and powerful steam engines in place of waterwheels meant that factories no longer needed to be sited by the fast-flowing rivers which had often confined them to areas remote from established centres of population.[5] As Sir Robert Peel reported to the Factory Acts Committee of Inquiry:

> large buildings are now erected, not only as formerly on the banks of streams, but in the midst of populous towns; and instead of parish apprentices being sought after, the surrounding poor are preferred . . .[6]

The work of James Watt on rotative motion was the technical key that had made this all possible. Until this breakthrough steam had been used to enhance water power rather than supersede it, beam engines being installed, for example, at Arkwright's mill, Cromford in 1780 to maintain supplies to the waterwheels. By applying steam alternately above and below the piston to produce a power stroke in both directions, Watt succeeded during 1781–2 in making his engine double-acting. In 1782 he took a patent on the 'sun and planet' motion which allowed rotative drive. Two years later, however, he patented the real breakthrough – parallel motion. The case was demonstrated in March 1786 at Albion Mill, where corn-grinding machinery was directly driven by steam power.[7] Wyatt, a friend of Boulton and Watt, had tried to interest various bodies such as the Victualling Office in the invention, but finding no response decided to build his own mill at the cost of £16,770 to establish the validity of his case.[8]

Once the initial capital cost of constructing

and equipping a mill[9] had been overcome, economies of scale and savings in power could be won by entrepreneurs from having as many processes as possible under one roof. This, in turn, stimulated innovation in each of the manufacturing processes to retain a co-ordinated flow throughout the factory. Hence, by 1823 Richard Guest could argue convincingly that:

the increasing number of steam looms is certain proof of their superiority over the hand looms ... It is a curious circumstance, that, when the cotton manufacture was in its infancy, all operations, from the dressing of the raw material to its being finally turned out in the state of cloth, were completed under the roof in the weaver's cottage. The course of improved manufacture which followed, was to spin the yarn in factories and to weave it in cottages. At the present time, when the manufacture has attained a mature growth, all the operations with vastly increased means and more complex contrivances, are again performed in a single building.... Those vast brick edifices in the vicinity of all the great manufacturing towns in the south of Lancashire, towering to the height of seventy or eighty feet, which strike the attention and excite the curiosity of the traveller, now perform labours which formerly employed whole villages. In the steam loom factories, the cotton is carded, roved, spun and woven into cloth ...[10]

On the same theme, Edward Baines observed in 1824 that 'each of the steam loom mills forms a complete manufacturing colony, in which every process from the picking the raw cotton to its conversion into cloth is performed; and on a scale so large that there is now accomplished in one single building as much work as would in the last age have employed an entire district'.[11] The number of worsted mills in Yorkshire rose from 54 in 1815 to 204 by 1835, their individual size probably being increased from the 1820s by the incorporation of power-loom weaving, so that those in 1835 employed on average 82 workers and used an average of 19 horse power.[12]

So long as demand for products rose, the owner of means saw sound financial reasons for increasing the size of his factory, limits being imposed by capital constraints, the ability of engines to work the machinery, transport networks to shift its goods, and the availability of skilled workers. The character of these restraints encouraged the erection of mills in major towns where communications were better, wealth concentrated and pools of labour at hand. This movement, as well as the growth in size of individual factories, did not escape the notice of contemporaries, Alexander Abram remarking of Blackburn that

the absorption of this once scattered manufacture into the factories involved a corresponding concentration of labour in the towns, and the migration of the weaving peasantry from the rural upland towns into the towns and villages of the valleys.[13]

At Blackburn, Butterworth added, 'in 1816 there was only one cotton mill in the town, and eight in the parish ... in 1838 the number of manufactories or concerns was 44, employing 10,460 hands'.[14] Once there, on show to the general public, some mill-owners must have felt the need to add an architectural gloss to their factories to advertise or raise the status of their businesses.

In America, too, this pattern of concentration could be observed. The country's first integrated textile concern (embracing all the processes from raw material to finished product) was erected by the Boston Manufacturing Co. at Waltham, their No. 1 Mill (1814–16) being able to card, spin and weave cloth. The inspiration of F.C. Lowell (1775–1817), who had surreptitiously toured England in order to discover the secrets of the power loom, it allowed co-ordinated production and resulted in economies of scale.[15] Externally bearing witness to the British practice, the buildings appeared as diluted Palladian architecture in the mould of Cressbrook or Matlock Mills. Labour-saving machinery, driven by steam power, encouraged the funding of substantial masonry mills in the United States during the 1820s. As they were constructed to create whole new settlements such as Lowell, Lawrence and Holyoke in Massachusetts or Manchester, New Hampshire, there was an increasing tendency for the simplicity and restraint of Palladian detail to be replaced by monumental buildings that reflected the various architectural movements sweeping through Europe. The Governor Harris Mill (1851), Harris, West Warwick, had a Greek Revival bell tower,[16] the Print Works (1853), Manchester, exhibited an Italianate staircase tower and deep corbelled frieze,[17] whilst Gothic influenced the Talbot Mill, North Billerica, built *c.* 1857, and Linwood Mill (1870), near Whitinsville, Massachusetts, took the Second Empire style for its model.[18] Nevertheless, as in Lancashire and Yorkshire, these features remained ornamental, intended to attract notice or outshine a neighbour, while the bulk of the mill remained a block whose shape and fenestration was determined by practical considerations of manufacture and cost.[19]

In Britain, Rykneld Mills may be quoted as an example of the way in which mills became larger under the influence of steam power. Distinguished by the scale and unrelieved monotony of its design, the factory comprised seven- and five-storey blocks (*c.* 1823) in Bridge Street, Derby.[20] These brick, fireproof buildings (possibly the silk-weaving and trimming premises erected by Messrs Peet and Thomas Bridgett & Co.) exhibited a sublimity and power which derived from their vastness and the lack of ornament or variation.

Notions of the sublime in architecture had, in fact, been analysed during the eighteenth century by Edmund Burke, whose *Philosophical Enquiry into the Origin of our Ideas of the Sublime and Beautiful* (1757) categorized the various qualities needed to produce this terror. Amongst those he listed were 'obscurity, power, privation, vastness, infinity, succession, uniformity, magnitude', and 'a quick transition from light to darkness'.[21] Mills and warehouses, many storeys high and of great length, blackened by smoke, pierced by regular rows of rectangular windows, fulfilled many of the demands of the sublime. Further, 'ancient heathen temples, which were generally oblong forms with a range of uniform pillars on every side', that Burke had selected to illustrate the nature of 'succession and uniformity', could on occasion serve as the basis for a factory - Marshalls' Mill, Leeds. Thus the sublime ranked alongside the 'Beautiful' (which

Burke argued was best represented by classical building), and the 'Picturesque', commonly manifested by Gothic structures. This first interpretation, as the following chapters will show, found a considerable following among industrial architects.

A building whose sublimity - emphasized by its awesome size, virtual absence of decoration, universal use of tough red brick and regular arrangement of windows - must have frightened its youngest employees was Sedgewick Mill (1818-20), Union Street, Ancoats. (Union Street is now called Redhill Street and the building is referred to as Union Mill.) Pyne, observing Messrs Murray & Co.'s and Messrs M'Connel & Kennedy's cotton factories, noted:

> In the external appearance of these buildings, we remark little else than their height. It is the interior which is most interesting. The hundreds of persons employed in them ... and the regularity of the process, strike a spectator with astonishment ...[22]

M'Connel & Kennedy had commissioned the mill in 1818 when James Lowe was engaged to erect an eight-storey, fireproof structure.[23] M'Connel & Kennedy were to supply all the materials for the building, while Lowe was to provide the equipment such as ladders and scaffolding. The active involvement of the owners in the mill's construction was by no means uncommon; during the erection of their 'Old Mill' (between September 1798 and January 1802 at a cost of £4,160) the spinners even had to supervise the provision of bricks.[24] An austere building, whose only decoration consisted of a bell cupola, it served as a smaller version of Sedgewick Mill.[25] A poem entitled 'The Cotton Mill', composed in 1821 by John Jones, one of their spinners, contained hyperbolic sentiments that must have been prompted by the offer of employment rather than the mill's exterior:

> Thy mills, like gorgeous palaces, arise
> And lift their useful turrets to the skies!
> See Kennedy's stupendous structure join'd
> To thine M'Connel - friends of human kind![26]

It was the sublimity and scale of these structures that most impressed the German architect, Karl Friedrich Schinkel (1781-1841), when he visited

27 Sedgewick Mill (1818–20), built for M'Connel & Kennedy, and Messrs Murrays' Mill, beside the Rochdale Canal in Ancoats, Manchester.

Ancoats in 1826, recalling of them that they stood 'as big as the Royal Palace in Berlin', but 'set up by a contractor alone without any architecture and made from red brick for the barest necessity only, make a rather gloomy impression'.[27]

Messrs Murray & Co.'s mill had been viewed in the early 1830s by an American, Zachariah Allen, who observed that the eight-storey brick buildings were arranged in the form of a hollow square entered through a great gate:

In the centre of this square is a sheet of navigable water bordered by a quay, on which canal boats may be seen discharging their freights of raw cotton and coals in the heart of the works, and receiving the packages of yarns. A tunnel or arched passage is made beneath the mill to connect this interior basin with one of the principal canals [the Rochdale] which traverses a considerable part of England.[28]

Practical considerations dictated the appearance of this 90,000-spindle mill, as in common with many Manchester manufactories 'nearly one half of the surface exterior walls' were composed of 'spacious glazed sashes, which are arranged in profusion to admit all the scanty light which a naturally hazy atmosphere, rendered still more obscure by smoke, will transmit'.[29] To increase Murrays' Mill's resistance to fire it had cast-iron columns and the timber ceilings were covered with sheet iron.[30]

John and Nathaniel Philip's linen tape mill (1823) at Upper Tean, Checkley was another substantial factory – four storeys and 27 bays in

28 Fishwick Mill (*c.* 1830), near Preston; the imposition and dominance of industry over agriculture depicted here reflected a measure of contemporary opinion.

length – driven by steam power. Its regular façade enlivened only by three symmetrically placed projecting bays (each three windows wide and topped by an angled pediment) fell within the established Palladian mould for mill design. The contractor had probably been James Trubshaw, a builder and engineer of Haywood, though George A. Lee had been consulted in the preliminary stages.[31]

Fishwick Mill (*c.* 1830) in Preston, built for the cotton spinners Swainson, Birley, Turton & Co., was another huge structure – 158 yards long, comprising some 44 bays, and seven storeys high[32] – whose scant adornment (a small cupola and a regular arrangement of windows) followed the accepted Palladian tradition. Ralph Orrell's Travis Brook (or Kingston) Mill (1834), Stockport, designed by William Fairbairn,[33] was noted for its structural innovations,

being an early example of the adoption of Hodgkinson's flanged beam in cast iron,[34] and may be quoted here as another large-scale town mill. This six-storey red-brick mill had two projecting wings (for storerooms, a counting house, rooms for winding the yarn on to bobbins and other miscellaneous tasks), with a central entrance reached between two small gatehouses.[35] The power looms were installed in the ground floor of the main block (later in the century they were housed in a separate shed to provide overhead lighting), the throstle-frames used for spinning the warp were placed in the first and second storeys, and the mules producing the weft in the fourth and fifth, whilst the preparation room, supplying material to those immediately above and below it, was on the third floor.[36] The attics were 'appropriated to the machines for warming and dressing the yarns for the power-looms'.[37] Not an inch of space had been wasted; even the staircase at the corner of each wing was horseshoe-shaped to accommodate a goods-lift in the central well.

Externally, adornment was limited to simple corner pilasters and restrained cornice. Unusually, the chimney, which had a classical base,

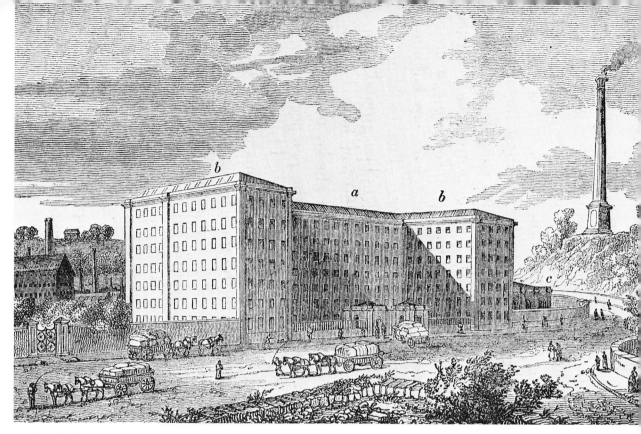

29 Orrell's Travis Brook Mill (1834), a mammoth factory with an attached engine house ('c') and a detached chimney.

into the hands of Messrs Fairbairn and Lillie, the eminent engineers of Manchester, it was too subject to the whims of the several individuals, often utterly ignorant of statics or dynamics, or the laws of equilibrium and impulse, who had capital to lay out in building a mill.[39]

was detached on a nearby knoll to increase the draught and reduce pollution, though its position gave it somewhat the air of a triumphal column. The overall treatment, which was much in keeping with the established pattern of industrial architecture (and conformed with the restraint and symmetry exhibited by the four-storey New Mill that Fairbairn had begun in 1825 for John Wood in Bradford),[38] was largely to be expected of a designer, like Bage, whose training and experience fell in the field of engineering, iron-founding and mechanics, rather than classical learning. Indeed, Andrew Ure, in his *Philosophy of Manufactures* (1835), which referred to the building as bearing comparison 'in respect of grandeur, elegance and simplicity with many aristocratic mansions', characterized mill architecture almost exclusively in engineering terms:

It had been ably begun by Mr Watt, but, till it fell

Sir William Fairbairn, born at Kelso in 1789,[40] had been apprenticed as a mechanical engineer to Percy Main Colliery, North Shields. After employment in London and at the Phoenix Ironworks, Dublin, Fairbairn moved to Manchester in 1813,[41] where in partnership with James Lillie, a former workmate, he set up as a consulting millwright. The breakthrough occurred in 1817, when having completed certain mechanical improvements to Messrs Adam and George Murray's mill, he was recommended to John Kennedy of M'Connel & Kennedy, then on the point of building a new mill. He recalled:

I laid down all his plans for the new mill to a scale, calculated the proportions and strength of the parts, fixed the position and arrangement of the different machines ... The erection of M'Connel and Kennedy's new mill was a great step in advance; we had now become engineers and millwrights of some consequence, and the complete and

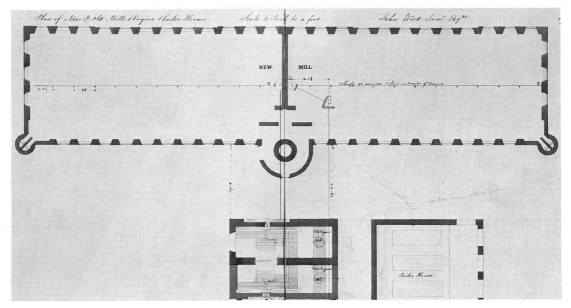

30 A plan prepared for Boulton & Watt of John Wood's New Mill (1825), Bradford. It was a fireproof building designed by William Fairbairn.

satisfactory execution of millwork established our characters as young men who were likely to introduce improvements in the construction of machinery, millwork and general mechanism of other branches of industry.[42]

Despite these assertions, it appears that Fairbairn and Lillie had not designed or completed the fabric of the mill. Construction was already well advanced by mid-1818 and the Manchester firm of J. & P. Sherratt cast the ironwork. The building in question was Sedgewick Mill, erected in 1818–20 under the superintendence of James Lowe (p. 54).[43] Yet following Kennedy's commission Fairbairn and Lillie's practice expanded. In 1829, they were employed by Henry and Edward Ashworth to convert a cotton manufactory and dyeworks at Egerton for spinning. One outside wall of the half-completed mill, which had been constructed three years before by the Swiss engineer Johann Georg Bodmer (1786–1864), was felled and the building doubled in width. In addition, Fairbairn and

Lillie installed a waterwheel 62 ft in diameter.[44] The architectural side of their practice even extended to include the design of Stalybridge Town Hall (1830–1).[45] About this time disagreement grew between the two partners, Fairbairn wishing to extend the scope of the business. Under the dissolution of the partnership in September 1832, Lillie was bought out and Fairbairn took sole control of the Canal Street Works in Ancoats.[46]

The business prospered and by the mid-1840s Fairbairn was employing over 2,000 workers. His career, including a knighthood in 1861 and a baronetcy in 1869, illustrated the growing importance of the consulting engineer and the range of tasks that such men performed. Fairbairn not only manufactured and fitted gearing for mills, he also constructed buildings, co-operated in experiments to improve the beams required for their structural framework, and combined this with the installation and design of waterwheels and boilers. In addition, he was a ship builder in iron, a bridge constructor, and also diverted part of his engineering workshops to the assembly of locomotives.

On completion, Shaddon Mill (1835–6), Junction Street, Carlisle, by the Manchester architect Richard Tattershall (c.1803–44), built for the firm of Peter Dixon, claimed to be the

31 Shaddon Mill (1835–6), Carlisle, built of local sandstone by the Manchester architect Richard Tattershall, and for a while the country's largest cotton mill.

largest cotton mill in England: 224 ft by 58 ft and 83 ft in height.[47] As if celebrating the factory's liberation from the restraints of water power, the red sandstone seven-storey block was identified by a tapered 300 ft chimney. Despite its size and the quality of the materials used, decoration remained at a bare minimum, the windows having flat frames and unmoulded architraves. The fireproof interior (iron columns and beams) had been the work of Fairbairn. Like Sedgewick Mill, Ancoats, or Fishwick Mill, Preston, Shaddon Mill was not situated in some

remote rural area, but to the south of old Carlisle at Denton Holme, a rising industrial suburb. Like the Strettons in Nottingham, Tattershall (born in Burnley and articled to William Hayley of Manchester, in whose office he remained until about 1830) was one of the first architects in general practice to seek industrial work. As well as designing churches, Unitarian chapels and public buildings, he built a number of cotton mills (including those for Samuel Brewis at Goulbourne) in Lancashire, and a warehouse behind the Royal Infirmary, Manchester, for George Faulkner.[48]

'A' Mill at Dean Clough, erected in 1840 for John Crossley & Sons, was not far from the centre of Halifax, and soon, by virtue of its size, encouraged the growth of an industrial community. Marked from a distance by a slender

32 'A' Mill at Dean Clough, Halifax. Built in 1840, it originally possessed a cupola over the central pediment and was six storeys with an attic.

chimney, the six-storey block (164 ft by 42 ft) operated on a scale that no waterwheel could manage. Outwardly it conformed to the dictates of restrained Palladianism. The angled pediment, topped by a bell cupola, was balanced by short projecting wings arranged ten bays from the central block and seven bays from the gabled ends. A similar building, 'B' Mill (209 ft by 42 ft), was erected in the following year.[49] Joseph Crossley (1813–68), son of the founder, who had entered the business at an early age, took a particular interest in building and machines and probably played a leading part in the design of 'A' and 'B' Mills.[50]

The Folly Hall complex of mills at Huddersfield may be taken to illustrate the strength of Palladian tradition and something of the social origins and attitudes of their designers, for No. 1 Mill (1825–7) and No. 2 Mill (1833) were both built by Joseph Kaye (1780–1858). Aged 19, he established a builder's business in Huddersfield and, though lacking formal education, decided to take on the role of architect as well.[51] The absence of an established professional body in what was a fast-growing industrial town presumably allowed him and others to win commissions for the design of churches, chapels and villas for prosperous entrepreneurs. Having constructed these two mills, Kaye did not sell them but let them to tenants, charging for floor space, power and, in a few cases, even the machinery.[52] Neither appears to have been fireproof, and the first was burnt down in 1844 and the second in 1856.[53] Both were rebuilt by Kaye, whose portrait (possibly by Samuel Howell, and the property of the Huddersfield Art Gallery) shows the new No. 1 Mill in the background. Situated on the Colne, the façade presented to the centre of Huddersfield seems to have received Kaye's greatest attention. For this elevation he employed dressed stone – he owned quarries at Sawood Marsh and Crosland Moor[54] – in a formal classical composition. A Venetian window was framed by a pedimented gable, while the cornice continued to form smaller pediments over the columns of round-arched windows that formed the projecting bays at each end. On this occasion iron beams and columns were employed for its internal structure. Thus it was that a man who had begun his career as a mason could end it as a builder, architect, mill-owner, stone-merchant, and lime-burner; in addition, Joseph Kaye was a maltster and brewer.

As already stated, industrial structures, like other types of building, reflected general changes in architectural thought rather than creating a separate and distinct tradition of their own, although at times they contributed to those mainstream developments. Bignold's Yarn Mill (1836),[55] Cowgate, Norwich (now Jarrold's Printing Works) helps illustrate this point. Designed by the local architect John Brown (1805-76), it consisted of a solid five-storey block 20 bays in length, enlivened by the addition of a semicircular turret (down which the bales were dropped) crowned with a dome. Piers running between the windows of the first three floors and linked together by brick arches strengthened the composition, while a recessed parapet sweeping

up to the tower completed the Palladian image.

The expansion of the textile industry and its demand for machinery and engines provided a stimulus to engineering firms, and one of the largest in Manchester was the Soho Foundry of Peel, Williams & Co. The factory, or its two principal buildings, exhibited Palladian principles in their symmetry and detail, one having an unusual curved central bay.[56] The works had in fact been erected for David Whitehead, but his death in 1807 prompted their sale three years later, when Peel, Williams & Co. purchased them. The advertisement for the sale provided a description:

> The foundry ... contains air-furnaces ... an excellent smithy and finishers' shop, and extraordinarily well lighted pattern-makers' and turners' shops extending 100 yards in length. Adjoining the foundry, is a most complete boring mill and turning shop

33 The Soho Foundry of Peel, Williams & Co.; the building on the left contained the foundry, pattern and turners' shops, while that to the right housed the boring mill.

... worked by an excellent steam-engine, of 18 horses power, which also works the blasts for the cupolas ...[57]

On visiting the site in 1821, Joshua Field of Maudslay, Sons & Field, sketched the foundry with its three cupola furnaces, boiler-making shop, forges and offices arranged around the four sides of a rectangular yard, with a wharf on the Manchester-Ashton-Stockport Canal.[58] Not only one of the leading engineering works in the city, it was also among the most architecturally distinguished.

Warehouses

As manufacturing units grew in size, whether ironworks, cotton mills or chemical plant, and the volume and range of their output expanded, so the need for larger and more efficient storage facilities increased, creating a demand for commodious, fireproof and secure warehouses. These, like factories, were now often sited in populous towns, as well as ports, and greater attention was paid not simply to their structural design but also to their external appearance.

The rising level of overseas trade meant that it was necessary both to increase the area of wharfage and to improve methods of receiving and storing goods, always attempting to prevent theft. In London the East and West India Dock Companies (p. 41) had obtained acts to construct non-tidal docks with adjacent warehouses; the whole surrounded by high walls. In order to cope with the flood of merchandise from the East, particularly tea, drugs and spices, the St Katharine Docks Co. was founded in 1825. The warehouses (1827-8), designed by Thomas Telford (1757-1835) and Philip Hardwick (1790-1870)[59] were unusual in that they abutted directly on to the moorings so that cargoes could be hoisted immediately without preliminary sorting on the quayside.[60] The upper storeys were, in part, supported by Greek Doric cast-iron columns, a fashionable choice but possibly one conditioned by practical considerations.

34 The last Telford warehouse (1827-8) at St Katharine Docks to be demolished; it reveals timber floors supported by cast-iron columns.

Their tapered profile and the absence of an ornate base meant that they were less of an obstruction to the movement of goods. W.S. Clark, the designer of the Bute Warehouse (1861), Cardiff, though selecting simplified Roman Doric columns to support the overhang, omitted the base in favour of a plain taper.[61] Again, the Pillar Warehouse (c.1849), Gloucester Docks, a similar red-brick structure, had been constructed with a row of cast-iron Greek Doric columns to support the storeys above the quayside. Internally, however, the St Katharine Docks' warehouses, which were initially timber-framed,[62] did not exhibit the same good sense, unlike Jesse Hartley's works for Liverpool Port (p. 116).

With a street-level stone arcade to protect pedestrians, the new Goree Warehouses (1810) at George's Dock, Liverpool, possibly by John Foster, consisted of a repeated series of column-like bays capped with angled pediments – an imposing zigzag line of sublime brick stores.[63] Clearly an effective design, it was repeated with minor variations, and later used by John B. Hartley (1814–69) at Hull, where the red-brick many-gabled warehouses (1851 and 1857) in Kingston Street offered an austere wall around the Railway Dock.[64] He sought to make these fireproof by the use of cast-iron columns and by covering the timber ceilings with sheet iron.[65] In 1845–6 Hartley had been responsible for the town's Princes Dock Warehouse in Castle Street, an unadorned three-storey brick building,[66] not distinguished in the manner of his father's commissions in Liverpool (p. 115). Port warehouses, usually located in poor neighbourhoods distinct from city centres and built for rough usage, in a sense formed a group united not only by sublime restraint but also by their role and situation.

The case of John Dobson (1787–1865) may be cited as a case of a classically schooled architect who, in establishing a considerable provincial practice, was on occasion drawn into the world of factories and warehouses.[67] Born in Chirton, North Shields, and having spent a year in London to study under the watercolourist John Varley, Dobson returned to Newcastle where 'he found that he was the only architect

in the county of Northumberland, as Mr Bonomi was the only architect in the county of Durham'.[68] Although primarily concerned with churches for the expanding industrial towns of the North-east and with modernizing castles for the local aristocracy, a good deal of his early work derived from the growth of trade in the region. Having designed Howdon-on-Tyne Docks in 1814, he built a warehouse at Broad Chare, Newcastle, in the same year, others following at Quayside for Mr Sorbie (1818), together with a large tobacco warehouse there in 1819. Dobson erected a glassworks for Mr Cookson in 1817, and though he had abandoned this form of commission by 1820, he subsequently built a number of warehouses at Sunderland Docks in 1850.[69] Dobson was also a distinguished station architect, responsible for Central Station, Newcastle, and one of the few educated designers who in the early part of the nineteenth century did not shrink from industrial work, though this must have been partly because of his situation distant from the fashionable London market.

A further example of the sublime, J. & R. Bush's Warehouse, Floating Harbour, Bristol, though exhibiting classical features (round-arched piers, a simple ashlar cornice and pediment), achieved its appeal by the robust handling of materials and subtle variation of uncomplicated elements.[70] Almost certainly by the City Architect Richard S. Pope (1791–1884),[71] who had in early life been a surveyor under Sir Richard Smirke for the Royal Mint and also come into contact with Cockerell, it was originally a tea warehouse but later served as a granary. Built in two sections (c.1832 and 1837), the first to third storeys formed a *piano nobile* linked together by an arcade that, through a variation of proportions, emphasized the central three bays. The eye's upward drift was arrested by the cornice and plain parapet which contained the narrow windows of the fourth storey. The warehouse was not fireproof, as cast-iron columns supported timber beams and floors.

Although constructed in the mid-nineteenth century, the various grain and general merchandise warehouses in James Street, Glasgow, had

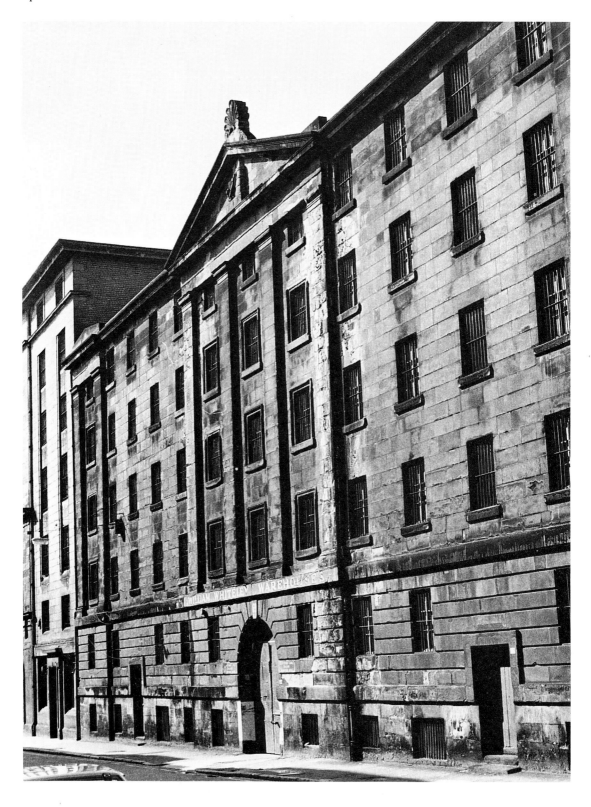

an architectural interpretation that lay in Palladian Britain. In its ordered symmetry No. 65–69–73 (c.1848)[72] was typical. In an elegant façade Doric pilasters supported a pediment containing a barrel and anchor device that acknowledged the building's purpose. That No. 44–46–54 (Warehouse No. 11) should have adopted a similar classical style when built in 1861 for Thomas Mann underlined a strong conservatism and sense of continuity characteristic of much Scottish architecture.

Georges Dock, Dublin, featured a number of ochre-brick and grey-granite warehouses (Stacks A, B and C), erected in c.1815–20.[73] Probably the work of John Rennie, their prison-like appearance (for they were designed to prevent the theft of their tobacco, wine and general merchandise) and sublime execution could have provided Hartley with a reference point when he came to design those warehouses needed in Liverpool directly across the Irish Sea, whilst their fire-resisting qualities would also have been

35 (*opposite*) A general merchandise warehouse at 65–69–73 James Street, Glasgow, built *c.* 1848 for Harvie & McGavin. Internally it was not fireproof, having timber floors supported by cast-iron columns.

36 'C' Stack at Georges Dock (*c.* 1815–20), Dublin, revealing tough granite facings and prison-like window grilles.

instructive. 'There is not one particle of wood', observed Wright in 1821,

> or other combustible matter. There are nine vaults beneath, which altogether afford perfect and convenient storage for 4,500 pipes of wine ... these vaults are lighted by means of thick lenses set in iron plates in the floor of the tobacco store ... the roof is supported by metal framework of an exceedingly ingenious construction, and, at intervals, long lanterns are inserted, the sashes of which are also metal; the entire frame work is supported by three rows of cylindrical metal pillars, 26 in each row; these rest upon others of granite ... All this iron work ... was manufactured by the Butterley-foundry in Derbyshire.[74]

Although sited at the confluence of the Shropshire Union Canal and the River Mersey, Telford's Great Warehouse (1830–3) at Ellesmere Port caught the eye not simply because of its great scale, but by the strikingly original design. Three identical arms, each supported by two graceful elliptical arches so that barges could be served directly below, stretched from a three-storey block over the basin.[75] The brick structure, with its limited use of stone dressings and virtual absence of ornament, had an appeal which derived from its overall shape and proportions.[76]

Inland, on waterways and near factories and ironworks, ever larger warehouses were required by the growth of industrial output. At Manchester the increased scale of operations may be illustrated by the Old Quay Company's New Botany Warehouse (1824) and the Victoria and Albert Warehouses, all situated in Chester Street,[77] together with Hall & Rogers' Rochdale warehouse (1836),[78] Tariff Street. Each of these, built of tough red brick and distinguished by the repetition of small round-arched windows, eschewed ornament, reinforcing a powerful image of sublimity, whilst the last had a double-arched loading dock for broad barges in keeping with those storehouses situated elsewhere in Manchester. The Great Warehouse (1838)[79] at Coalbrookdale, a timber-floored building with cast-iron columns erected for the storage of castings, illustrates the architectural use of cast iron not simply for window frames but sills and lintels, and for the ornate clock tower which was added in 1843.

The promoters of the first railway companies, like the canals before them, saw their principal

37 A substantial brick warehouse, dated 1836, for Hall & Rogers in Tariff Street, Manchester. The twin shipping holes (it was formerly served by the Rochdale Canal), concealed by the building in the foreground, have now been infilled.

function as the transport of merchandise, and hence produced a new generation of warehouses. The earliest included those built beside the Liverpool Road Station in Manchester.[80] There is a possibility that Thomas Haigh, a Liverpool architect and surveyor, who subsequently performed much work for the railway company, had produced the plans. David Bellhouse, a timber merchant and builder (and possibly the father of David, the ironfounder) obtained the tender to erect the buildings. Completed in 1830, they fell into an established pattern of warehouse design: ten terraced bays linked together by angled pediments, symmetrically placed pilasters inserted between every two bays, restraint in decoration and a limited use of stone. Structurally, they were timber-framed except at the cellar level where wooden posts gave way to cast-iron columns. This range of warehouses implies, therefore, that the coming of the railways did not cause a hiatus with architectural precedents. They stand as an example of continuity at the head of a tradition evolved by the canals and maritime ports.

The great majority of early nineteenth-century mills and warehouses, and particularly those constructed on a large scale, fell into the restrained Palladian mould, but there did exist, as a portent for the future, a small number of important exceptions where architects had been employed. Often, as will be seen, these exhibited features of the then-popular Greek Revival.

The Greek Revival

Although its antecedents in Britain date back to the 1750s, the Greek Revival did not achieve maturity until the 1820s, when it came to the fore in fashionable building.[81] Part of the rise of neo-classicism, the movement reached its zenith around 1829, though it subsequently retained a lasting hold in Scotland.[82] However, industrial buildings did not yet occupy a place in the forefront of architectural change; instead, as before, they followed behind, picking up developments in style and adapting or modifying them to their own circumstances. Occasionally, of course, a commission such as the St Katharine Docks or

Vanbrugh's work for Woolwich Arsenal, through the skill of its designer or the generosity of its patron, would rank amongst the best of the period; yet for the moment these were exceptions. The days when factories and warehouses would consistently make significant contributions to the body of architectural theory were still to come.

An example of the Greek Revival filtering into industrial architecture may be identified in the Globe Works (c.1825), Green Lane, Sheffield.[83] Belonging to Messrs Ibbotson Brothers, manufacturers of fenders, saws, files and edge tools, it formed a dignified classical monument. The pedimented wings in dressed stone balanced a central projecting bay enlivened by Ionic pilasters, though the Greek theme was not faithfully reproduced, as the ground-floor windows were round headed. In fact, one of the earliest cases of Greek Doric being applied to a humble working building was Sir John Soane's (1753-1837) brick barn, Solihull (1794).[84] Starkly detailed, simply executed, it probably owed more to Soane's own original style than to Greek classicism (though he had visited Paestum in 1779) and can be compared in execution to his stables (1814-17) for the Royal Hospital, Chelsea.[85]

The Hope Foundry (c.1812), Mabgate, Leeds, exhibited the influence of the Revival in its gateway, which featured tapered pilasters and ornamental sculpted heads.[86] Similarly, the Shropshire Union Canal Company's Shrewsbury Warehouse (1835), built by Fallowes and Hart of Birmingham, offered a stuccoed Greek Doric entrance to Howard Street.[87] Like the Water Street Bridge (1829-30) in Manchester (see p. 84), which carried the Liverpool & Manchester Railway on two rows of fluted cast-iron Greek Doric columns,[88] the London & Greenwich Railway's Spa Road Bridge (1834-5) adopted a Revivalist stance. Designed by Lt. Col. George Landmann, RE (1779-1854), the company's engineer, each side was supported by four fluted Doric columns.[89] While the Spa Road Bridge held a brick-arched viaduct, the Water Street Bridge consisted of cast-iron beams with brick arches sprung from lateral girders (like so many factory floors). The cast-iron

38 The Globe Works (*c.* 1825), Sheffield, a formal but elegant example of industrial architecture blackened by over a century of use.

parapets were decorated with recessed Doric pilasters. Suffice it to say that the adjacent station in Liverpool Road, 'a neat and commodious building with a Grecian front',[90] though limited in its architectural expression, also adopted this style.

Finally, it was significant that two of the principal termini in the early railway schemes had been influenced by the Greek Revival: the Euston Propylaeum and Curzon Street.[91] Built by the London & Birmingham Railway and designed by their surveyor Philip Hardwick, they greeted passengers and symbolized the company's aims. At Euston (1836–8) he erected a massive gateway supported by fluted Doric columns, while in Curzon Street (1838) a more conventional three-storey office block and booking hall enlivened by Ionic columns was built.

Both were executed in dressed stone on a grand scale and the monumental interpretation of classicals models could, in part, have been planned to allay the fears of travellers about to embark on a novel and possibly frightening form of transport. A contemporary report observed of Euston that:

> We here behold the full majesty and severity of the order exhibited upon such a scale that renders it truly imposing ... We have the effect not only of magnitude, as well as forms, but that also arising from breadth of light and shade, heightened by that of great depth, and the contrast of perspective.[92]

Of course, the Greek theme continued to be adopted long after it had fallen from widespread popularity, and was favoured by some station architects: Leicester's Campbell Street Station (1840),[93] by the local architect William Flint (1801–62), a two-storey stone building, was entered through a Greek Doric portico; Thomas Moore's Monkwearmouth Terminus (1848) featured an Ionic portico,[94] while Ashby-de-la-

39 Curzon Street Station (1838), a massive Greek Ionic booking hall by Philip Hardwick to greet passengers travelling by the London & Birmingham Railway.

Zouch Station (1849) by Robert Chaplin, another fine stone structure, had been enlivened by Doric columns, pilasters and decorative wreaths.[95] The style continued to be expressed in Glasgow's commercial buildings, where Alexander 'Greek' Thomson (1817–75) specialized in its execution.[96]

Gasworks

Whilst it may be true that the huge gasometers, refineries and mechanized coke-handling apparatus of the late nineteenth century did not generally present great opportunities for architects, their earlier small-scale counterparts, which could be contained within more conventional structures, produced a number of pleasing designs. The Warwick Gasworks (c.1822), situated, possibly for reasons of safety and smell, on the town's perimeter at Saltisford,[97] was clothed in restrained Palladian garments. Its twin gasholders, housed in symmetrical octagonal towers and topped by louvred lanterns, were linked by a central entrance building. Blind arches to the stuccoed road façade gave a decorative finish to this ornate balanced composition. However, the building could scarcely be recognized for what it was, since an unwise safety regulation demanded that gasholders, as potentially explosive vessels, had to be encased in brick. A slightly less ornamental version was constructed at Mill Holme, Northampton, in 1824, where again twin linked octagonal holders fronted the retort house behind.[98] The gasholder, incorporated in the extensions to Bean Ing Mill of 1824, designed by Fairbairn, was apparently a brick octagon surmounted by an iron dome.[99] Palladian models dominated Canon's Marsh Gasworks (1819) at Bristol, where a symmetrical office building, entered by

40 The Warwick Gasworks at Saltisford (*c.* 1822);
motivated by a desire to protect the nearby
inhabitants from explosions, the gasholders were
encased in brick, a precaution which could, in fact,
have produced even greater devastation.

41 The Edinburgh Gasworks (1825–6) at Tanfield
beside the Water of Leith, a fanciful design with no
obvious industrial references.

an Ionic porch, was lit by Venetian windows.[100]

An original and exciting design was produced by William Burn (1789–1870) for the Edinburgh Gas Works (1825–6), in Tanfield beside the Water of Leith.[101] Although this appears to have been his only industrial commission in a career that specialized in country houses, he created a striking composition. In contrast to the Warwick and Northampton examples, the gasholders, like giant dovecotes, were said 'to represent a Moorish fortress',[102] though their restraint and lack of obvious ornament placed them within the Georgian tradition of industrial buildings. Schinkel, on visiting the Edinburgh Gasworks in 1826, remarked:

> This is an excellent institution. Sir Walter Scott outlined the plan for the whole, the architect William Burn executed the building with great refinement of construction. The two sketches [by Schinkel] explain the frontal view of the gasholders and the central building together with the details of the roof construction, and the iron railings which surround the gasholders.[103]

More conventional in adopting a classical theme were the Kendal Gasworks (1825), whose small stone façade was enlivened by two Tuscan columns supporting the motto *Ex fumo lucem*.[104]

As engineers came to appreciate that brick

casings were in fact a source of potential danger, so gasholders were constructed naked. One of the earliest, and the oldest now surviving, was erected at Fulham, where the Imperial Gas Light & Coke Co.'s No. 2 holder (1827–30) was supported by a circle of cast-iron guides.[105] These pyramid-shaped brackets, internally reinforced by rings of diminishing size, were a device later to be adopted for the brackets supporting the roof of King's Cross Station (p. 81). In its economical refinement No. 2 has an appeal that contrasts sharply with its neighbour No. 3, which featured highly ornate composite columns, typical of late-nineteenth-century holders.

Burn was not the first architect commissioned to design a gasworks, for in 1823 the Imperial Gas Light Co. in London had invited Francis Edwards (1784–1857) to draw up plans for their Hoxton offices and plant.[106] Significantly, this appears to have been Edwards' first independent commission in a career that was not characterized by industrial work. He was responsible for all the company's buildings from its incorporation in 1823, except during the last few years of his life when he was employed as a consulting architect. An engraving by Thomas Shepherd entitled *Gasworks near the Regent's Canal* (see fig. 42) is thought to depict the scene, in which case this was another symmetrical classical composition, possibly stuccoed. Two linked rectangular blocks (joined by a pedimented office) were enlivened by central chimneys executed as if triumphal Roman Doric columns.[107] In the early

42 A gasworks beside the Regent's Canal; it could possibly have been the Imperial Gas Light Co.'s Hoxton plant.

stages, when gas lighting was novel and considered to be hazardous, the directors presumably wanted to present a secure and familiar image to their public.

Ironworks

During the period 1800–1835, plant in the iron industry experienced few dramatic technical changes, increases in output being achieved for the most part by a duplication of furnaces and foundries. Limitations of size and the relatively embryonic nature of the processes allowed ironmasters some scope to consider the architecture of their offices, blowing houses and blast furnaces. At Rhymney, the Bute Ironworks' three blast furnaces were regarded as having 'a somewhat pretentious style of architecture, having a front of Egyptian design'.[108] Based on a temple, reputedly the ruins of Dendera, the plan accommodated the three furnaces, each shaped as a massive pylon linked together by high-level arches and topped by a continuous frieze which formed the charging platform.[109] Regarding the composition as 'a great departure from the limestone furnace character of the early works', Wilkins observed in 1903 that the subject, apparently designed by M'Culloch:

> at the time (1828) attracted considerable notice, and engravings appeared in engineering magazines, with comments, and the expression of hope that there would be in future some attempt at Classic ornamentation, instead of the plain architecture, old fashioned almost to severity, of literally the 'old school'.[110]

Less distinguished architecturally were Merthyr Tydfil's two mighty ironworks, Cyfarthfa and Dowlais, where the blast furnaces were more simply constructed of local dressed stone.[111] But here even the standard blast furnace reflected in diluted fashion the architectural principles of the day. The tapered circular form of the stack, with the need to have a restricted throat, meant that the column and plinth formed ideal models for the blast furnace. The Dowlais Iron Co. introduced a design in the mid-1840s which had good-quality stone

facings, a dentil cornice to support the charging platform, and a decorative string course situated in the lower half of the column. No. 12, 38 ft square at the base, and erected in 1851, stood as a fine example of this type.[112] Similarly, a furnace at the Coltness Works had a dressed-stone outer skin and a simple cornice beneath the balcony; its base of rusticated stone formed a plinth for the shaft above, being entered through round arches accentuated by voussoirs.[113] 'Until a comparatively recent period', remarked Truran in 1855, 'the bottom was invariably formed of large blocks of coarse sandstone. Great expense was incurred in quarrying, dressing and setting the blocks in their respective stations.'[114] The quality of the ashlar that had been used for the façade of the twin blast furnaces erected by the Blaenavon Ironworks encouraged its stripping at the turn of the nineteenth century to provide a source of stone to build the nearby St Peter's Church. While medieval masons selected dressed stone for fortresses so that they might better resist the impact of missiles, the adoption of this material in blast furnaces, rather than brick or rubble, revealed a concern with appearances and an appreciation of their impact on the local landscape. The four furnaces of Ynysfach (one with a cast-iron key plate bearing the date 1836 and the initials of William Crawshay II)[115] and their blowing engine houses of sandstone rubble and ashlar quoins were so solidly constructed as to have survived in the Merthyr district.

The company's stables, erected in 1820, were among the Dowlais Iron Works' finest architectural monuments. The authorship of this Palladian building is not known,[116] though Edward Heycock, the Shrewsbury architect, was commissioned to produce designs for the neighbouring Market House.[117] His elevations for the two-storey entrance buildings, distinguished by a Greek Revival clock tower, were not effected when the Market House was constructed in 1847.[118] While puddling furnaces, rolling mills and coke ovens did not lend themselves to such treatment, Josiah Guest's home, Dowlais House (1817–18), situated in the middle of the works and entered through a Doric porch, had an unpretentious classical appearance.[119]

43 No. 12 blast furnace, built in 1851 for the Dowlais Iron Co., near Merthyr Tydfil.

The British Ironworks (1826), Abersychan, near Pontypool, was designed by Decimus Burton (1800–81), but with the exception of several warehouses in London – for Gilpin & Co. (1830–4), Hebbert & Co. (1822–48) in Pall Mall, and a storehouse for the Grenadier Guards, Westminster (c.1830) – appears to have been an aberration undertaken very early in a career which later included many country houses, churches and the Athenaeum Club (1829–30).[120] At Abersychan the architect was responsible for the central gateway flanked by pairs of pedimented pavilions and linked together by arcades, which presumably contained the puddling furnaces and the mills that rolled the rounds, squares and flats. The blast furnaces, situated behind this row of buildings (in plan like a Georgian country house), seem to have conformed to a more typical pattern of design.[121]

As in the eighteenth century, when Vanbrugh designed the Royal Arsenal, it generally remained the case that leading architects would consider industrial commissions only if they carried some special distinction. The Royal Mint (1804–9), a secure foundry, fell into this category. Matthew Boulton, writing to Rennie, the engineer responsible for the structural elements, suggested that

> the buildings [or rather the façade] should be simple and strong ... the front which may be simple, elegant in the Wyattistic style ... Mr Wyatt may design the ornamental part, but I must sketch the useful.[122]

In the event Samuel Wyatt was discharged in 1794 for neglecting his duties,[123] and James Johnson, architect to the Barrack Department of the War Office, produced the elevations featuring a central pediment, supported by six attached Tuscan columns.[124] After his death in 1807, Robert Smirke (1780–1867) completed the classical stone façade, and the two lodges (1809–11) on the street.

Transport: canals and railways

Industrialization could proceed in Britain only so long as improvements in transport kept pace with the needs of an expanding manufacturing sector. In the eighteenth century this had been achieved by turnpiking the roads and by the construction of canals, while increasing congestion in the nineteenth century encouraged the promotion of pioneer railways. The major engineering features which offered architectural scope included tunnels and aqueducts or viaducts. Many canal tunnels, often bored through remote outcrops, received scant treatment in local brick or stone with little or no attempt to add adornment. Like the canal bridges, any appeal they held derived from the skill of the builder or the quality of the available materials. The late-eighteenth-century brick footbridges over the Oxford Canal, or the stone ones on the Thames and Severn, provide pleasing examples of vernacular architecture.[125]

Nevertheless, some tunnels and aqueducts, as structures requiring engineering expertise and likely to attract the eye, earned the detailed consideration of an engineer or architect. Among the finer portals are those to the Islington Tunnel (1819–20), by James Morgan,[126] where an elliptical arch bore some resemblance to Vanbrugh's entrance to the Great Dial. Flanked by Doric pilasters, it may originally have been stuccoed. The eastern portal of the Sapperton Tunnel (1789)[127] on the Thames and Severn Canal, engineered by Josiah Clowes, by contrast offered a richer classical façade. Flanked by Roman Doric columns, decorative niches and a simple cornice, its elegant design was atypical of canal architecture.

Because they were viewed by so many more people and because the public's expectations had changed, railway tunnels and bridges, in contrast with those on canals, were often considered respectable architecture. Amongst the earliest was Isambard Brunel's (1806–59) western portal to Box Tunnel (1841),[128] finished in dressed Bath stone with a projecting cornice, balustrade and decorative quoins. The fact that the line was broad-gauge, and so wider than most, added to its imposing presence. The tunnels leading to Edge Hill Station in the Chatsworth Street cutting of the Liverpool & Manchester Railway followed the Moorish theme adopted by the adjacent arch leading across and down to the tracks.[129] The portals topped by a simple battlement were balanced on each side by two brick chimneys (1830–2) executed as triumphal columns – apparently Roman Doric. The arch behind, more highly detailed than the tunnels, exhibited Turkish touches, its architect being a Mr Foster of Liverpool[130] – presumably John Foster of Lawton Street.[131]

Some contemporary artists chose canal aqueducts as subjects for illustrations, and many had, indeed, been finely executed. The Marple Aqueduct (1794) on the Peak Forest Canal (promoted by Samuel Oldknow), engineered by Benjamin Outram (1764–1805), consisted of a triple-arched structure pierced by circular openings and emphasized by tapered pilasters.[132] Although not a great work of architectural orthodoxy, it nevertheless created an unusual

44 The eastern portal of the Islington Tunnel on the Regent's Canal.

and exciting picture. More conventional, and in keeping with the restrained classical architecture of the region, was Rennie's Dundas Aqueduct (1800) for the Kennet and Avon Canal Company.[133] A symmetrical, ordered Roman Doric design, it must, like the canal bridges in the town itself, have been inspired by the classical splendour of Bath. Thomas Telford's Chirk Aqueduct (1796–1801), on the Ellesmere Canal, and the adjacent 19-arch viaduct (1848) for the Chester & Shrewsbury Railway, by Henry Robertson (1816–88),[134] may be selected to illustrate the continuity between the two forms of transport.[135] Both were solidly constructed of undressed stone, their similar rhythm of arches

(the viaduct was, however, higher than the aqueduct) breaking across the Ceiriog valley in a powerful succession of arched piers. The aqueduct had, in addition, served as a proving ground for James Parker's 'Roman' cement, which Telford had used for the trough because of its putative watertight properties.[136] The builder employed for both the Chirk and the Pontcysyllte Aqueducts (1795–1803), John Simpson (1755–1815), was described by Telford as 'a treasure of talents and integrity'.[137]

Summary

If viewed from a purely stylistic standpoint, the period 1800–1835 saw no startling innovations in industrial architecture; factories, ironworks and warehouses did not ring great changes in principles of design. Churches, country houses and public buildings remained the media in which the leading architects worked with enthusiasm and inspiration. Young men, engineers, the unskilled and builders were commonly called upon to execute industrial structures. Yet the concentration and growth of manufacturing enterprise in certain regions during these three decades created the conditions for the rise of the specialist factory architect. Writing in 1843, George Dodd suggested that:

> the circumstance of the cotton manufacture having become so firmly located in Lancashire has exerted a powerful influence on the settlement of machinists, millwrights and engineers in that quarter; otherwise, London would perhaps still have maintained a pre-eminence in these departments.[138]

These were the forerunners of the firms of civil engineers and architects that built up considerable practices in the middle and latter decades of the nineteenth century. Not far distant was the day when mills would catch the eye not simply as places where hundreds of workers toiled using novel machinery, but as buildings whose very appearance offered an interest of their own.

The application of steam engines to processes formerly driven by waterwheels was of fundamental importance. The potential power of steam combined with its reliability allowed manufacturers to duplicate or install heavier machinery. This, in turn, resulted in bigger buildings. The experimental work of Hodgkinson in collaboration with Fairbairn meant that manufacturers could put greater reliance on large iron-framed structures which were also more resistant to fire. The expertise required to bring these elements together also encouraged the rise of specialist engineers, builders and architects.

Notes

1 *The Mirror of Literature, Amusement and Instruction*, 10 January 1829; Herbert Spencer, *London's Canal*, London (1976), pp. 65–6.
2 See p. 74.
3 PRO, Rail 860/18 Regent's Canal Company General Committee Minute Book 1820, 12 May 1820, p. 63; 14 June 1820, p. 88.

4 The present structure was, in fact, faithfully reconstructed, the whole having been demolished by a powder barge exploding in October 1874; *Illustrated London News*, Vol. LXV, No. 1833, 10 October 1874.
5 Joseph Nasmith, *Recent Cotton Mill Construction and Engineering*, Manchester (c.1895), p. 8.
6 Quoted from B.H. Thwaite, *Our Factories, Workshops and Warehouses, their Sanitary and Fire-Resisting Arrangements*, London (1882), p. 10.
7 BRL, Boulton & Watt Collection, Portfolio 152, numerous plans of the engine, gearing and two sets of stones, 1786; Hills, *Power in the Industrial Revolution*, op. cit., p. 142; Asa Briggs, *The Power of Steam*, London (1982), p. 56.
8 Robinson, op. cit., p. 45; Roll, op. cit., p. 110; Skempton, op. cit., pp. 59, 69.
9 John Crabtree, *A Concise History of Halifax*, Halifax (1836), p. 305; John James, *History of the Worsted Manufacture in England*, London (1857), pp. 621–2.
10 Richard Guest, *Compendious History of the Cotton-Manufacture*, Manchester (1823), p. 47.
11 Edward Baines, *History, Directory and Gazetteer of the County Palatine of Lancaster*, Vol. I, Liverpool (1824), p. 118.
12 D.T. Jenkins and K.G. Ponting, *The British Wool Textile Industry 1770–1914*, London (1982), p. 31.
13 Wm. Alexander Abram, *A History of Blackburn, town and parish*, Blackburn (1877), p. 230.
14 Edwin Butterworth, *A Statistical Sketch of the County Palatine of Lancaster*, London (1841), p. 9.
15 Steve Dunwell, *The Run of the Mill*, Boston, Massachusetts (1978), pp. 30–3.
16 Martha and Murray Zimiles, *Early American Mills*, New York (1973), p. 134.
17 Coolidge, op. cit., p. 100.
18 Zimiles, op. cit., pp. 135, 137.
19 See also J.B. Armstrong, *Factory under the Elms: A History of Harrisville, New Hampshire*, MIT (1969) for comparative developments in woollen mills, particularly the construction of Granite Mill in 1846–7 (p. 29) and New Mill in 1867 (p. 124).
20 Nixon, *Industrial Archaeology of Derbyshire*, op. cit., pp. 248, 199.
21 Edmund Burke, *A Philosophical Enquiry into the*

Origin of Ideas of the Sublime and Beautiful (1757), edited by J.T. Boulton, London (1958), pp. 57-80.

22 *A Century of Fine Cotton Spinning 1790-1906, McConnel & Co Ltd*, Manchester (1906), p. 11; W.H. Pyne, *Lancashire Illustrated*, London (1831), p. 70.

23 C.H. Lee, *A Cotton Enterprise 1795-1840, A History of M'Connel & Kennedy, Fine Cotton Spinners*, Manchester (1972), p. 102.

24 *Ibid.*, pp. 101-2.

25 *A Century of Fine Cotton Spinning, op. cit.*, p. 10 and plate.

26 Quoted from Lee, *op. cit.*, opposite p. 1.

27 *AR*, Vol. XCVII, May 1945, L. Ettlinger, 'A German Architect's Visit to England in 1826', p. 133.

28 Zachariah Allen, *The Practical Tourist, or Sketches of the State of the Useful Arts, and of Society*, Vol. I, Providence (1832), p. 129.

29 *Ibid.*, p. 122.

30 LivRO, *Goad's Plans of Manchester*, Vol. II, No. 235, January 1927.

31 Robert Sherlock, *The Industrial Archaeology of Staffordshire*, Newton Abbot (1976), pp. 60-3.

32 Edward Baines Junior, *History of the Cotton Manufacture in Great Britain*, London (1835), plate opposite p. 185; Nikolaus Pevsner, *A History of Building Types*, London (1976), p. 279, plate 17.14; William A. Shaw, *Manchester Old and New*, Vol. II, London (1894), p. 17.

33 Andrew Ure, *The Cotton Manufacture of Great Britain*, Vol. I, London (1836), p. 296.

34 Binney, *Satanic Mills, op. cit.*, pp. 62-3.

35 R.A. Hayward, *Sir William Fairbairn*, Manchester [n.d.], pp. 5-7.

36 Andrew Ure, *The Philosophy of Manufacturers*, London (1861), pp. 112, 385; Norman Longmate, *The Hungry Mills*, London (1978), pp. 42-3.

37 Ure, *Philosophy, op. cit.*

38 BRL, Boulton & Watt Collection, Portfolio 508, plans dated 1833.

39 Ure, *Philosophy, op. cit.*, p. 32.

40 *B*, Vol. XXXII, No. 1647, 24 August 1874, Obituary, p. 724; *MPICE*, Vol. XXXIX (1874-5), Memoir, pp. 251-63.

41 Axon, *Annals of Manchester, op. cit.*, pp. 342-3;

Samuel Smiles, *Industrial Biography*, London (1863), pp. 305-6, 313.

42 William Pole (Editor), *The Life of Sir William Fairbairn, Partly Written by Himself*, London (1877), p. 115.

43 Lee, *op. cit.*, p. 102.

44 Rhodes Boyson, *The Ashworth Cotton Enterprise*, Oxford (1970), pp. 19-21.

45 Colin Cunningham, *Victorian and Edwardian Town Halls*, London (1981), pp. 254-5.

46 R.A. Hayward, *Sir William Fairbairn*, Manchester [n.d.], p. 2.

47 Robert M. and Francis Bancroft, *A Practical Treatise on the Construction of Tall Chimney Shafts*, Manchester (1885), p. 49; N. Pevsner, *BoE, Cumberland and Westmorland*, Harmondsworth (1967), p. 103; J.D. Marshall and Michael Davies-Shiel, *The Industrial Archaeology of the Lake Counties*, Newton Abbot (1969), pp. 97-8.

48 Wyatt Papworth (Editor), *The Dictionary of Architecture*, Vol. VIII, London (1892), 'T', p. 11; Colvin, *op. cit.*, p. 597.

49 R. Bretton, *Crossleys of Dean Clough* (from *THAS* Parts I-VI, 1950-4), p. 79.

50 *Ibid.*, p. 82.

51 *HE*, Vol. VII, No. 348, 27 March 1858, Obituary, p. 2; *HC*, 17 April 1852, p. 5.

52 *Old West Riding*, Vol. 4 (1984), E.A.H. Haigh, 'Joseph Kaye – A Builder of Huddersfield', p. 31.

53 *The Huddersfield and Holmfirth Examiner*, Vol. VI, No. 281, 8 November 1856, p. 8.

54 KLH, Local Newspaper Cutting, 5 October 1918, Letter from Lt. Col. Sir Albert Kaye Rollit.

55 Brockman, *op. cit.*, pp. 27-8; Bracegirdle, *op. cit.*, p. 197.

56 MCL, Maureen Hamilton, 'An Aspect of Technology and Transport ... Peel, Williams & Co. of Ancoats' (handwritten study); Print, fMSC, 113, 105.

57 *Manchester Mercury*, 23 January 1810; A.E. Musson, *Business History*, Vol. III (1960), 'An Early Engineering Firm: Peel, Williams & Co. of Manchester', p. 12.

58 *Ibid.*, p. 14.

59 *MPICE*, Vol. XXXIII (1871-2), Obituary Philip Hardwick, p. 215.

60 Jane Fawcett (Editor), *Seven Victorian Architects*, London (1976), Hermione Hobhouse, 'Philip and Philip Charles Hardwick', p. 34.

61 John B. Hilling, *Cardiff and the Valleys*, London (1973), pp. 48-9; *The Historic Architecture of Wales*, Cardiff (1976), pp. 143-4.

62 GLC, Drawings No. 3196, No. 2024/1-4, Internal constructional details.

63 J. Quentin Hughes, *Liverpool*, London (1969), p. 36; Ritchie-Noakes, *Historic Waterfront, op. cit.*, pp. 27, 140.

64 *MPICE*, Vol. XXXIII (1871-2), Obituary J.B. Hartley, pp. 216, 217; N. Pevsner, *BoE, Yorkshire: York and the East Riding*, Harmondsworth (1972), p. 278.

65 LivRO, *Goad's Plans of Hull*, No. 10, revised 1952.

66 *Ibid.*, p. 278.

67 *B*, Vol. XXIII, No. 1145, 14 January 1865, Obituary, p. 27.

68 *Ibid.*

69 Lyall Wilkes, *John Dobson, Architect and Landscape Gardener*, Stocksfield (1980), pp. 124-5.

70 Andor Gomme, *Bristol, an Architectural History*, London (1979), pp. 361-2; T.H.B. Burrough, *Bristol*, London (1970), p. 57.

71 *B*, Vol. XLVI, No. 2146, 22 March 1884, p. 426.

72 John R. Hume, *The Industrial Archaeology of Scotland, No. 1, The Lowlands*, London (1976), pp. 172-3.

73 Correspondence with Dublin Port and Docks Board; Revd G.N. Wright, *An Historical Guide to Ancient and Modern Dublin*, London (1821), pp. 314-15; LivRO, *Goad's Plan of Dublin*, Vol. II, Nos. 10 and 11, October 1906.

74 *Ibid.*, pp. 314-15.

75 N. Pevsner, *BoE, Cheshire*, Harmondsworth (1971), p. 217; Robert Harris, *Canals and their Architecture*, London (1980), pp. 145-50.

76 Unfortunately it was not a fireproof structure and was gutted in 1970, to be subsequently demolished.

77 Stephen Wilkinson, *Manchester's Warehouses, their History and Architecture*, Manchester [n.d.], pp. 3-4.

78 Robert Furneaux-Jordan, *Victorian Architecture*, Harmondsworth (1966), p. 38.

79 W. Grant Mutter, *The Buildings of an Industrial Community, Coalbrookdale and Ironbridge*, London (1979), p. 17.

80 Fitzgerald, *Liverpool Road Station, op. cit.*, pp. 36, 42-3.

81 J. Mordaunt Crook, *The Greek Revival*, London (1972), pp. xi, 107.

82 *Ibid.*, pp. xi, 67-8, 110-11, 127.

83 N. Pevsner, *BoE, Yorkshire, West Riding*, Harmondsworth (1959), p. 471.

84 Brockman, *op. cit.*, pp. 18, 20; N. Pevsner and Alexandra Wedgwood, *BoE, Warwickshire*, Harmondsworth (1966), p. 402.

85 H.-R. Hitchcock, *Architecture: Nineteenth and Twentieth Centuries*, Harmondsworth (1977), pp. 97-8.

86 Derek Linstrum, *Historic Architecture of Leeds*, Newcastle (1969), p. 33.

87 Richards, *Functional Tradition, op. cit.*, pp. 36-7.

88 Fitzgerald, *op. cit.*, pp. 22-5.

89 John Gloag and Derek Bridgewater, *A History of Cast Iron in Architecture*, London (1948), p. 168; R.H.G. Thomas, *London's First Railway*, London (1972), pp. 14, 30-1, 36-7; *DNB*.

90 J. Everett, *Panorama of Manchester and Railway Companion*, Manchester (1834), p. 197.

91 Fawcett, *op. cit.*, Hobhouse, p. 40.

92 *The Civil Engineer and Architect's Journal*, Vol. I (1837-8), Ralph Redivivus, 'The Railway Entrance, Euston Square', p. 276.

93 J.D. Bennett, *Leicestershire Architects 1700-1850*, Leicester (1968), plate 8; G. Biddle and Jeoffry Spence, *The British Railway Station*, Newton Abbot (1977), p. 21.

94 David Lloyd and Donald Insall, *Railway Station Architecture*, Newton Abbot (1978), pp. 35, 42-3; Bracegirdle, *op. cit.*, p. 36, plate 11 (b); Gordon Biddle, *Victorian Stations*, Newton Abbot (1973), p. 31.

95 Marcus Binney and David Pearce, *Railway Architecture*, London (1979), p. 210; Biddle, *op. cit.*, p. 32.

96 Ronald McFadzean, *The Life and Work of Alexander Thomson*, London (1979).

97 Brook, *op. cit.*, pp. 156-7.

98 D.E. Roberts and J.H. Frisby, *The Northampton Gas Undertaking 1823-1949*, Leicester (1980), pp. 7-8.

99 Linstrum, *West Yorkshire, op. cit.*, p. 292.

100 N. Pevsner, *BoE, North Somerset and Bristol*, Harmondsworth (1958), p. 429.

101 James Grant, *Cassell's Old and New Edinburgh*, Vol. III, London (1883) pp. 87, 89; Dyos and Wolff, *Victorian City*, Vol. II, *op. cit.*, p. 440.

102 Grant, *op. cit.*, p. 87.

103 Ettlinger, *op. cit.*, p. 134.

104 N. Pevsner, *BoE, Cumberland and Westmorland*, Harmondsworth (1967), p. 257.

105 E.G. Stewart, *Historic Index of Gasworks ... in the area served by the North Thames Gas Board 1806-1957*, London [n.d.], p. 41.

106 Colvin, *op. cit.*, p. 190.

107 Thomas H. Shepherd, *Metropolitan Improvements; or London in the Nineteenth Century*, Vol. I, London (1828), p. 161; Dean Chandler, *Outline History of Lighting by Gas*, London (1936), p. 49.

108 J. Lloyd, *The Early History of the Old South Wales Ironworks*, London (1906), p. 129.

109 E.E. Edwards, *Echoes of Rhymney*, Risca (1974), pp. 20-1; Hilling, *Cardiff and the Valleys, op. cit.*, p. 47.

110 Charles Wilkins, *The History of the Iron, Steel, Tinplate, and Other Trades of Wales*, Merthyr Tydfil (1903), p. 187.

111 D. Morgan Rees, *Mines, Mills and Furnaces, An Introduction to the Industrial Archaeology in Wales*, London HMSO (1969), pp. 72-3.

112 William Truran, *The Iron Manufacture of Great Britain*, London (1855), p. 19, plate 2.

113 William Fairbairn, *Iron, its History, Properties and Processes of Manufacture*, Edinburgh (1861), pp. 46, 63.

114 Truran, *op. cit.*, p. 20.

115 Rees, *op. cit.*, p. 73; Hilling, *op. cit.*, p. 44.

116 Huw Williams (Editor), *Merthyr Tydfil: 1500 Years* (1980), 'Dowlais Stables', p. 54.

117 GRO, D/DG Plans 89, 90 and 91 (Dowlais Market House, signed Edward Heycock).

118 *Merthyr Historian*, Vol. III (1980), John Owen, 'Industrial Archaeology in the Merthyr Tydfil District', plate 13.

119 John A. Owen, *A History of the Dowlais Iron Works*, Risca (1975), p. 24, plates opposite pp. 16 and 48.

120 *B*, Vol. XLI, No. 2029, 24 December 1881, Obituary, pp. 779-80; Colvin, *op. cit.*, pp. 110-13.

121 D. Morgan Rees, *Historic Industrial Scenes, Wales*, Ashbourne [n.d.], plate 12.

122 Quoted from Tann, *op. cit.*, p. 161.

123 Robinson, *op. cit.*, p. 44.

124 Sir J. Craig, *The Mint*, London (1953), p. 270; Colvin, *op. cit.*, p. 322.

125 Harris, *op. cit.*, pp. 112-20, opposite p. 65.

126 GLC, Islington Box No. 7.

127 Harris, *op. cit.*, pp. 122-3, 205.

128 Bracegirdle, *op. cit.*, p. 49

129 Paul Rees, *Industrial Archaeology Review*, Vol. II, No. 1 (1977), 'Chatsworth Street Cutting', pp. 38-40; *Railways Began Here*, Liverpool (1980), pp. 1, 6, 7.

130 Everett, *Panorama, op. cit.*, p. 199.

131 Edward Baines, *Gazetteer of Lancaster, op. cit.*, Vol I. p. 358.

132 Klingender, *op. cit.*, p. 81, plate 36.

133 Bracegirdle, *op. cit.*, pp. 19-21, plate 5(b).

134 *Journal of the Iron & Steel Institute*, part 1 (1881), Obituary, p. 219.

135 Dyos and Wolff, *op. cit.*, p. 428; J.B. Hilling, *The Historic Architecture of Wales*, Cardiff (1975), pp. 146, 147.

136 *AR*, Vol. CXIV, December 1954, R.J.M. Sutherland, 'Telford', p. 391; Kenneth Hudson, *Building Materials*, London (1972), pp. 47-8.

137 Colvin, *op. cit.*, p. 543.

138 George Dodd, *Days at the Factories*, London (1843), p. 14.

FOUR

Iron and Romantic classicism

1835-55

Two major themes influenced industrial building in the period 1835-55: the increasing application of iron, and the rise of neo-classical architecture. Although, of course, cross-currents flowed between them – many iron structures exhibited Renaissance forms and certain *palazzo* buildings made extensive use of iron in their construction – the two were often difficult to reconcile. And, indeed, they drew contemporaries into much dispute. The difficulty in resolving this dichotomy springs, in part, from the nature of these twin movements. The story of iron was largely a technical one, whose characters were engineers or embryonic scientists, telling of a gradual revolution in building method, while neo-classicism, dominated by academically educated architects, was most conspicuous in halls, government offices and gentlemen's clubs. That there existed links between them – especially in the field of city warehouses and stations – has not always been fully appreciated.

Iron and glass

Against a background of architectural ideas in flux, important advances in foundry and engineering knowledge created exciting possibilities for structural innovation. The need for the development of the single-span arch was both created by the Industrial Revolution and resolved by its progress. The first major example of iron used in a structural way had been the Iron Bridge (1777-81) near Coalbrookdale, designed in essence by Thomas Farnolls Pritchard (1723-77), a Shrewsbury architect and the son of a joiner. Erected by Abraham Darby III (1750-91),[1] the ironfounder, and composed of five cast-iron ribs linked at the apex, it spanned the River Severn in a semicircular arch 100 ft across and 45 ft high.[2] However, the brittleness of cast iron and the cost of making the stronger wrought iron (even after Henry Cort's puddling process of 1784) meant that the constructional use of ferrous metal had been restricted throughout the eighteenth century.

In fact, the earliest buildings to employ iron for architectural effect (rather than for structural purposes, as in many factories) were not industrial in their function. Markets, particularly those designed by Charles Fowler (1791-1867) – including Covent Garden (1828), Hungerford (1831-3) and Exeter (1837-8)[3] – and glasshouses earned this distinction. Fowler had also built the Conservatory (1827-30) at Syon House, which featured a glazed dome 38 ft in diameter.[4] At Chatsworth Joseph Paxton (1803-65), the Duke of Devonshire's former head gardener, in attempting to devise a practical method of covering glasshouses, produced a ridge-and-furrow system of wood and glass. In 1836-40 he erected the Great Stove, whose central nave spanned 70 ft, though its main ribs were of laminated timber.[5] The involvement of Decimus Burton in its design, like Hardwick's work on Hartley's docks or Thompson's collaboration with Stephenson at Derby Tri-junct Station,[6] was explained, as 'the assistance of an architect will be needed only when a work of great magnitude is to be undertaken, or when doubts arise concerning a particular feature'.[7] Possibly because he had helped with the Great

Stove's architectural details, Burton was then invited to prepare plans for the Palm House (1844-8) at Kew. With the help of Richard Turner, who had previously built a glasshouse at Glasnevin, near Dublin, Burton designed a broader structure whose wrought-iron ribs spanned a central area 100ft wide and 138ft long.[8] The Kew and Chatsworth examples, therefore, demonstrated to engineers how large spaces could be enclosed without an internal confusion of columns and buttresses. The factory roof, the train-shed and the covered market could all borrow from these glasshouses. At Liverpool's Lime Street Station (1849-50), for instance, Richard Turner with Joseph Locke (1805-60) erected at a cost of £15,000 a single-span train-shed 153ft across, supported by a series of massive Roman Doric columns, its wrought-iron sickle girders having been rolled in the former's Hammersmith Works, Dublin.[9]

The culminating achievement of this architecture of glass and iron fell to Paxton, who won the competition to design a hall for the Great Exhibition of 1851.[10] Contemporary photographs reveal the Crystal Palace (1850-1) to have been a magnificent glasshouse on a scale far larger than anything before. A building 1,848ft by 408ft with an internal gallery, it boasted a dominating central transept with a span of 72ft, which rose 108ft from the ground. Adopting in the main the materials employed for the Great Stove, Paxton selected cast iron for the columns and girders (supplied by Fox, Henderson & Co. of Birmingham), though the transept ribs and most of the glazing work remained timber. The working details were drawn up by [Sir] Charles Fox (1810-74),[11] while George Henderson (1783-1855) organized the production of the ironwork.[12] The ridge-and-furrow technique devised at Chatsworth was successfully repeated.[13] The use of prefabricated sections enabled the Crystal Palace to be moved to Sydenham in 1852-4, where it was reconstructed on a more ambitious scale. An anonymous 'engineer' fired by these developments wrote to *The Builder* in 1856 to say:

At present there is a shaking amongst the dry bones

of architecture; and we have preachings, denouncings and prophesyings, revivals and new creations ... Iron and glass are to supersede all other kinds of material; and not only are exhibitions and museums to be constructed of these materials but even whole town communities are to be roofed beneath glass ...[14]

Of importance for the future, however, were the opinions of Pugin and Ruskin, who, in arguing that such structures did not constitute architecture, called the Crystal Palace respectively a 'glass monster' and a 'cucumber frame'. *The Ecclesiologist*, whilst admiring the 'unprecedented internal effects', 'an effect of space' and 'a general lightness and fairy-like brilliance' concluded that 'it is not architecture; it is engineering of the highest merit and excellence ...'[15]

Moreover, it is possible that the twin train-sheds at King's Cross Station (1850-2), the work of Lewis Cubitt (1799-1883) and his engineer relation Joseph Cubitt (1811-72), owed a debt to Paxton's central transept. Although these were wider at 105ft, like the Great Stove, the ribs were made from laminated timber deals.[16] The use of these materials, in fact, dated back to the 1830s. Laminated timber arches had been used by Benjamin Green and his brother in the North-east for railway bridge construction, notably the Ouseburn and Withington Dean viaducts. The idea was again adopted by John Hawkshaw (1811-91) in 1849 for the West Riding Union Railway and appears to have stimulated a number of mill architects to employ the same device for roof structures – Buttershaw Mills and Ripley's Spring Mill, both in Bradford. Weakened by exposure to steam and smoke, the ribs at King's Cross had to be replaced in 1869-70 by steel principles, though Cubitt's decorative cast-iron shoes, which held them, remained in place.[17] The simplicity of these brackets, together with the lack of obvious ornament elsewhere, resulted in a building whose structure directly dictated the final form. King's Cross Station had an austere appearance. Ruskin preferred this, and claimed that

another of the strange and evil tendencies of the present day is to the decoration of the railroad station ... There was never more flagrant nor impertinent folly than the smallest portion of ornament in anything concerned with the railroads ... Railroad architecture has or would have a dignity of its own if it were only left to its work.[18]

Matthew Digby Wyatt (1820–77), Brunel's assistant for Paddington Station (1852–4),[19] who had previously worked for Paxton on the Crystal Palace as the superintendent architect, wrote in 1851 that he hoped 'the novelty of its [Paddington's] form and details ... will exercise a powerful influence on national taste'. Its three train-sheds (68 ft, 102 ft and 72 ft wide respectively)[20] were linked by two transverse transepts (forming a path for the locomotives to be turned about), which accentuated the length

breadth of this vast hall. Paddington, like the Crystal Palace, exhibited a range of unorthodox detailing – octagonal columns and Saracenic motifs. Fox, Henderson & Co. had again been employed to supply the cast-iron columns with their elaborate capitals.[21] They also applied the construction techniques perfected at the Crystal Palace to their design for Oxford's London & North Western Railway Terminus (1851–2).[22] Based on the flat-roofed aisles that flanked the main transept, this ridge-and-furrow train-shed may, through its various pedigrees, be seen as the descendant of Paxton's Victoria Regia Lily House (1849) – a small glasshouse with a ridge-and-furrow roof supported by wrought-iron girders and cast-iron columns.[23] On a much larger scale, Fox, Henderson & Co. made the sickle girders used for the 211 ft-span train-shed erected for New Street Station (1850–4), Birmingham, to the design of E.A. Cowper (1790–1852), the engineer, and William Baker.[24] Significantly, its office façade and hotel, by William Livock, the London architect, offered a

45 The ribs supporting one of the naves at Paddington Station (1852–4). Matthew Digby Wyatt was responsible for the details; Burke's principles of succession, uniformity, vastness and infinity are well illustrated here.

restrained *palazzo* exterior, its lower storey consisting of an arcade of Doric pilasters.

Stations and exhibition halls were not the sole application for these improved engineering and founding methods. The rotunda was selected as the basis for a number of industrial buildings. Several railway companies erected sheds on a circular plan, including that at Gorton, designed for the Sheffield & Manchester Railway in the early 1840s by Richard Peacock (p. 100). The architects were Weightman & Hadfield, assisted by the engineer Alfred S. Jee (1816–58), who was also responsible for the Dinting Viaduct, and the Woodhead and first Standedge Tunnels.[25] The Gorton shed was a cast-iron structure based on a central column with radiating bars to support an uncomplicated tie-beam roof. It probably owed a debt to the roof structures worked out at Derby Tri-junct Station (1839–41), where three tie-beam, cast-iron sheds had been designed by Robert Stephenson (1803–59), assisted in the detailing by Francis Thompson.[26] The central span of 56 ft at Derby represented an advance on the earlier but similar structure at Euston (1835–9), also by Stephenson, but only 40 ft wide. Another rotunda, Camden Town Engine Shed (1847), by Robert B. Dockray (1811–71) under Stephenson, was a larger and architecturally more satisfying design than Gorton. The Roundhouse, as it was also known, 160 ft in diameter, had a roof supported not by a single column but by an inner circle (40 ft across) of 24 cast-iron pillars in an attempt to produce a fireproof building.[27] The roof rose to a point, in contrast with Gorton's depressed centre and ring of ventilators. The outer walls were constructed from light-yellow brick and regularly reinforced by buttresses, topped with a simple dentil border. However, the growth in the number and size of locomotives using the railway soon rendered the Roundhouse inadequate and, like the rotunda at Leeds and Derby, it was replaced by a more conventional form of engine shed.

The forty years following the Crystal Palace witnessed the construction of ever larger train-sheds and market-halls – enclosed spaces of greater area. In 1865, for example, William Barlow (1812–92) erected the world's largest single arched structure at St Pancras from wrought-iron ribs, his train-shed being 243 ft across. It relied, nonetheless, on tie bars, concealed below the rail deck, connecting the spring lines of the arch. Manchester Central (1876–80), by Sir John Fowler (1817–98), though slightly narrower, dispensed with the latter and took advantage of the self-equilibriating properties of the arch form supported by brick buttresses. These structures did not commonly reflect engineering achievements in their outward form, however. Such iron halls as they contained were hidden behind masonry so that the second half of the nineteenth century was not especially distinguished by architecture in glass and iron. H.-R. Hitchcock has argued with force that:

> to a certain extent metal literally 'went underground' as new types of foundations were evolved for taller and heavier buildings; but more generally metal structure was masked with stone or brick … When the use of exposed metal and glass became significant again in the nineties that use was to be a major constituent of general architectural development …[28]

Thus it can be concluded that the 1840s and early 1850s existed as a first-base towards a summit in the use of structural iron. Nevertheless, it would be wrong to suggest that this was a conscious attempt to revolutionize architecture. The authors of these glasshouses, exhibition- or market-halls and train-sheds, mostly engineers and builders, were simply exploiting the new materials that industrialization had made available in an attempt to cover sites as cheaply and efficiently as possible. Questions of decoration, often entrusted to aspiring architects, remained subsidiary to the central engineering problems. In the cases of Paddington Station or the Crystal Palace, the team responsible for the building's design and execution was led by an engineer, specific tasks being undertaken by an architect. Later in the century, when roles had become more closely defined, engineers commonly received instructions from architects who had been entrusted with the overall commission and provided the structural parameters within which they were to work. For St Pancras Station, Barlow, consulting engineer to the Midland Railway, designed the monumental train-shed, while Sir George Scott produced the plans for the hotel that also formed the entrance to the platforms.

As a postscript to this section, it should be added that parallel and related advances occurred in the structural design of factories and warehouses. The development of the fireproof mill, a feature of the late eighteenth century, continued in this period as experiments were undertaken to discover the properties of different types and shapes of iron beams. Based on the work of Thomas Tredgold (1788–1829) and the Manchester physicist, Eaton Hodgkinson (1789–1861), these tests allowed engineers to erect buildings of greater size with safety. For 'the very frequent use of iron beams for supporting the floors of the factories, and of other places crowded with people', Hodgkinson argued, 'renders it extremely desirable that best information should be obtained with respect to the strength of this material'.[29] He also perceived the constructional advantages of such improvements, adding that:

> if by an alteration from the usual shape, the same strength could be obtained with a smaller quantity of metal, the expense would be reduced; and the material rendered even more capable of bearing more pressure, by having less to support its own weight. It may be stated in illustration of this remark, that there are usually upwards of 100 tons of metal in the beams supporting the floors of a factory.[30]

His investigations revealed that if the bottom flange were increased in size and an upper one added (so that their areas were in the proportion six to one), the strength of a cast-iron beam was 'overwhelmingly' improved.[31] That enabled engineers to erect buildings with columns spaced at 20-ft intervals, instead of 14 ft as commonly practised. 'This power of enlargement', Fairbairn, a friend and collaborator of Hodgkinson, recognized:

> occurred most opportunely, as the amplification, or rather longitudinal extension, of some of the principal machinery in cotton mills at that particular period, necessitated a considerable increase in the width of mills. Such moreover, was the confidence inspired by this improved section that I have myself constructed buildings from six to seven storeys in height, and 52 ft wide, with only one row of pillars down the centre of each room and two beams across, each 26 ft span.[32]

It appears that George Stephenson's Water Street Bridge (1829) offered the first application of Hodgkinson's flanged beams (these having been cast at Fairbairn and Lillie's foundry),[33] which predated their use in the construction of Travis Brook Mill (1834).[34] Although Hodgkinson's experiments increased the strength of these beams, the innate characteristics of cast iron meant that they remained brittle and any imperfections which lay concealed beneath the surface could cause them to break without warning. The sudden collapse of mills or their complete destruction by fire could, on occasion, be blamed on the properties of cast iron. For these reasons Fairbairn recommended 'the advantages of wrought-iron beams or joists in substitution of the more cumbersome and uncertain ones of cast iron now in general use'.[35] The superior tensile strength of wrought-iron beams and the vastly reduced likelihood that they would contain flaws were compelling reasons for their employment in fireproof factories. Further, with wrought-iron beams, Fairbairn suggested that mills 65 ft in width could be built with only a single row of internal columns.[36] Yet the greater cost of wrought iron, which required puddling and rolling, meant that its introduction appears to have been uncommon for mills (an exception being the use of fabricated wrought-iron beams at Ripley's Mill, Bradford) though more popular in warehouses. Many factories, even in the second half of the nineteenth century, were constructed with cast-iron beams, which were thought by some to be more rigid,[37] as well as cheaper.

Amongst the subsequent applications of Hodgkinson's theory, which had been studied by the directors of the Chester & Holyhead Railway, may be included the Britannia Bridge (1845–50) by Robert Stephenson and Francis Thompson. Fairbairn, the consultant engineer, recommended the use of wrought-iron plates[38] hand-riveted together to form tubes (widest span 463 ft) supported by three stone piers with twin entrance abutments.[39] Although the decorative pairs of lions (by sculptor John Thomas) were Nubian and contemporaries believed the bridge to be Egyptian in style, this was a misreading of Thompson's intentions. If anything, the restraint exhibited by the piers was slightly Italianate, while their bold prison-like grills had a sublimity which complemented the strength of the iron box girders.

Much attention has been focused on iron and its contribution to industrial buildings, but it should not be forgotten that without corresponding advances in the manufacture of glass many of the examples already listed could have proved prohibitively expensive. The rapid and relatively inexpensive construction of the Crystal Palace could not have proceeded without the introduction of the cylinder process for making sheet glass. Importing the innovation from France, Chance Brothers of Smethwick could tender successfully for 900,000 square feet of glass, as well as the further $\frac{3}{4}$-million square feet needed in the rebuilding at Sydenham.[40] The repeal of excise duty on glass in 1845 and the production of cylinder glass and plate glass by the casting process meant that architects had some of the constraints of price or shortages lifted in the design of buildings with large window areas.

Neo-classicism

The mid-1830s, under the leadership of Sir Charles Barry (1795–1860) and C.R. Cockerell (1788–1863), witnessed a move away from Greek models to those of Italy. These were executed, not with strict regard to rules of symmetry and proportion as in the Palladian period, but freely, so as to allow fuller reign to the emotions. In this Romantic era, buildings, no longer ruled by the refined dictates of reason, drew upon Roman examples in an attempt to create vital and original designs. This gradual reappraisal of classical principles was accompanied by an undermining of the hierarchy of decorum.

In the increasingly eclectic climate some argued that particular styles, rather than degrees of interpretation, were fitted to particular types of buildings. In 1851 a Mr Anderson, lecturing at Glasgow, asked:

> whether the style for houses in town is not the Palladian; whether for public monuments commemorative of conquests and triumphs, the Doric; whether the Gothic is not the appropriate one for religious structures and whether for country mansions the Elizabethan should not be preferred.[41]

This weakening of the hierarchy, combined with the migration of industry into major provincial towns and the progressive social elevation of businessmen, meant that factories and warehouses were increasingly dressed in fashionable clothes, with architects, rather than builders, employed to cut and shape the material.

One of the major advances in neo-classical architecture, and one that was to exert a great influence on the appearance of city warehouses, resulted from Barry's successful entry in the competition for the Travellers' Club (1830–2).[42] Drawing on the Renaissance merchant houses and warehouses that enlivened Italy's commercial centres,[43] and possibly in particular Raphael's Pandolfini Palace, Florence,[44] Barry chose a *palazzo* composition. For the Travellers' Club exhibited a block-like unity and regular fenestration surmounted by an accentuated cornice. Followed in 1838–40 by its neighbour, the Reform Club – based upon Antonio da Sangallo's Farnese Palace (1513–34), Rome[45] – these two provided architectural paradigms for the next twenty years, influencing the design of public buildings, offices and many warehouses.[46]

When Barry executed the Manchester Athenaeum (1837–9) in the *palazzo* manner, this encouraged others to adopt the style nearby in the city's commercial quarters, for Edward Walters (1801–72), the local architect who came to dominate warehouse building there, had just begun to experiment with this Renaissance theme. Making restrained use of the *palazzo* vocabulary, his Cobden Warehouse (1839), 16 Mosley Street, remained, because of its limited scale, something of a trial. Walters had, in fact, studied the Mannerist palaces of Alessi at Genoa when he had been sent by Sir John Rennie to supervise the construction of a Turkish ordnance plant.[47] On these travels he met Richard Cobden who persuaded him to leave his native London and set up practice in Manchester where, as industrialization proceeded, a host of lucrative commissions arose. In 1845, at a time when *The Builder* observed that 'the greatest change in the architecture of Manchester is apparent in the warehouses',[48] he built the Schwabe Warehouse, also in Mosley Street,[49] of good red brick with stone dressings. In its execution he worked out the essential features of his style: a definite rhythm of windows and hoists enlivened by bold and varied fenestration. The windows, larger and more closely spaced than academic tradition permitted, had to provide adequate light by which the cloth could be examined, finished and packaged, while the solid definition of the detailing – surrounds, entrances and cornices – ensure they would survive the effects of Manchester's erosive and sooty atmosphere.[50] An editorial in *The Builder* commented on the high standards of construction, adding that 'very considerable sums of money are spent on the warehouses in Manchester and in many cases they display not only sound construction, extending to rendering them fireproof, but good taste'.[51]

J. Brown & Son's Warehouse (1851-2), Portland Street,[52] by Walters, represented a triumph of the style, executed in a richness hitherto considered inappropriate for such a role. 'So pleasing in design and so original in treatment' was this edifice, believed *The Builder*, 'that the old-fashioned Manchester warehouse style was discarded, and Italian Renaissance buildings became the fashion.'[53] It was powerfully framed vertically by rusticated piers at each corner, whilst a horizontal emphasis had been provided at the base by double-height arches from basement to ground floor, and above by a strong cornice and balustrade which concealed a top-lit attic. Further, Walters exaggerated the decorative elements to keep them in proportion with the rest of the warehouse – this having the added advantage of combating the deadening effect of industrial grime.

Remaining in Manchester until 1865, Walters' success did not divert him from warehouse commissions (completing them at Nos 34, 10 and 12 Charlotte Street in 1860), though he included a bank and several stations amongst his later works.[54] The subsequent development of his practice revealed something of the status attached to the warehouse architect, albeit one that designed smart 'city' versions, for the two pupils whom he admitted to the partnership (Thomas Barker and George Ellis) preferred to undertake commercial projects and were responsible for the Manchester Stock Exchange, Briton Insurance offices and stations on the Lancashire & Yorkshire Railway.[55]

John Edgar Gregan (1813-55),[56] a local architect who died young, was responsible for an outstanding warehouse design on the corner of Portland and Parker Streets.[57] Erected in 1850 and untypically faced with Yorkshire stone, it offered a simple but effective contrast to Walters' more exuberant commissions.[58] Using the *palazzo* formula in the three main storeys, Gregan accentuated alternate bands of windows by simple frames and angled pediments. The base provided by the linked ground basement windows, and the shorter fifth-floor windows below the cornice, completed the building's business-like appearance.[59] As the firm, Thornton & Co., that occupied the warehouse had extensive dealings with America, the upper storeys contained a series of counting houses for visiting merchants' use, while the lower floors consisted of stores, offices, sale and sample rooms.

Part of Manchester's market in textile warehouses was captured by Edward Salomons (1828-1909). A pupil of Gregan, he had originally been employed in his father's merchant business before choosing architecture as a career.[60] One of his earliest commissions after starting his own practice in 1852 was for Daniel Lee & Co. – 'so bold and striking a building that it was a bitter disappointment to its author that it

46 A warehouse erected on the corner of Portland and Parker Streets, Manchester, by J.E. Gregan and illustrated in *The Builder* for August 1850.

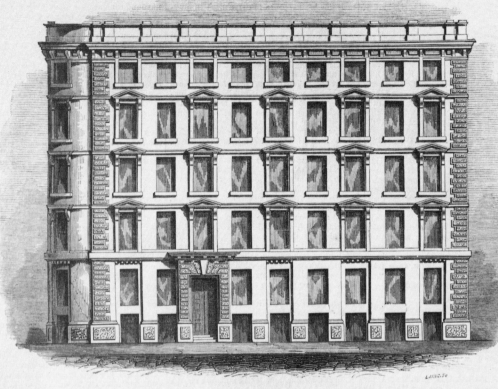

ELEVATION.

10   5   0   10   20   30 FEET

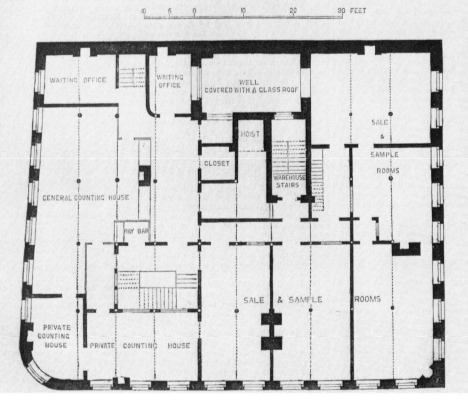

47 The imposing entrance to Daniel Lee & Co.'s warehouse (1856), designed by one of Manchester's leading architects, Edward Salomons. Note the variety of the deeply profiled windows.

did not bring him fame and the rush of employment that follows fame'.[61] Erected in 1856 at the junction of Fountain Street and Spring Gardens,[62] it did help establish Salomons in the city, though apparently not beyond south Lancashire. Subsequently he designed warehouses (including one in Manchester's Oxford Street for Nathan & Sons and that at 12 Dalton Street in 1865), several theatres, synagogues and the Reform Club (1870) in Manchester,[63] selecting a different style to suit the respective building types.[64]

The largest and most imposing warehouse in Manchester was Henry Travis and William Mangnall's design of 1856-8.[65] The sheer size of S. & J. Watts & Co.'s warehouse[66] dictated that the roofline be broken at regular intervals by large ornate dormer windows which towered above the surrounding buildings. The principal elevation possessed a wide range of Renaissance and classical features, each of its six storeys having different window surrounds and ornaments. Far more than any of Walters' compositions, it exhibited a great richness (with a Derbyshire stone façade to Portland Street) and could have passed, in scale and grandeur, for a palace; indeed, today it serves as a majestic hotel. *The Builder*'s contemporary judgement was mixed:[67]

> There is novelty in the main forms, and the use of the details of the Renaissance; but novelty is present mainly, and in predominance over that beauty which is equally or more important ... The building, then, has the effect which follows from great dimensions - aided by what will always result from good stone - an effect which cannot but be in a certain sense impressive ... The length of the principal front of this building is about 300 feet ... and in height reaches upwards of 100 feet.

However, Victorians remained impressed, and an 1888 survey of the city judged Travis & Mangnall's creation as having 'no rival of its class in the Kingdom',[68] though in function it was more akin to a wholesalers than a factory being 'stocked with Manchester goods of every description, together with every conceivable article appertaining to the silk, mercery, drapery, hosiery, and haberdashery businesses'.[69]

The palatial quality of some of these textile warehouses was further demonstrated when one in Aytoun Street was converted in 1880 as a luxury hotel, The Grand.[70] Designed in 1867 for A. Collie & Co. in a rich Italianate manner of Darley Dale stone, its architects were Alexander W. Mills (1812/3-1905)[71] and James Murgatroyd (1830-94). Mills, born in London, had started in Bunning's office but on completing his articles he moved to Manchester to work for Richard Tattershall.[72] In 1838 when Bunning, who was to remain in the capital, suggested that they become partners, Mills took charge of a new Manchester office. On Bunning's retirement in 1853, Mills took his pupil, Murgatroyd, into the partnership; it was in their office that Edgar Wood was to train.[73] As general practitioners they were responsible for the LNWR's London Road Station, a number of workhouses and the redesigning of the Royal Exchange.

Thus Manchester, having provided the environment for the adoption of *palazzo* architecture, witnessed a considerable step forward in industrial building. The wealth of warehouse owners and their desire for social and commercial status resulted in a number of outstanding designs, or, as *Building News* suggested:

> as we now boast merchant 'princes', it was, of course, to be expected that their regalia ... would be palatially housed and that a certain architectural ambition should have become blended with prosperity.[74]

This development received the critical approval of an editorial in *The Builder* for 1858 which argued that:

> all that deserves to be aimed at, is an expression *consistent with* the purpose ... We would not have a lunatic asylum look like a prison, or a church like a theatre ... We may, as to these warehouses, at least ask to be shown what is the character proper for buildings which are allied to retail shops, more

48 The grandeur and sheer scale of S. & J. Watt's warehouse in Portland Street, Manchester.

than to the class of wholesale stores of heavy goods. Granaries, or the warehouses of a seaport might properly be required to appear very different to them externally.[75]

In this judgement the author was not strictly accurate. For as will be seen in the cases of Nottingham and Bradford, many of these warehouses were more akin to factories than shops, as they performed a number of finishing processes in addition to their packing and sales functions. It was their situation in financial and commercial quarters, rather than at the dockside or close to factory gates, which had prompted architectural embellishment, together with the need to impress visiting clients. This combined with an association of ideas – that they were seen to resemble the merchant houses of Renaissance Italy – explained the adoption of the *palazzo* style.

The Lace Market, Nottingham's warehouse area, came to be dominated by the local architect Thomas Chambers Hine (1813-99), in the same way that Walters rose to prominence in Manchester. A former pupil of Matthew Habershon (1789-1852), his works included the Great Northern station at Nottingham and the buildings on the line from there to Grantham, the design and restoration of some 30 to 40 parish churches in the Midlands, numerous houses and some 'thirty of the principal warehouses and factories associated with the lace and hosiery manufacture in this town'.[76] The finest of his warehouses was probably the one for Messrs Adams & Page, on the corner of Broadway and Stoney Street. Completed in 1854-5,[77] it comprised a central entrance beneath a column of bay windows and topped by an elaborate balustrade and decorative pediment. The E-plan, together with the quality of materials used (red dressed bricks with Ancaster and Matlock stone dressings) did not, however, win universal acclaim.

49 Messrs Adams & Page's warehouse (1854-5) by T.C. Hine in the Lace Market, Nottingham.

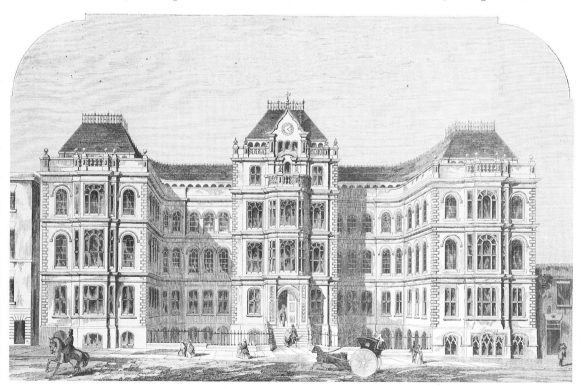

The editor of the *Nottingham Review* referring to its 'odious windows and ugly doorways', suggested that 'a man may ... ask what sort of exhibition this new Nottingham will make when its irregular streets are fully occupied by their equally irregular edifices?'[78] His opinions have not stood review and the warehouse's striking elevation, with its overtones of French Empire style, can now be seen to have represented a major contribution to the city's architecture.

Like so many Manchester warehouses, this too was in effect a factory as well as a storehouse. The lace was machined in these buildings before being packaged and dispatched, whilst rooms were also allocated for the inspection and sale of samples. Thomas Adams' evangelical faith and philanthropic disposition prompted the provision of a chapel (distinguished at the base of the right-hand wing by incongruous Gothic tracery windows), library and classroom, together with a separate dining building.[79] It is interesting to note that the adjacent warehouse of 1855 for Messrs Birkin, also by Hine, had a stone tablet above the entrance containing the architect's, owner's and builder's initials accompanied by a crossed trowel and hammer.

An earlier warehouse commission (Hine & Mundella's Hosiery Factory, Station Street), erected in 1851, may be quoted as an example of architectural continuity. This five-storey factory, though exhibiting features of Hine's personal style – an elaborate Dutch gable and bay windows over a Doric entrance – had yet to abandon the more rigid, restrained Palladian model revealed by the use of simple regular windows arranged in a symmetrical pattern.[80] A short description in *The Builder* – 'the principal entrance to the building is through a recessed portico in the circular corner at the intersection of the two streets and, which, with the staircase and offices on the same, connect the warehouses and factory together'[81] – constituted one of the earliest references to an industrial building in this journal published since 1842, and reflected the gradual acceptance of the warehouse into the world of architectural respectability.

One of the finest groups of city warehouses survived almost undisturbed in Bradford's 'Little Germany'. Taking its name from the continental businessmen who had settled in the district, it consisted, as James observed in 1866, of 'numerous merchants' and manufacturers' warehouses, which ... may vie in external architecture with the most splendid of their kind in the kingdom. They are, indeed, palatial structures, and add greatly to the appearance of the town'.[82] These were the work, as in Manchester or Nottingham, of a few architects' practices (Milnes and France, Lockwood and Mawson, together with Andrews and Delaunay) that specialized in these types of building. However, among the first to be built on a grand scale in the *palazzo* style was one in Hall Ings for Milligan, Forbes & Co. (1852–3), designed by William Andrews (1804–70) and Mr Delaunay (d.1864), a Frenchman articled in Manchester, whom he had taken into partnership in 1848.[83] This elegant four-storey stone structure exhibited a variety of closely-spaced window surrounds set within a frame provided by accented quoins, bold string courses, a rusticated ground floor and a simple dentil cornice.[84] The site cost about £7,000 and the building itself a further £20,000. Different types of woollen cloths were stored in the first three floors and basement, whilst goods received from dyers were examined, measured and folded in the fourth storey before being consigned below.[85]

As in other industrial towns, most of these warehouses performed more than a simple storage role. Finishing and distribution operations were all contained within their mannered ashlar walls. Merchants purchased cloth directly from the loom and took responsibility for all subsequent processes, sending cloth out to be dyed after an initial inspection.[86] *The Builder*, describing a Bradford warehouse, summarized its various functions:

> The basement floor of each consists of piece-rooms and blanket-stores; on the ground floors are the counting houses, grey-rooms and packing shops. The three intermediate floors are occupied as goods, stock and sale rooms; and the top floor as making up rooms. Hoists worked by steam power communicate with each storey.[87]

Clear natural light by which to inspect the

material in all its stages, in an age of poor artificial substitutes, determined the need for many large windows on all floors and the provision of a central well. Hence the departure from the generous spacing demanded by the historic *palazzo* model.

Eli Milnes (1830–99), regarded as the leading warehouse architect in Bradford, designed some of the finest buildings in the town.[88] A local man, he had been articled to Walker Rawstorne (d.1867) of Bradford, subsequently entering into partnership with John Dixon (d.1854), but after Dixon's death,[89] he admitted Charles France (1833–1902) to the firm in 1863; his own son, Charles E. Milnes, becoming a partner in 1888. Both Rawstorne and Dixon had already entered the warehouse market, the former constructing them for Russell Douglas & Co. and Oxley & Co. in Leeds Road during 1844, and the latter for Leo Schuster (1838) in Charles Street and for John Haigh & Co. and Frederick Schwann & Co., Hall Ings, both in 1849.[90] Milnes' practice prospered on the back of the town's growing commercial and business community and included Priestley's warehouse (1867), 66 Vicar Lane, where he produced a slightly austere corner block, the entrance on the angle, in which a variety of recessed windows were placed between a tapered plinth and machicolated cornice.[91] The relative simplicity of this *palazzo* warehouse and that which he had erected at 53–55 Leeds Road in 1859–62,[92] contrasted with the richness of the one he built in Peel Place (1862), costing £12–13,000, where a greater variety of window surrounds suggested an owner with a generous purse and a desire to impress.[93] The tendency towards a profusion of ornament and fuller architectural treatment, often on a large scale, occurred as a feature of the late 1860s and 1870s in Bradford and elsewhere (p. 150 ff).

A certain continuity there, as in Lancashire (p. 192), was provided by the building contractor, who, if he were successful, could almost monopolize the market for the execution of industrial commissions in certain districts. McKean Tetley's home-trade warehouse in Peel Square had, for example, been erected by one of the town's master builders, Archibald Neill

(1825–74).[94] Born in Musselburgh, he came to Bradford in 1851 to supervise the construction of the Lancashire & Yorkshire Railway's goods warehouse in Vicar Lane on behalf of his brother, a Manchester contractor. Although subsequently involved with other types of building (workhouses, hotels, stations, banks and villas), he continued to erect warehouses including Carver's (1869), Vicar Lane; Leo Schuster's (1873), Leeds Road; E.B. Behrens' (1873), Peckover Street; and that for Law & Russell (1874), Vicar Lane.[95] Neill also won part of the contract for Saltaire Mills and the model village and constructed the Alston Works (1865), Thornton Road, for Isaac Holden. His firm was among the earliest integrated contractors in Yorkshire. Employing as many as 1,400, the business embraced every operation from the quarrying of stone at Wrose and Calverley to the most detailed joinery and plumbing work. Neill himself patented machinery to notch floor beams for joists, and for the dressing of stone.[96]

For Glasgow's mercantile and commercial quarters a similar story unfolded. Yet those city warehouses at 81 Miller Street (1849–50), designed by James Salmon (1805–88)[97] and executed in a modified Palladian manner, exhibited something of the conservatism of Scottish architects.[98] The symmetrical and ordered arrangement of Georgian fenestration was disturbed only on the ground floor, where a row of round-headed windows lit the offices. The restraint evident in No. 81 contrasted with the exuberance and vitality of No. 37 Miller Street (1854).[99] This warehouse, designed by Alexander Kirkland (c.1824–92) in Venetian Renaissance style, created a sense of movement by the range of ornament and variety of windows, capped by a light cornice and parapet. Both buildings, like so many of Manchester's city warehouses, reflected the status of their merchant owners and for clients gave their businesses an aura of respectable solidity – in the manner of the splendid offices commissioned by insurance companies later in the century.[100]

The *palazzo* formula could be adapted to suit the demands of a railway terminus, though this did not commonly occur. London Bridge Station

50 Priestley's warehouse, 66 Vicar Lane, Bradford, designed by Eli Milnes in 1867. One of the simplest façades in Little Germany, but dignified and exhibiting stonework of high quality.

(1844–5),[101] built by Henry Roberts (1803–76),[102] a former pupil of both Charles Fowler and Sir Robert Smirke, together with Thomas Turner, gained the approval of the *Illustrated London News*:

> the Italian *palazzo* style ... is the prevailing one in the company's buildings; the choice having been determined by the convenience of its general arrangement, its cheapness and the suitability of its picturesque decorations to the bustling character of a railway site ... the campanile made here to serve the useful purpose of a clock tower is certainly a striking and appropriate feature.[103]

Possibly the irregular or extended shapes demanded of the station militated against *palazzo* compositions which required an upright and compact block.

Industrial Italianate

Whilst the *palazzo* model could be effectively adapted to city warehouses or, rarely, station booking halls, the less orthodox demands of factories meant that, if they were intended to be architecturally distinguished, then the looser dictates of the Italianate style were commonly observed. One of the best-known examples of the latter's use in mill design occurred at Saltaire, which may also serve as an illustration of the acceptance that industrial structures had earned over the previous half century.

Henry F. Lockwood (1811–78)[104] and his partner William Mawson (1828–89)[105] planned a huge alpaca mill and model town for their owner Sir Titus Salt. The mill (1850–3), one of the first industrial buildings to be illustrated in *The Builder*[106] (which had earlier suggested that

51 Saltaire Mills (1851–3); the round-arched windows beside the central entrance formerly lit the two engine houses.

its 'walls look more like those of a fortified town than a building destined to the peaceful pursuits of commerce'),[107] possessed an imposing southern façade (six storeys and 545 ft in length) dominated by two Italianate towers. The main entrance was enlivened by a curved pediment with scrolls, and the 250 ft chimney resembled a great campanile, the whole being constructed of local dressed stone. Its popularity with many was reflected in John James' comments, who having referred to Saltaire as a 'palace of industry', added:

> Whether this colossal structure be contemplated with respect to the magnificence and appropriateness of its architecture, the notable excellence and ingenuity of the machinery ... it certainly, as the largest and best contrived of factories, stands supremely at the head of those in the worsted department.[108]

Again, Fairbairn had been the consulting engineer, responsible for its fireproof interior (cast-iron columns and beams with hollow brick arches to reduce the weight of the floors)[109] and the arrangement of the spinning and weaving machines – the drives in the weaving shed being placed beneath the floor for safety.[110] To facilitate the manufacturing process, the single-storey shed with its north-facing lights, which housed the power looms, was adjacent to the multi-storey spinning mill. A debt to the past, and this was scarcely unique, may be discerned in the ordered symmetrical plan to which both mill and town were erected, while the twin loggia

52 The ground plan of Saltaire Mills taken from *The Builder*, August 1854.

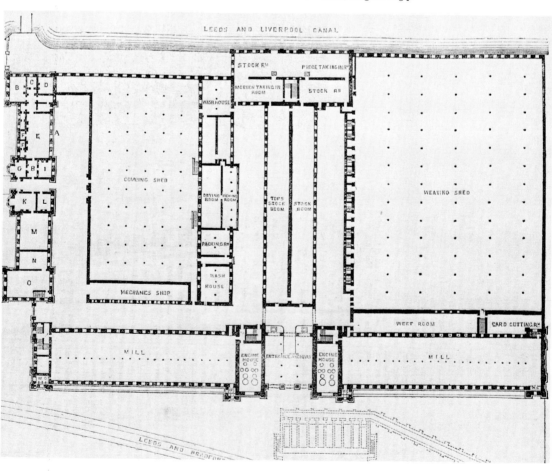

towers formed an essential part of the former's balanced composition.[111]

Although Lockwood and Mawson earned a considerable volume of industrial commissions, their practice, like so many other provincial firms engaged in factory design, had a general character. Indeed, a contemporary report remarked that during the period 1850–80 when 'the majority of the buildings in the centre of the city were erected – they appear to have been virtually the architectural dictators of Bradford'.[112] Lockwood, a native of Doncaster, trained in London as a pupil of Peter Robinson (1776–1858) and, having superintended the rebuilding of York Castle, moved to Hull to set up his own practice. Here he was joined by William Mawson who had completed his articles with Chantrell & Dobson, the Leeds architects. After Lockwood and Mawson transferred to Bradford in 1849, the local Board of Guardians provided them with one of their first commissions – a workhouse – although the partnership was soon to benefit from the prosperity of the textile trade.[113] Once established, however, Lockwood returned to the capital in 1874 and opened an office at 10 Lincoln's Inn to be more readily able to compete for the most prestigious prizes. The firm's industrial expertise gained them an international dimension, as continental nations anxious to learn from British experience appointed architects from Lancashire and Yorkshire. Lockwood and Mawson designed works for M. Scheppers Loth in Belgium and others at Asnières, near Paris, Dusseldorf and Alsace. When William Mawson retired in 1886 the practice was kept going by his younger brother, Richard Mawson (1834–1904), who as a 'young architect of special talent' had been admitted to the partnership at an early age.[114] It seems that Richard, a man of artistic ability, designed many of the buildings, while William, who was of a more practical disposition, ran the business and performed much arbitration and valuation work, one of his final tasks being the conversion of Manningham Mills into a limited liability concern.

Other mills that exhibited Italianate features, though to a lesser degree, and constructed on a smaller scale than Saltaire, included Black Dyke Mills, Queensbury, Copley Mills, Akroydon, Haley Hill Mill and Dean Clough Mills, both in Halifax. Whilst the main five-storey block (No. 16, or Victoria, Mill) at Black Dyke possessed a definite Italianate exterior and tower – it dated from c.1857 – the earlier entrance lodge (c.1842–8), situated between the mechanics' shop and the counting house in Brighouse Road, stood as an example of architecture in transition.[115] The arrangement was Palladian – a basket arch surmounted by a dentil pediment and bell cupola – but the freer handling suggested the Renaissance style that was to appeal to so many mill-owners and architects.

Copley Mills, when enlarged for Colonel Edward Akroyd (1811–87) in 1847, followed the earlier Palladian tradition established there in the simple repetition of forms and absence of obvious external ornament.[116] However, this expansion of capacity was accompanied by the completion of a triumphal arch: an imposing stone gateway enlivened by Roman Doric pilasters and an angled pediment.[117] Its clock and bellcote marked shifts and the lodge recorded movements of goods and the number of hours worked by employees. The Italianate tower that dominated the river end of Copley Mills could have been added in 1865. Akroyd, like Salt, believed that a businessman's duties extended beyond the factory walls and he, too, constructed a number of houses for his workforce, the local architect, W.H. Crossland (1823–1909), being employed to design the village.[118] Sir George Gilbert Scott had been approached by Akroyd and recommended that his former pupil Crossland adapt the plans and carry them into effect. Work started in 1861 and some 350 houses of varying size were erected at Akroydon.[119] Speaking specifically of New Lanark, Zachariah Allen declared that the 'plan of building up a village, as well as the manufactory, is termed, in England, the "colonizing system", and is not much relished by manufacturers, who dislike such heavy investments in real estate, amounting to nearly as much as the fixtures and machinery of an equal manufactory in Manchester'.[120] An entrepreneur, therefore, who was prepared to spend precious capital on housing was also likely to believe that the architecture of his buildings was worth some consideration – Salt, Owen, Cadbury and Lever were men of this class. Haley Hill Mill (1836), nearby in Halifax, was another Akroyd project, and when it was enlarged in 1856 the earlier simple pattern of building was imitated.[121] A feature of this and Copley Mill were the rounded bays that fronted the projecting staircase towers.

'Among the factories of Halifax', observed James in 1857, 'are two of the largest establishments of their kind in the kingdom, namely Mr Akroyd's for damasks, &c., and Messrs Crossley's (at Dean Clough) for carpets'.[122] John Crossley & Sons, having successfully mechanized their carpet-weaving process, undertook a major expansion programme at Dean Clough, building two six-storey blocks ('D' and 'E' Mills) between 1854 and 1857.[123] Designed by Roger Ives, a local architect, the Italianate detailing received fullest attention in the corner towers and staircase bays, the windows and remainder showing only minimal adornment (p. 59). Other mills followed – 'F' in 1858, 'G' in 1867 and 'H' in 1869 – so that by 1885 there were eight, together with three weaving sheds, which led an observer to comment:

> There is little of the picturesque about them. There is no unity of structure. They comprise a series of establishments varying in every element of size and are thus in striking contrast to the Saltaire works. The difference is easily accounted for. Saltaire is the creation of a manufacturer who had attained success and reconstructed his works as a whole in the height of his success, and was thus able to pay attention to detail, to architectural embellishment, and to adapt every portion of his gigantic work to the special uses to which it was attended. The Dean Clough Mills, on the other hand are clustered round the site ... on which the first mill occupied ... and as one mill after another has been built ... they are thus a record of a continuous progress.[124]

The later mills were designed by another local architect, F.W. Petty.

To demonstrate the widespread appeal of Italianate models J. Whitmore's (now H.T.H. Peck's) spinning factory (c.1848), West Bridge,

Leicester may be quoted. Constructed from local red brick, this tall mill with its loggia staircase tower and restrained cornice revealed less emphasis in its detailing than the public buildings erected in the town by its architect, William Flint (1801–62).[125]

Although less susceptible to such treatment, a few ironworks of the period were erected in an Italianate style. The Round Oak Iron Works, Brierley Hill, built in 1857 for Lord Ward, was designed to be a model of its kind, no expense being spared in the construction and equipment.[126] The main building (480 ft by 138 ft), which housed the puddling furnaces and rolling mills, was open on two sides, with louvred ventilators in the roof to reduce the working temperature and facilitate the movement of metal.[127] The brick walls that formed the other two sides, like the twin warehouses and the central entrance, had been executed in an Italianate manner with round-arched windows or blind arcades enlivened by stone quoins and a dentil border. Similarly John Brown's Atlas Ironworks in Savile Street East, Sheffield, which were acquired in 1856, had Italianate entrance buildings and offices.[128] Elsewhere in the town the Sheaf Works (probably built in the 1820s for William Greaves),[129] situated near the terminus of the Sheffield Canal possessed an elegant four-storey office block and store whose classical proportions and detailing typified much of the town's better industrial building at the time.[130] The Green Lane Works (1860) of Hoole & Robson, though not Italianate, exhibited classical features, being entered through a tripartite triumphal arch enlivened by relief panels of Vulcan and Art over the pedestrian gates.[131] A clock in an ornate timber cupola announced the time to the workforce. Alfred Stevens became director of design there in 1849 and was responsible for shaping their products: grates, firebacks and ornamental ironwork. At Rotherham the Holmes Works, Steel Street, erected in 1842 by Peter Stubs, the file maker, offered an exceptional example of the successful importation of classical principles into an integrated steelworks. The works were entered through a triumphal gateway that could have graced a mansion. The six cementation furnaces (distinguished by their bottle-shaped chimneys and neat stone caps) were arranged in two rows of three, linked together by a single-storey building with three gabled ends.[132] Its symmetrical arrangement, pedimented entrance and blind arcade revealed that classical features could be sensitively applied to a steelworks in an effective and appropriate fashion without impairing its practical operation.

A few port warehouses adopted the Italianate theme, and the Ivory House, or 'I' Warehouse (1852), by George Aitchison Senior (d.1862),[133] at St Katharine Docks, exhibited continuity with Telford's earlier structures in the use of stock brick and exposed iron columns, although the clock tower and range of window forms revealed a richer interpretation. Yet the ordered symmetry of the block, the lightness of touch and some of the detailing harked back to the eighteenth century.

However, it seems that the Ivory House was something of an exception, as a number of warehouses erected along the Thames in the mid-Victorian period retained an adherence to the classical tradition. Several of those constructed on the south bank in Southwark were the work of the Allen, Snooke and Stock partnership. The founder, George Allen (1798–1847), who practised in Tooley Street and had been a pupil of James Elmes (1782–1862), winning the Royal Academy's Silver Medal in 1820, was 'extensively employed in valuations, building of warehouses and other works'.[134] He designed Fenning's Wharf (1836), a four-storey warehouse, much in the tradition of Alexander at London Docks, with a balanced composition of segment-headed windows and hoists set above the round arches of the ground floor. Decoration was limited to rusticated quoins and a shallow pediment to the elevation facing London Bridge. Allen's warehouse commissions also included those for Mr Aldis Humphery on the north side of Southwark Cathedral in 1838, Cotton Wharf for Messrs Scovell, Jopping's Wharf (after 1843) and Davis's Wharf.[135] Henry Stock (1824/5–1909),[136] a pupil of Allen, entered the office in 1840, and when the latter died, he took over the

business in partnership with William Snooke (d.1883). Snooke, who 'devoted most of his attention to the surveying part of the business' (Stock carrying out the architectural work), also took over Allen's post as District Surveyor for Rotherhithe and Hatcham.[137] The firm of Snooke and Stock continued to earn fees from warehouse commissions and, following in the style of Allen, designed massive classical structures that relied for effect upon simple variations in composition rather than a profusion of ornament.

Among their finest work must be included Hay's Dock. 'E', 'C' and part of 'B' blocks (c.1856–7), each of five storeys of brick with stone or stucco dressings, were formally treated; a continuous round-arched arcade supported a main order retained by a succession of pilasters linked together by semicircular heads and surmounted by a simple cornice and parapet. The Tea Auction Room, centrally placed in Counter Street, was indicated by a paired window and angled pediment. John Humphery, for whom the wharf was built, had married two sons to daughters of William Cubitt (1785–1861), the contractor, and his firm undertook its erection. The various fireproof floors, described in 1857 by James Loveday,[138] consisted either of stone and brick arches, concrete and slate, or asphalt and brick, some with timber floorboards. Snooke and Stock were also responsible for those warehouses on the western side of Hay's Dock that had to be replaced after the great Tooley Street fire of 1861. Although the firm developed as a general practice, they were responsible for a number of industrial and commercial projects, including various factories for Peek, Frean & Co., Bermondsey (1898–1906); Paul's Wharf for Alex. Cowan & Sons, Upper Thames Street; and workshops in Childers Street, Deptford.

The Italianate villa provided a suitable model for railway booking halls, and vice versa. J.C. Loudon's *Encyclopaedia of Cottage, Farm and Villa Architecture* (1842) contained several designs for cottages that had, in fact, been copied from existing stations.[139] However, of the many examples which this period of railway speculation produced, Chester Station (1847–8) by

Francis Thompson was outstanding.[140] Executed in local red brick with stone dressings, the particularly long façade was successfully broken by twin projecting blocks, each with a central balconied window and corner loggia towers. Others of comparable quality included Sir William Tite's (1793-1873) Southampton Terminus (1839)[141] whose *palazzo*-like three-storey block was entered through a rusticated round-arched arcade; and in the capital, the London & Southampton Railway built Nine Elms Station (1837-8), also by Tite, with a stuccoed façade dominated by a fine arched entrance.

Engineering works

One of the most successful works of the mid-nineteenth century was established by James Nasmyth (1808-90), who had initially set up as a mechanical engineer and machine-tool maker in a floor of an old mill in Dale Street, Manchester.[142] To expand, in 1836 he moved to an undeveloped site at Patricroft. Timber workshops were assembled so that interruptions to production would be minimized; although the slow pace at which Bellhouse erected the buildings meant that a number of orders had to be cancelled.[143] The situation was alleviated when the Birleys, Manchester cotton manufacturers, who saw advantages in having a tied engineering works, agreed to provide financial backing for his new enterprise. By the end of 1837 Hugh Birley and his younger brother, Joseph, had invested £4,883 in the business. Caution led them to insist that the Bridgewater Foundry be so designed as to permit conversion to cotton spinning should it get into difficulties.[144] Accordingly, when the temporary buildings were replaced by masonry, a five-storey factory (100 ft by 60 ft) known as the 'mill building' was completed in 1838. It was constructed of brick made from clay that lay just beneath the surface at Patricroft. Resembling a Palladian spinning mill, the particular feature was a corner staircase tower topped with a decorative cap. Such a multi-storey structure was unsuitable for forge and foundry work, so that:

> the top and fourth storeys are used as pattern stores, the third storey is given up partly to brass-

finishers and the template-makers, whilst another portion is used as the erecting shop. One end is used for erecting cotton presses, which are long kinds of machines, and to make room for them a part of the floor above has been cut away, and the lifting crane used in connection with the work is fixed to the joists of a third floor.[145]

Apart from these difficulties, the foundry was laid out so that goods could move from one production process to another with as little diversion as possible. The other buildings were one-storey sheds linked by railway tracks. These had a classical appearance (pilasters between the windows and a simple cornice) while the chimney had a pedestal decorated with angled pediments.[146] Nasmyth, who was prone to exaggerate his achievements, wrote that he, together with an assistant, John Clerk, had designed the structures. Clerk had formerly worked for Fairbairn and Lillie and was foreman of the pattern-making department. 'I found him', recalled Nasmyth:

> of great use in superintending the erection of the additional workshops which were required in proportion as our business extended. He made out full-sized chalk-line drawings from my original pencil sketches on the large floor of the pattern store, and from these were formed the working drawings for the new buildings.[147]

His autobiography does not record whether an architect was employed. He may have sought advice from his friend Fairbairn, but as with so many industrial enterprises of the time, construction, layout and operation methods were subject to experiment.

The Gorton Foundry of Beyer, Peacock & Co. was also an enterprise in which the first partners played a major part in the design of the buildings. Charles Beyer (1813-76), who in 1854-5 planned and erected the Gorton works, had travelled to England from Saxony to study textile machinery and had eventually joined the Manchester drawing office of Sharp, Roberts & Co. After they re-entered the locomotive market, he became their chief engineer, but in 1853 left to set up on his own. In the following year Beyer formed a partnership with Richard Peacock (1820-89), locomotive superintendent of the

Manchester & Sheffield Railway, and they began to make their own engines.[148] By 1887 the Gorton Foundry occupied 22 acres and a contemporary account observed:

> having so admirable a site at their command, the founders were enabled to lay out their works upon a plan which would afford the greatest amount of room in the many departments.[149]

The works were arranged in three main avenues, the eastern one (123 ft in length) being divided into two storeys and serving as a pattern-making shop, general smithy and boiler shops. The locomotive-erecting shop occupied the centre avenue, and the iron foundry with its overhead cranes lay to the west – both were 163 ft long. A block to the south contained the forge and wheel-making shop.

When Nettlefold & Chamberlain, the Birmingham manufacturers of woodscrews, decided to build new premises in Heath Street, Smethwick, adjoining a canal arm, they judged that the success of the enterprise in part depended on having safe and efficient plant. Accordingly, the Heath Street Works, begun in 1854 (consisting then of two linked one-storey sheds, 219 ft long and 50 ft wide), were designed with cellars to house the shafting, with band holes for the belting. Normally this dangerous machinery was installed at roof level with consequent safety risks. Externally the factory, executed in alternate bands of red and blue engineering brick (a local tradition), had a restrained Italianate appearance created by a succession of round-arched recessed panels along the length of the mill. That the London architect, Thomas Chatfeild Clarke (1829–95) was responsible for the extension of the works (around 1863) was certain, and he may too have designed the original 1854 buildings. His appointment presumably had been influenced by the fact that Nettlefold and Chamberlain both followed Unitarianism, while Clarke in 1862 designed the Unity (Unitarian) Church at Islington, and in 1859 had married a daughter of J.S. Nettlefold.[150] Not a specialist industrial architect, he did nevertheless design a number of warehouses, including those on the Thames for the West Kent Wharf; the Dublin

and Leith; and the Glasgow Wharf.[151] In 1880 Clarke produced the plans for Nettlefolds' new Birmingham offices in Broad Street, together with a new mill there in 1882.[152] When the Heath Street woodscrew plant expanded during the nineteenth century, similar building methods and materials were employed in a style contiguous to that of the founding period. The use of recessed panels there, as in other industrial structures, although primarily for decoration, also resulted from sound business considerations. In an age when labour was comparatively cheap and economies needed to be exercised over materials, considerable savings could be made on bricks without dangerously weakening the building's structure.

On the opposite side of Heath Street was the Patent File Co.'s Birmingham Works – later the Imperial Mills of Nettlefolds Ltd. Built in 1864, it was among the finer examples of industrial architecture in the Smethwick area. In its use of different-coloured materials and attention to detail, the one-storey street façade was distinctive. The central entrance with linen-fold gates was surmounted by an ornate Dutch gable into which were set the company's shield and a date plaque.[153] This building contained the various offices, stores, fitters' and smiths' shops, whilst the cutting and pickling shops, rolling mills and engine house were situated behind in plainer sheds. The machinery and furnace plans were signed by S.H.F. Cox, agent and contractor, Sheffield, The architect was Robert C. May (1829–83) of Westminster.[154] He was, in fact, a civil engineer much concerned with railways, whose other work included gasworks at Cuckfield and Ashford. He also designed the aqueduct and South Eastern Railways' waterworks at Hastings. The Smethwick file works appears to have been his only true factory commission and, if judged by its appearance and the prosperity of its later occupants, it was a success.

The Egyptian movement

The Romantic environment in which neo-classical architecture flourished also generated an interest in ancient Egypt. Although never as popular as Roman or Greek models, the movement did, nevertheless, find adherents throughout Britain, and, as the example of the Bute Ironworks has shown, also in industry. Probably the best-known, and certainly one of the outstanding factory designs of the period, was Marshalls' Temple Mills (1838–40) in Leeds.[155] Joseph Bonomi (1796–1878), the architect, who had spent ten years in Egypt studying archaeological sites, allowed no restraint in the execution of this one-storey stone mill. The offices, which were set back from the road, appeared as

an ancient temple, and the adjacent spinning shed was dominated by a row of massive columns with papyrus-leaf capitals; the Nubian theme continued in the obelisk-shaped chimney. Whilst Temple Mills was one of the few factories to be executed in this style, its sublime treatment was in tune with much industrial architecture. The solidity, black coating of grime and seemingly endless repetition of forms instilled something of Burke's qualities of 'vastness, infinity, succession and awe'.

In its planning James Marshall, son of John Marshall II, had a considerable influence; he argued successfully with his father for the adoption of a single-storey mill, as against the conventional multi-storey building:

53 The principal entrance and office building of Temple Mills (1838–40), Leeds. An unusual but outstanding example of industrial architecture.

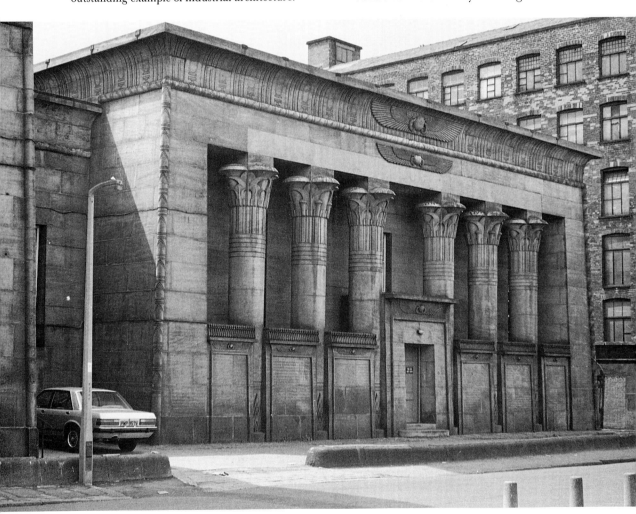

In no case could the one-storey be more expensive than the six-storey. We have a model one third the full size and 6 ft high by 24 ft each way put up on boards ... by which we can compare accurately the light given by the two plans of mill. Light by the skylights [of the one-storey mill] though only half the area of the other windows is clearly and decidedly better and more uniform and there is no difficulty from the shadows from it being too vertical ... The concentration of the one storey plan I still think a great advantage for the arrangement of work, overlooking, etc.[156]

Natural illumination was, in fact, provided by 65 glass domes. The factory, described by Disraeli in *Sybil* as 'one of the marvels of the district' had been scrupulously laid out:

a single room [396 ft by 216 ft], spreading over nearly two acres, and holding more than two thousand work-people. The roof of groined arches, lighted by ventilating domes at the height of eighteen feet, was supported by hollow cast-iron columns, through which the drainage of the roof was effected. The height of the ordinary rooms in which the work-people in manufactories are engaged is not more than nine to eleven feet; and these are built in storeys, the heat and effluvia of the lower rooms communicated to those above, and the difficulty of ventilation insurmountable. At [Marshalls], by an ingenious process, not unlike that which is practised in the House of Commons, the ventilation was carried on from below, so that the whole building was kept at a steady temperature.[157]

Attention to detail included installation of a forced warm-air system and channels set into the floor filled with water to maintain the humidity necessary in the flax-spinning process.[158]

The total bill for the mill came to £27,443, which was reckoned to be the same as that for a multi-storey fireproof structure, Marshall adding that 'the cut stone front . . . had greatly enhanced the cost, and that being the first building of the kind erected in the neighbourhood of Leeds, it had naturally been more expensive than others would be'.[159] Apparently the decision to adopt a single-storey building had been inspired by a weaving shed constructed by a Mr Smith of Deanstone which relied on a similar structure.[160] The advantages of such a plan were declared to be:

convenience of supervision, facility of access to the machines, the power of sustaining uniformity of temperature and moisture, the absence of currents of air which are so objectionable in other mills, the simplicity of the driving gear, and the excellent ventilation which is so desirable for the health of the workpeople.[161]

However, single-storey sheds were not commonly adopted for spinning though considered suitable for weaving. A multi-storey mill required less land and could be built more cheaply, whilst different operating criteria ruled in the case of weaving (p. 163).

Among the other structures to exhibit Egyptian characteristics may be mentioned Brunel's Wharncliffe Viaduct (1838), Hanwell, which carried the Great Western Railway on a series of massive tapered brick piers, their simple stone capitals shaped in a Nubian fashion.[162] Its name, and the coat-of-arms, derived from the Earl of Wharncliffe, the chairman of the committee who had steered the Railways Bill through the Lords. Brunel's original designs for the Clifton Suspension Bridge (1829) revealed that the piers at each side were to have been decorated with Egyptian motifs, though as executed by W.H. Barlow only the pylon shape was retained, in a modified form.[163]

The fact that, in common with other building types, the Egyptian movement achieved only a limited following, reinforces the argument that industrial architecture did not develop in a vacuum, and was not responsible for the creation of a distinct 'functional tradition' which may be traced in an unbroken line through to the modern period; industrial buildings, once admitted within the sphere of architectural respectability, reflected and responded to fashion just as palaces, churches and public buildings mirrored, heralded or actually introduced changes in popular taste.

Summary

The development of neo-classical architecture in Britain corresponded with a period when building in iron and glass reached a premature peak. This summit was partly the result of

54 The influence of the Egyptian movement may be detected in the shape of the stone capitals and brick piers supporting the Wharncliffe Viaduct (1838) by Brunel. The scale of this structure was among the novelties introduced by the railways.

improvements in the production of cast and wrought iron, combined with advances in engineering science, pioneered by empiricists such as Hodgkinson and Fairbairn. The continued advance of industrialization demanded novel structures (train-sheds, larger halls, mills and warehouses) for which these new materials were particularly suited. The 1840s and 1850s witnessed an important matching of technical achievement, consumer demand and popular taste. Just as in sixteenth-century Florence Giorgio Vasari had written *The Lives of the Artists*,[164] so in mid-nineteenth-century England Samuel Smiles, a barometer of public opinion, wrote *The Lives of the Engineers*.[165]

Although Gothic architecture had done much

to establish itself by 1850 (see following chapter), the predominant style was Italianate, and its historical associations with successful trade and finance had secured it a virtual monopoly amongst industrial buildings. The *palazzo* form adapted well to city warehouses, while substantial mills such as Saltaire, Dean Clough and Black Dyke took a looser Italianate model, thereby establishing a tradition that was to continue long after the style had fallen from more general favour.[166]

It was as if designers (whether architects or engineers) were travelling along separate paths; the architects experimenting with Renaissance models, and the engineers seeing ever greater applications for their new materials and structural understanding. For the moment the two remained parallel developments and it was really not until the late nineteenth century that close co-operation resulted in the creation of original designs. J.B. Bunning's (1802–63) Coal Exchange of 1846–9 illustrates this divergence.[167] Although strictly speaking a commercial building, its industrial associations and actual composition revealed much of these conflicting contemporary attitudes. Situated in the City of London and performing an important business role there, its exterior of dressed stone was appropriately executed in the *palazzo* manner. Yet these outer garments, so fitted to its function and situation, belied its interior structure. Inside a glazed cast-iron rotunda rose the entire height of the Exchange, taking industry as its decorative theme. The columns, brackets and railings that formed its circular galleries were of iron cast to resemble twined lengths of thick rope, in robust patterns of which *The Builder* remarked, 'the less said the better'.[168] The spaces between the ribs were filled with porcelain panels illustrating mining scenes and fossil plants found within coal seams. Victorians at the mid-point of the nineteenth century were prepared, at a pinch, to accept iron and glass for interior decoration, but would not countenance its use to determine the final form of a prestigious building set in the heart of the nation's commercial capital. It was a compromise solution to a conundrum that was not to be resolved until the very end of the century.

Notes

1 Thomas Tredgold, *Practical Essay on the Strength of Cast Iron and other Metals*, London (1842), p. 10; Barrie Trinder, *The Iron Bridge*, Ironbridge Gorge Museum Trust (1979), pp. 3–5; Stuart Smith, *A View from Ironbridge* (1979), Introduction by Barrie Trinder, pp. 4–5; John Gloag and Derek Bridgewater, *A History of Cast Iron in Architecture*, London (1948), p. 82.

2 John Smith, 'A Conjectural Account of the Erection of the Iron Bridge' (typescript, North East London Polytechnic, 1979), pp. 7–8.

3 *AR*, Vol. 135, No. 805, March 1964, Jeremy Taylor, 'Charles Fowler: Master of Architects', pp. 177–80.

4 *Ibid.*, p. 176.

5 George F. Chadwick, *The Works of Sir Joseph Paxton 1803–1865*, London (1961), p. 95.

6 See pp. 83, 116 respectively.

7 *Magazine of Botany*, Vol. VIII (1841), 'Garden Architecture', p. 107.

8 *B*, Vol. VI, No. CCLVIII, 15 January 1848, p. 31.

9 *MPICE*, Vol. IX (1849–50), Richard Turner, 'Description of the Iron Roof over the Railway Station Lime-Street, Liverpool', pp. 205–8; *B*, Vol. 7, No. CCCXLVI, 22 September 1849, p. 454; Carroll L.V. Meeks, *The Railroad Station*, Yale (1956), p. 39; Dixon and Muthesius, *op. cit.*, p. 100.

10 Chadwick, *op. cit.*, pp. 104–5; *MPICE*, Vol. IX (1849–50), p. 233.

11 *MPICE*, Vol. XXXIX (1874–5), Obituary Sir Charles Fox, p. 265.

12 C.H. Gibbs-Smith, *The Great Exhibition of 1851*, London HMSO (1981), pp. 13–15.

13 *MPICE*, Vol. X (1850–1), William Cubitt, 'On the Construction of the Building for the Exhibition of the Works of Industry of all Nations in 1851', pp. 127–91.

14 *B*, Vol. XIV, No. 692, 10 May 1856, p. 264.

15 *Ecclesiologist*, Vol. XLI (1851), 'The Design of the Crystal Palace', p. 269.

16 *B*, Vol. IX, No. 459, 22 November 1851, p. 731.

17 Meeks, *op. cit.*, pp. 21, 40, 63; Hitchcock, *Early Victorian Architecture*, *op. cit.*, pp. 555–7.

18 John Ruskin, *The Stones of Venice*, Vol. I, London (1851), pp. 110–11.

19 *AR*, Vol. 109, No. 652, April 1954, H.-R. Hitchcock, 'Brunel and Paddington', pp. 245–6.

20 Binney and Pearce, *Railway Architecture*, *op. cit.*, p. 30.

21 *AR*, April 1954, Hitchcock, *op. cit.*, p. 246.

22 Hitchcock, *Nineteenth and Twentieth Centuries*, *op. cit.*, p. 186.

23 Chadwick, *op. cit.*, p. 101.

24 *B*, Vol. XII, No. 581, 25 March 1854, p. 158; Hitchcock, *Early Victorian Architecture*, *op. cit.*, pp. 563–4.

25 Gloag and Bridgewater, *op. cit.*, p. 170; *MPICE*, Vol. XVIII (1858–59), pp. 193–6.

26 Meeks, *op. cit.*, p. 38.

27 *B*, Vol. 4, No. CCII, 19 December 1846, 'Important Works on the Birmingham Railway', pp. 602–3; Richards, *Functional Tradition*, *op. cit.*, pp. 168–9; Gloag and Bridgewater, *op. cit.*, p. 171.

28 Hitchcock, *Nineteenth and Twentieth Centuries*, *op. cit.*, p. 170; see p. 173.

29 *Memoirs of the Literary and Philosophical Society of Manchester*, Second Series Vol. V, London (1831), Eaton Hodgkinson, 'Theoretical and Experimental Researches to ascertain the strength and best form of Iron Beams', p. 407; see also Tredgold, *Strength of Cast Iron, op. cit.*

30 *Ibid.*, p. 408.

31 Fairbairn, *Application of Cast and Wrought Iron*, *op. cit.*, pp. 5–6, 29; see also *Memoirs of the Literary and Philosophical Society of Manchester*, Second Series Vol. VI, London (1842), W. Fairbairn, 'An Experimental Inquiry into the strength and other properties of Cast Iron, from the various parts of the United Kingdom', pp. 171 ff.

32 *Ibid.*, p. 30.

33 Fitzgerald, *op. cit.*, p. 24.

34 Binney, *Satanic Mills, op. cit.*; R. Fitzgerald, 'Structural Development', p. 63.

35 Fairbairn, *Application, op. cit.*, p. vi.

36 *Ibid.*, p. 76.

37 *TM*, Vol. XVII, 15 May 1891, p. 228.

38 Fairbairn, *Application of Cast and Wrought Iron*, *op. cit.*, pp. 104–5.

39 R.A. Buchanan, *Industrial Archaeology in Britain*, London (1980), p. 314; Hitchcock, *Early Victorian Architecture, op. cit.*, pp. 518–20.

40 McGrath and Frost, *Glass in Architecture, op. cit.*, p. 45.

41 Quoted from A.L. Osborne, *English Domestic Architecture*, London (1967), p. 282.

42 Hitchcock, *Nineteenth and Twentieth Centuries*, *op. cit.*, p. 115.

43 Peter Murray, *The Architecture of the Italian Renaissance*, London (1969), pp. 63 ff.

44 *Ibid.*, p. 148.

45 *Ibid.*, pp. 166–9; Hitchcock, *op. cit.*, p. 116.

46 In 1849 *The Builder* published various *palazzo* windows, elevations and cornices as 'Hints for Street Architecture', Vol. 7, No. CCCXVIII, 10 March 1849, p. 114; *ibid.*, No. CCCXXIII, 14 April 1849, p. 172.

47 *B*, Vol. XXX, No. 1519, 16 March 1872, Obituary of Edward Walters, pp. 199–200; Hitchcock, *Early Victorian Architecture, op. cit.*, p. 387.

48 *B*, Vol. III, No. CXLV, 15 November 1845, p. 548.

49 *B*, No. 1519, *op. cit.*, p. 200; Hitchcock, *op. cit.*, p. 388.

50 *B*, Vol. XXIV, No. 1218, 8 July 1866, 'Decay of Stone'. Dr Angus Smith, investigating the air in the centre of Manchester, discovered as much as 25 parts of sulphuric acid in 100,000 parts of atmosphere. Other injurious chemicals included carbonic and nitric acids, ammonia salts and salt, p. 421.

51 *B*, Vol. VI, No. CCCIV, 2 December 1848, p. 577.

52 *AR*, Vol. 105, No. 625 (1949), H.-R. Hitchcock, 'Victorian Monuments of Commerce', p. 64; *Early Victorian Architecture, op. cit.*, pp. 390–1.

53 *B*, No. 1519, *op. cit.*, p. 200.

54 *Ibid.*, pp. 200–1.

55 *The Architect's Engineer's and Building-Trades' Directory* (1868), pp. 99, 110, 142.

56 *B*, Vol. XIII, No. 640, 12 May 1855, J.E. Gregan's Obituary, p. 222.

57 Hitchcock, *op. cit.*, pp. 389–90.

58 Nicholas Taylor, *Monuments of Commerce*, RIBA London (1968), p. 49.

59 *B*, Vol. VIII, No. CCCXCV, 31 August 1850, pp. 409, 414.

60 JRL, 1/1/14 Presidents of the Manchester Society of Architects, collected by John Holden, 1897, Edward Salomons, President 1871–3; 1892–4.

61 MCL, Newspaper Cuttings 1903–9, Vol. 7, *MG*, 15 May 1906; *City News*, 19 May 1906, p. 21.

62 LivRO, *Goad's Plans of Manchester*, Vol. I, No. 11, 1938.

63 Burnett Tracy, *op. cit.*, p. 219; Cecil Stewart, *Index to Principal Buildings and their Architects*.

64 *B*, Vol. LXVIII, p. 759.

65 William E.A. Axon, *The Annals of Manchester*, Manchester (1886), p. 274; *A New Directory of Manchester and Salford*, Manchester (1853), pp. 213, 320, 373; *Slater's General and Classified Directory . . . of Manchester and Salford*, Manchester (1852), pp. 5, 282.

66 T. Swindells, *Manchester Streets and Manchester Men*, Vol. II, Manchester (1907), p. 18.

67 *B*, Vol. XVI, No. 784, 13 February 1858, 'Art and Buildings at Manchester', p. 98.

68 *Manchester of Today*, London (1888), p. 161.

69 *Ibid.*

70 *B*, Vol. XXVI, No. 1334, 29 August 1868, p. 640.

71 *MG*, 2 January 1906, Obituary.

72 JRL, 1/1/14 A.W. Mills, President 1869–71; James Murgatroyd, President 1873–5.

73 *TLCAS*, Vols. 73 and 74 for 1963–64, Manchester (1966), J.H.G. Archer, 'Edgar Wood: A Notable Manchester Architect', p. 154.

74 *BN*, Vol. 5, 22 July 1859, p. 675.

75 *B*, Vol. XVI, No. 784, 13 February 1858, p. 97.

76 *BN*, Vol. 59, 1 August 1890, p. 166.

77 *B*, Vol. XII, No. 611, 21 October 1854, pp. 546–7.

78 Quoted from Roy A. Church, *Economic and Social Change in a Midland Town, Victorian Nottingham 1815–1900*, London (1966), p. 228.

79 *Ibid.*, pp. 290–1.

80 *Ibid.*, p. 52; *B*, Vol. IX, No. 454, 18 October 1851, p. 656.

81 *Ibid.*, p. 656.

82 John James, *Continuation and Additions to the History of Bradford*, London (1866), p. 244.

83 *BO*, Vol. XXXI, No. 1578, 5 May 1864, Obituary, p. 4; John S. Roberts, *Little Germany*, Bradford (1977), pp. 7, 9.

84 *AR*, No. 625, Hitchcock, *op. cit.*, pp. 63, 67.

85 BL, 'Bradford Weekly Telegraph', Vol. II, 1883–9, *Illustrated Weekly Telegraph*, Vol. XI, No. 4163, 8 May 1886, p. 147; LivRO, *Goad's Plans*, Bradford, Vol. I, No. 9, 1929.

86 Roberts, *op. cit.*, p. 14.

87 *B*, Vol. XX, No. 1028, 18 October 1862, p. 750.

88 *BO*, Vol. LXVI, No. 11532, 9 December 1899, p. 7; *B*, Vol. LXXVII, No. 2969, 30 December 1899, Obituary, p. 613.

89 *BO*, Vol. XXI, No. 1069, 31 August 1854, Obituary, p. 5.

90 Linstrum, *op. cit.*, pp. 375–6, 383.

91 Roberts, *op. cit.*, p. 29; *Supplement to the Warehouseman and Draper*, 30 September 1899, 'Bradford and its Manufactures', p. 17.

92 *Ibid.*, pp. 23, 25.

93 *B*, No. 1028, *op. cit.*, pp. 750–1.

94 *BO*, 25 May 1874, Obituary.

95 BL, *Illustrated Weekly Telegraph*, Vol. XL, No. 4165, 22 May 1886, p. 149.

96 Roberts, *op. cit.*, pp. 129–30.

97 *B*, Vol. LV, No. 2371, 14 July 1888, Obituary, p. 31.

98 Andor Gomme and David Walker, *Architecture of Glasgow*, London (1968), pp. 108–9.

99 *Ibid.*, p. 111.

100 Alfred Waterhouse's superb offices (1891–3) for the Refuge Assurance Co. in Manchester, and the Prudential Assurance Co., or the Liver Building (1908–11) by Walter Thomas for the Royal Liver Friendly Society.

101 Meeks, *op. cit.*, plate 21; Pevsner, *Building Types, op cit.*, p. 227.

102 *The Architect's Directory* (1868), p. 133; *DNB*, Vol. 16, p. 1266; Roberts was assisted by Thomas Turner (Biddle, *op. cit.*, p. 33) and George Smith (1783–1869) in N. Taylor, *Monuments of Commerce, op. cit.*, p. 13.

103 *Illustrated London News*, Vol. 55, 3 February 1844, p. 75.

104 *B*, Vol. XXXVI, No. 1851, 27 July 1878, Obituary, p. 788; *BO*, Vol. XLV, No. 4856, 23 July 1878, p. 3.

105 *BO*, Vol. LVI, No. 8215, 27 April 1889, Obituary, p. 7.

106 *B*, Vol. XII, No. 602, 19 August 1854, pp. 437–9.

107 *B*, Vol. X, No. 508, 30 October 1852, p. 694.

108 John James, *History of Worsted Manufacture in England*, London (1857), pp. 467, 469.

109 Thwaite, *op. cit.*, pp. 208–9.

110 William Fairbairn, *Application of Cast and Wrought Iron*, *op. cit.*, pp. 157–8, 161–2; W. Pole (Editor), *The Life of Sir William Fairbairn*, London (1877), p. 327.

111 BL, *Illustrated Weekly Telegraph*, Vol. XL, No. 4134, 17 October 1885, p. 83.

112 BL, Newspaper Index, Lockwood and Mawson.

113 *BN*, Vol. XXXV, 26 July 1878, Obituary, p. 91; *The Architect's, Engineer's ... Directory* (1868), p. 124.

114 *B*, Vol. LXXXVII, No. 3228, 17 December 1904, Obituary, p. 641; *Yorkshire Daily Observer*, Vol. LXXI, No. 13,096, 12 December 1904, p. 6.

115 Eric M. Sigsworth, *Black Dyke Mills, A History*, Liverpool (1958), pp. 178, 179; *Supplement to the Warehouseman and Draper, op. cit.*, p. 14.

116 Linstrum, *West Yorkshire, op. cit.*, pp. 134-5.

117 CCL, H, Newspaper Cuttings (1942-6), 17 October 1938, p. 111; (1965), 1 March, p. 37.

118 *B*, Vol. XXI, No. 1045, 14 February 1863, pp. 109-10; *BN*, Vol. LVIII, 7 February 1890, Obituary, p. 221.

119 RIBA Biography File, W.H. Crossland; William Grime, *Rochdale Observer*, 21 August 1971, p. 10.

120 Allen, *Practical Tourist, op. cit.*, Vol. II, Boston (1832), p. 355.

121 N. Pevsner, *BoE, Yorkshire, The West Riding*, Harmondsworth (1959), pp. 239-40.

122 John James, *History of Worsted Manufacture, op. cit.*, p. 621.

123 Linstrum, *op. cit.*, p. 379.

124 R. Bretton, *Crossleys of Dean Clough* (from *Transactions of the Halifax Antiquarian Society*, Parts I-VI, 1950-4), p. 78.

125 J.D. Bennett, *Leicester Architects 1700-1850*, Leicester Museums (1968), plate 10.

126 W.K.V. Gale, *Historic Industrial Scenes, Iron and Steel*, Hartington (1977), plates 33, 34.

127 *PIME*, Vol. XI (1860), Frederick Smith, 'Description of the Round Oak Ironworks', pp. 211, 216, plate 43, fig. 1.

128 *DBB*, Vol. I (1984), p. 476.

129 K.C. Barraclough, *Sheffield Steel*, Sheffield (1976), p. 62.

130 *Ibid.*, pp. 20-1.

131 Pevsner, *Yorkshire, West Riding, op. cit.*, p. 470; Hitchcock, *Early Victorian Architecture, op. cit.*, p. 526.

132 Barraclough, *Sheffield Steel, op. cit.*, pp. 27-8; Arthur Rastrick, *Industrial Archaeology*, London (1973), p. 48, plates 5a and 5b. Sadly the Works were demolished in 1969-70.

133 Dixon and Muthesius, *op. cit.*, p. 252; Bracegirdle, *op. cit.*, p. 68, plate 19(b).

134 *B*, Vol. V, No. CCXXX, 3 July 1847, Obituary, pp. 311-12.

135 E.W. Brayley, *Topographical History of Surrey*, Vol. V, London (1841-8), pp. 356, 373; Colvin, *op. cit.*, p. 40.

136 *B*, Vol. XCVI, No. 3464, 26 June 1909, Obituary, p. 766.

137 *B*, Vol. XLIV, No. 2090, 24 February 1883, Obituary, p. 240.

138 John Harvard Library, Southwark, Local Studies Library, James T. Loveday, *Loveday's London Waterside Surveys*, London (1857), p. 5.

139 Meeks, *op. cit.*, p. 45.

140 *Ibid.*, p. 67, plate 63; Biddle, *Victorian Stations, op. cit.*, p. 52.

141 Biddle and Spence, *op. cit.*, p. 22.

142 *The Engineering and other Industries of Manchester reprinted from 'The Ironmonger'*, London (1887), p. 60.

143 *BH*, Vol. XXIII (1981), J.A. Cantrell, 'James Nasmyth and the Bridgewater Foundry: Partners and Partnerships', p. 348.

144 *Ibid.*, p. 349.

145 *Engineering and other Industries, op. cit.*, p. 60.

146 Samuel Smiles (Editor), *James Nasmyth, Engineer, An Autobiography*, London (1883), plates facing pp. 205, 216.

147 *Ibid.*, pp. 220-1.

148 R.L. Hills, *Beyer, Peacock, Locomotive Builders of Gorton, Manchester, A Short History*, Manchester (1982).

149 *Engineering and other Industries, op. cit.*, p. 47.

150 *B*, Vol. LXIX, No. 2735, 6 July 1895, Obituary, p. 15.

151 *The Architect's, Engineer's ... Directory* (1868), p. 105.

152 Nettlefolds Ltd, Directors' Minute Book, No. 1, 1880-1886, 20 April 1880, p. 7; 2 May 1882, p. 154.

153 The Patent File Co. Ltd, Birmingham, Drawing No. 15, Front Elevation, Robert C. May, March 1864.

154 *The Engineer*, Vol. LIV, 4 August 1882, p. 89; *MPICE*, Vol. LXXIII (1883), Obituary, pp. 376-8.

155 *AR*, Vol. 119, No. 742, May 1956, Nikolaus Pevsner and S. Lang, 'The Egyptian Revival', p. 244.

156 Quoted from W.G. Rimmer, *Marshalls of Leeds, Flax Spinners 1788-1886*, Cambridge (1960), p. 203.

157 Benjamin Disraeli, *Sybil, or the Two Nations* (1845), Harmondsworth (1980), p. 225.

158 Linstrum, *op. cit.*, p. 290; Derek Fraser (Editor), *A History of Modern Leeds*, Manchester (1980), p. 149.

159 *MPICE*, Vol. II (1842), James Combe, 'Description of a Flax Mill recently erected by Messrs Marshall and Co. at Leeds', p. 145.

160 *Ibid.*, p. 143.

161 *Ibid.*, pp. 142–3.

162 Klingender, *op. cit.*, p. 109; J.P.M. Pannell, *Man the Builder*, London (1964), p. 115.

163 Burrough, *op. cit.*, p. 48.

164 Giorgio Vasari, *The Lives of the Artists*, 2nd Edition, Florence (1568), Harmondsworth (1965).

165 Samuel Smiles, *The Lives of the Engineers*, 3 Vols, London (1861–2).

166 See Manningham Mills (1871), p. 145.

167 *B*, Vol. XXI, No. 1083, 7 November 1863, pp. 782–3; *AR*, Vol. CI, No. 605, May 1947, H.-R. Hitchcock, 'London Coal Exchange', pp. 185–7.

168 *B*, No. 1083, *op. cit.*, p. 783.

FIVE

The Gothic Revival
1835–55

Although a minority of Gothic buildings – sometimes the result of eccentricities – had been erected during the latter part of the eighteenth century, they did not often conform to the dictates of the picturesque. Symmetrically planned, with an ordered arrangement of doors and windows, they failed to exhibit the 'intricacy' and 'variety' that Uvedale Price pointed to as characteristic of this style of architecture.[1] Picturesque Gothic, as described by Pugin and the Ecclesiological Society, flowered in England from the 1840s, when it was particularly favoured by church architects. Whilst it acquired a following amongst country-house designers, the Gothic style failed to exert a profound influence upon industrial building in this period: factories, warehouses and works in general rarely displayed Gothic features and were only occasionally executed in the picturesque manner. This comparatively short chapter seeks to explain the failure of early Gothic to appeal to entrepreneurs and those to whom they granted architectural commissions.

Eighteenth-century industrial Gothic

Among the very few eighteenth-century mills with Gothic details was Sutton Mill, near Mansfield, which was said to have cost £6,000 for Samuel Unwin to build.[2] This four-storey cotton spinning factory (erected in 1771 but enlarged sometime before 1784) was distinguished by simple battlements and pointed windows, though its overall plan remained symmetrical, according to Palladian rather than picturesque principles. It employed a windmill to pump water back to the nine-acre reservoir that supplied the water-wheel. In the detailing and execution Bow Bridge Mills (*c.*1825), Tudor Road, Leicester, for William Kelly, followed in a similar pattern.[3] Although it had battlements, lancet windows and quatrefoil recesses, this braid factory also had matching wings, a central entrance and bell cupola, which reiterated the earlier tradition of factory-building. One of the few industrial buildings of this period constructed in a truly Gothic manner was Kings Mills on the River Trent near Castle Donnington. Water-powered, they were used by Samuel Lloyd to grind flint, alabaster and dyewoods and to make plaster, glaze, Paris white and other colouring materials.[4] They had, in fact, been erected in the 1790s by the landlord, the Hastings family, who having rebuilt their nearby mansion, Donnington Hall, in the Gothic style, decided that the estate would be improved if its mills conformed to this Arcadian image. Whether William Wilkins (1751–1815), a Gothicist, who had designed the Hall,[5] also worked on the watermill, is unclear. The watermill, soon to be called 'the chapel', bore some resemblance to a church, featuring a row of lancet windows with tracery and decorative finials, while the gabled residence nearby was christened 'the priest's house'. When extensions were made in 1817 to the watermills at Bromley-by-Bow, the decorative clock tower with its bell cupola had Gothic windows, in contrast to the earlier House Mill (p. 16). Nevertheless, most factories and mills in this period exhibited classical, rather than Gothic, features, and almost all were Palladian in their interpretation.

Gothic detailing was possibly more commonly adopted in the eighteenth century by canal companies than by mill-owners, as a number of lock houses and bridges were constructed in this style. The turret-like two-storey circular stone cottages erected by the Thames & Severn Canal Company had simple lancet windows and entrances, as well as pointed roofs.[6] The Staffordshire & Worcestershire Canal Company built similar brick towers, with battlements, to house their lock keepers. Elsewhere, the Rochdale Canal Company constructed stone entrance buildings and offices in Dale Street, Manchester at the turn of the century, with walls capped by battlements,[7] though the round-arched doorway and Georgian windows did not complete the medieval image. In 1800 the Grand Junction Company erected an ornate Gothic bridge over their canal at Cosgrove, Northamptonshire, its design being enlivened by ogee-headed niches, blank arches and quatrefoils.[8] The comparative popularity of the style with waterway companies could have resulted from its Arcadian associations. Attractive canal banks and locks were probably regarded as more suitable for Gothic features than the polluted districts of industry.

Gothic was only rarely adopted for factories even in the early nineteenth century when its features were worked into essentially Palladian structures to add variety. The Warwick Gasworks (c.1822) and the Cannon Ironworks (1816), Chesterfield,[9] for instance, though having blind pointed arches, were both restrained,

55 The Castle Grinding Mill at Sheffield – not a truly picturesque example of industrial Gothic.

symmetrical buildings whose Gothic elements merely served as decoration. Similarly, the mock battlements that enlivened the centre portion and twin staircase towers of Fishwick Mill (c.1830) could have been but a whim, as the overall design was Palladian.[10] Castle Mill, Sheffield, a factory rented out for grinding and polishing cutlery, fell into this mould, its ordered composition had simply been given a medieval gloss by the addition of turrets.[11] Much the same could be said of the Seven Wharf Building (pre-1849), Ironbridge, a one-storey red-brick warehouse.[12] Although it exhibited battlements and lancet windows and its twin chimneys had mock arrowloops, this detailing remained only surface-deep, as the regular and symmetrical arrangement of doors and windows placed it in the classical rather than the picturesque tradition, influenced by the popularity of the Gothic image.

Picturesque Gothic

'In Gothic buildings', argued Uvedale Price (1747–1829), 'the outline of the summit presents such a variety of forms, of turrets and pinnacles, some open, some fretted and variously enriched, that even where there is an exact correspondence of parts, it is often disguised by an appearance of splendid confusion and irregularity'.[13] Such characteristics, he believed, distinguished the picturesque from both the beautiful (symmetrical, classical structures) and the sublime. In other words, to apply Gothic features to a rigid ordered framework was not sufficient; these towers, windows, entrances and so forth had to be arranged in such a manner that they created diversity, excitement and surprise; asymmetry and irregularity were the hallmarks of the picturesque. Yet it was not until the 1840s and the public debate stirred by A.W.N. Pugin (1812–52) and the Ecclesiologists that picturesque Gothic came to the fore in architectural thought. Drawing upon English medieval examples, Pugin argued that 'pointed architecture', hitherto much neglected, should be regarded as the basis for church, collegiate and civil building.[14] Whilst this assertion may seem to have little

bearing on industrial building, the arguments which supported his beliefs did, in fact, explain why mills and warehouses were initially overlooked by the Gothic Revival.

Central to Pugin's philosophy was the principle outlined in *Contrasts* (1841), that a building's 'fitness' should determine its ultimate form:

> It will be readily admitted that the great test of architectural beauty is the fitness of the design to the purpose for which it is intended, and that the style of a building should so correspond with its use that the spectator may at once perceive the purpose for which it is erected.[15]

In a sense, Pugin supported a kind of hierarchy of decorum when he argued that:

> The scale of propriety in architecture must always be regulated by purpose, and to illustrate this more fully, I will divide edifices under three heads – Ecclesiastical, Collegiate, and Civil. The greatest privilege possessed by man is to be allowed, while on earth, to contribute to the glory of God.[16]

For him cathedrals and churches occupied the highest place in a ranking of architectural commissions. Civil and domestic building concerned Pugin least, and his efforts in this area focused on a critique of the Italianate style. For industrial buildings (a subject which he virtually ignored) only passing scorn was evinced, in his claim that 'England is rapidly losing its venerable garb ... Factory chimneys disfigure our most beautiful vales.'[17] In *Contrasts* Pugin included two engravings that were designed to illustrate the rape of Christian Gothic building. The first showed a Catholic town in 1840 whose panorama was dominated by tall, austere warehouses and a gasworks, pottery and ironworks, together with Non-conformist chapels. The foreground contained a Benthamite jail and a small Gothic church mutilated by classical and Palladian additions; in the distance 'St Maries Abbey', another medieval building, lay in ruins. The contrasting plate for 1440 revealed the town in all its Gothic splendour, a walled city whose skyline was broken by the many spires and towers of churches and chapels, unaffected by the evils of industrialization.[18]

In summary, Pugin claimed that a building's

purpose critically determined the style of architecture that should be adopted. He was in some ways a functionalist, positing two 'great rules for design':

> ... there should be no features about a building which are not necessary for convenience, construction or propriety; second, that all ornament should consist of the enrichment of the essential construction of the building.[19]

Given that industrial buildings, in his eyes, occupied a place at the bottom of the architectural ladder, and that their purpose was merely to manufacture goods, he could conceive of no need to treat them in an elevated manner, and regarded them as unworthy of the attentions of an architect well versed in the principles of English medieval construction.

In 1843, Pugin's third major study, *An Apology*

for the Revival of Christian Architecture in England, made direct reference to railway stations, a number by then having been constructed in the Gothic style, like Brunel's symmetrical train-shed and offices at Bristol Temple Meads (1839–40). Whilst admitting that a station might receive such elevated treatment, he criticized some of those already erected: 'at Rugby, because Rugby School, as rebuilt lately, has had battlements and turrets, the old station had four half-turrets with the best side turned out, and a few sham loop holes'.[20] (Rugby Station had been

56 On the left of the picture are examples of Gothic railway architecture advocated by Pugin in his *Apology for the Revival of Christian Architecture in England* (1843), whilst the classically inspired versions on the right only won his disapproval.

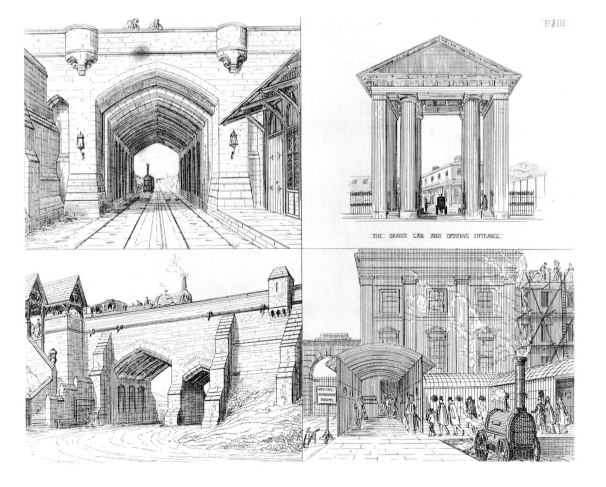

designed by the London & Birmingham Railway's architect, George Aitchison Senior.) Accordingly, he proposed a design that required Gothic vaults, buttresses and massive walls, and would have equalled in expense the existing structure that he ridiculed. He was still more contemptuous of the Euston Arch and the Curzon Street Terminus, viewing them as 'two gigantic piles of unmeaning masonry' which served as 'a striking proof of the utter disregard paid by architects as to the *purposes* of the building they are called upon to design'.[21] It was not that as stations *per se* they were unfitted to receive the attention of an architect, rather that in his eyes these elevations were inconsistent with their function. 'Architectural skill', Pugin suggested:

> consists in embodying and expressing the structure required, and not disguising it with borrowed features. The peasant's hut, the yeoman's cottage, the farmer's house, the baronial hall, may each be perfect in its kind.[22]

His dislike of industrialization and admiration of Catholic society in medieval England revealed itself in the examples employed in this passage; no mention was made of the weaver's terrace, the mill-owner's mansion or the miner's tenement.

Nevertheless, Pugin's comments may be seen to have influenced some station architecture, including that at Perth (1848) by Sir William Tite and H.A. Hunt's Stoke-on-Trent Station (1847–8), together with Battle (1852) for the South Eastern Railway,[23] where William Tress, a pupil of Tite and designer of several Italianate versions, produced a Gothic booking hall whose structure and execution fulfilled Pugin's demands. The viaduct commissioned by the Manchester, South Junction & Altrincham Railway at Deansgate presented the city with an enduring medieval monument. Designed by William Baker and dated 1849, the cast-iron parapets and brackets featured lancet arches, while the supporting brick and stone piers were castellated. The ironwork had been produced by E.T. Bellhouse (d.1880) of the Eagle Foundry, Manchester, a former apprentice of Fairbairn and a manufacturer of prefabricated warehouses and homes.[24]

On the subject of the use of iron Pugin held equally forthright opinions. 'When viewed with reference to mechanical purposes', he asserted, 'it must be considered as a most valuable invention but it can rarely be applied to ornamental purposes'.[25] Because he opposed iron's use when disguised by paint or other coverings as a deception, it could only be incorporated in an exposed state. Yet its great strength, in comparison with stone, meant that 'to be consistent the mullions of cast-iron tracery must be reduced as to look painfully thin, devoid of shadow and out of all proportion to the openings to which they are fixed'.[26] Hence his objections to the adoption of iron in architecture were theoretical, rather than structural, and centred on its fitness. Concluding that 'the external and internal appearance of an edifice should be illustrative of, and in accordance with, the purpose for which it is destined',[27] and placing industrial buildings low in his order of priorities, Pugin was probably unconcerned whether they featured iron decoration or not, such matters being far from his passion for medieval ecclesiastical architecture.

Yet the arguments of Pugin and the Ecclesiological Society, powerful as they were, and reflecting a measure of popular taste, cannot provide the whole explanation for the comparative absence of Gothic in industry. The established appeal and associations of the Italianate, which followed more directly from the Palladian tradition, led mill-owners or their appointed architects to think first of Renaissance models. The picturesque, requiring irregular and intricate compositions, for which Gothic was particularly suited, had little attraction for the designers of factories and warehouses, whose requirements at this stage could be satisfied by box-like structures of regular dimensions.

Early nineteenth-century industrial Gothic

One important feature of the Gothic Revival which was to have wider repercussions concerned the related demand in the 1840s for simple and heavy masses in building – an inheritance from the sublime. For example, Pugin, who had already laid great stress on the selection of stone and its arrangement,[28] had suggested this approach in his revisions for Rugby Station. The emphasis on massiveness was particularly apparent in the work of Anthony Salvin (1799–1881) who designed a number of country-house 'castles' – at Peckforton (1844–50), Cheshire, and Alnwick (1854–65).[29] That this represented an innovation may be confirmed by examination of the earlier writings of Uvedale Price, who had sought to avoid 'greatness of dimension' or 'lumpish appearance' in his advocacy of lightness, variety and intricacy.[30]

Although not an academically-tutored architect, nor a member of the Ecclesiological Society, Jesse Hartley (1780–1860), civil engineer and superintendent of Liverpool's Port,[31] adopted many of the qualities urged by Pugin: massiveness, fitness of materials and designs for their purpose and a reference to English medieval building, though the last characteristic applied specifically to his port furniture and walls, rather than to his warehouses, which were closely related to the London dock tradition.

Appointed early in 1824 as dock surveyor, his early work, a form of apprenticeship in Liverpool, consisted of repairs and alterations.[32] The Albert Dock (1841–5), covering seven acres, Hartley's first major commission, comprised a non-tidal basin surrounded on all four sides by brick warehouses.[33] Greek Doric cast-iron columns, in various groupings, supported a beam carrying the four floors above (as at St Katharine Docks), while in the space between these groups – the same distance as between the outer

57 Albert Dock (1841–5), a non-tidal basin surrounded on all sides by brick fireproof warehouses.

two columns – an elliptical brick arch rose gently to the height of the first storey.[34] Although he had written to Philip Hardwick in 1834 for advice and adopted the successful layout devised for St Katharine Docks, the final design was clearly Hartley's.[35] It was significant, however, that Hardwick had been selected to design the Albert Dock offices (1846–7), for which he devised a simple, two-storey classical block entered through a Tuscan portico. Presumably Hartley, as a young engineer, was not considered qualified by the Trustees to undertake the execution of a conventional office building, and Hardwick was also entrusted with the design of the dock's classical clock tower, which, surmounting one of the warehouses, bore little affinity to the architecture below. Hartley did, in fact, modify Hardwick's offices by the addition of a second storey. The portico's four columns, its entablature and pediment were all surprisingly of cast iron, though they had been manufactured so as to resemble stone.

Because merchants had been slow in Liverpool to adopt the fireproof structures devised for mills, the port developed a poor reputation among insurers.[36] In order that the warehouses at Albert Dock should combine 'security from fire with stability and economy' Hartley submitted costings for several types of structure: cast-iron beams with brick arches, flagged floors and timber beams covered with sheet iron.[37] Although the building itself could be made fireproof, the merchandise that was to be stored in these warehouses remained inflammable and this, as Hartley argued in May 1843, influenced his recommendations:

If the floors are constructed wholly of iron or wholly of brick, any fire that might occur originating amongst the goods might I imagine from these floors being air tight be got under before much damage could be done to them, otherwise should the ironwork be brought to a red heat or approaching thereto the expansion would be such as to throw out the walls and completely destroy the building. In the common mode, however, of constructing warehouses the timber floors, I am of opinion, tend to accelerate their destruction more than the goods that are stored within them.[38]

Should a timber floor need to be covered with sheet iron, then cost dictated that a structure of iron beams and brick arches be preferred.[39] Prices ranged from £33 10s per sq yd for a scheme with a 'common warehouse floor as used in Liverpool' to £70 14s for a proposal with an iron framework to support iron plates covered with sand and flagstones. In the event, the warehouses Hartley erected around the Albert Dock had cast-iron columns and beams with brick arches and tiled floors, and were roofed with galvanized iron plates riveted to wrought-iron supports.[40]

At Stanley Dock (1850–7) Hartley erected a row of warehouses of similar external appearance, except that the cast-iron columns supporting the upper floors lacked entasis, having a concave line up to their Doric capitals.[41] Also designed for the storage of flammable materials (spirits and tobacco), these five-storey buildings were of iron and brick, the use of timber being everywhere avoided.[42]

Aesthetically of greater appeal than the warehouses were the docks themselves, their walls, gatehouses and quays. In 1848 *The Builder*, on visiting Liverpool, observed that 'the enclosure walls, river wall, lofty clock-tower, and other buildings, are all constructed from Galloway granite, and seem built for futurity'.[43] The castellated masonry walls and towers (intended to prevent pilfering and sufficiently solid to resist the battering of wagons and carts) which linked together the various docks and wharves, revealed Hartley's architectural skills at their height. Constructed from grey granite – he had opened a quarry at Kirkmabreck, Kirkcudbrightshire, specially to supply the stone[44] – the variously shaped blocks were meticulously fitted together and dressed with the strength of abstract sculpture. His style may have owed a debt to Thomas Harrison (1744–1829) who designed the Grosvenor Bridge over the Dee at Chester which Hartley erected in 1827–32, 'his consent to undertake the work being given, on the condition that no alteration should be made in the external design of the architect … but that the interior and all practical points should be left to him'.[45] The castellated offices – at

58 The northern range of warehouses to Stanley Dock (1850–7). The intricately arranged granite blocks that Hartley employed to form the quayside are also visible.

Salisbury Dock (1848), the Victoria Tower (1848) and the hydraulic accumulator tower at Canada Dock – recalled Salvin's castles.[46] Yet at root Hartley's cyclopean building was highly individualistic, based upon an empathy with the materials, the docks' practical function and a desire to create resilient, dramatic shapes; it must have owed something to his father's trade as a stonemason. If certain industrial buildings were the best representatives of the sublime in British architecture then included amongst these must be the work of Hartley. Contemporaries appreciated the quality of his work, an editorial in *The Builder* for 1859 asserting that 'so long as Liverpool endures, there will be samples of his masonry in existence equal to anything of the kind the world has yet seen'.[47]

Hartley's son, John, who had worked in his office at Liverpool and succeeded him there,[48] resigned as engineer to the Hull Dock Co. in 1858 to take up a similar post in Birkenhead.[49] Although his father refused to be associated with the project, J.B. Hartley proceeded to assist with the construction of a deep-water basin and docks there. Possibly the most enduring feature of his work was the accumulator tower (1863) to provide power for the gates and bridge, whose castellated stone exterior stood in direct comparison with those on the other bank of the Mersey.[50]

The application of Gothic in this innovative phase was not, however, limited to port architecture. The notion that lime kilns, like many

59 A gatekeeper's lodge, by Hartley, near Stanley Dock, Liverpool.

early blast furnaces, resembled turrets in a line of fortifications was developed by Richard Kyrke Penson (1816–86), the Welshpool architect better known for his churches and schools. At Llandybie near Ammanford alongside the limestone quarries, in 1856, he erected a row of stone kilns elaborated by buttresses rising to form a lancet arcade and topped by a corbelled brick parapet.[51] He was a devotee of the style and the Gothic detailing was pure ornament, having no practical influence on the working of the kilns.

Although peripheral to this study of industrial buildings, the pumping station, in function similar to the engine house of a mill, received comparable architectural attention. An outstanding example, erected to fill the reservoirs in Green Lanes, Harringay, followed in the robust Gothic manner adopted by Hartley in Liverpool. Designed by W. Chadwell Mylne (1781–1863), engineer to the New River Co., and executed in 1854–6,[52] this pumping station was based on Stirling Castle, its individual corner towers being respectively a winding staircase, a stand pipe and a flue. In tune with the fortress theme, the solid buttressed brick walls of the keep were lit by narrow Gothic windows. It demonstrated how a traditional composition, then entering a second period of popularity, could be adapted and enlivened in a rather eccentric fashion to perform a modern role.

Summary

The paucity of Gothic industrial buildings in the period up to the mid-nineteenth century was the result both of theoretical debate and practical considerations. The Italianate, as a natural successor of the Palladian tradition, adapted well to the box-like structures that mills and warehouses demanded, while its commercial associations provided a philosophical appeal. When businessmen selected the Gothic it was often for

their private houses rather than their factories; Willersley Castle, overlooking the River Derwent, Richard Arkwright's mansion erected in 1789–90,[53] and Cyfarthfa Castle, built in 1824–5 at a cost of £30,000 for William Crawshay II, the Merthyr ironmaster,[54] both fell into this category. In each case the entrepreneur had no hesitation in commissioning an architect to design the mansion – Willersley Castle was by Thomas William (d.1800)[55] and Cyfarthfa by Robert Lugar (c.1773–1855), who dedicated his *Villa Architecture* to Crawshay.[56] Neither Arkwright nor Crawshay, however, would have automatically thought of calling on the services of an architect when extensions were required to their textile mills or ironworks. Indeed, William Crawshay I, father of William II, who remained head of the firm, fiercely objected to the purchase of the land for Cyfarthfa Castle in 1820 and its subsequent construction, because it depleted valuable capital reserves necessary to buttress the business during the slumps which characterized the iron industry, and also because the acquisition was simply governed by a desire for social advancement.[57]

Railway stations, the truly novel building type of the era, attracted the attention of Gothic designers almost to the same degree as the rival Italianate, but until a further loosening and broadening of contemporary architectural thought, industrial buildings were not prominent in the Gothic Revival. The career of George Kemp (1759–1844), author of Edinburgh's picturesque monument to Sir Walter Scott (1840–4), illustrated this theme, according to Samuel Smiles. Born the son of a Scottish shepherd, Kemp trained as a carpenter and, falling in love with Gothic architecture, took every opportunity provided by his trade to sketch medieval buildings throughout Northern England. 'His skill as a mechanic', wrote Smiles, 'and especially his knowledge of mill-work, readily secured him employment wherever he went'.[58] That Kemp, the Gothicist, had no apparent desire to design mills reflected first the low standing of industry and secondly the view that such buildings, as rectangular blocks, were not suited to the style.

Notes

1 Uvedale Price, *An Essay on the Picturesque*, London (1796), pp. 25-6.

2 Chapman, *Early Factory Masters, op. cit.*, pp. 130-2.

3 D.M. Smith, *Industrial Archaeology of the East Midlands, op. cit.*, pp. 52, 198.

4 Humphrey Lloyd, *The Quaker Lloyds in the Industrial Revolution*, London (1975), pp. 251-2, Plate 33.

5 G. Richardson, *New Vitruvius Britannicus*, Vol. II, London (1808), pp. 31-5; Colvin, *op. cit.*, p. 674.

6 Harris, *Canals and their Architecture, op. cit.*, p. 137.

7 *Rochdale Canal* (pamphlet), pp. 3, 20.

8 N. Pevsner, *BoE, Northamptonshire*, Harmondsworth (1973), p. 159.

9 See p. 35 and p. 69 respectively.

10 Baines, *Cotton Manufacture, op. cit.*, opposite p. 185; see p. 56.

11 Charles Tomlinson, *Cyclopaedia of Useful Arts, Mechanical and Chemical*, Vol. I, London (1854), p. 484; SYCRO, Pen and wash drawing of Castle Mills by William Flockton, *c.* 1830-40.

12 W. Grant Mutter, *The Buildings of an Industrial Community*, London (1979), pp. 16-17; *Country Life*, 23 June 1977, Tony Aldous, 'An Industrial Story told with Skill', p. 1740.

13 Price, *op. cit.*, p. 64.

14 A.W.N. Pugin, *The True Principles of Pointed or Christian Architecture*, London (1841), *passim*.

15 A.W.N. Pugin, *Contrasts*, London (1841), p. 1.

16 Pugin, *True Principles, op. cit.*, p. 50.

17 *Ibid.*, p. 70.

18 Pugin, *Contrasts, op. cit.*, Plate I; Kenneth Clark, *The Gothic Revival*, London (1962), pp. 146-7; Phoebe Stanton, *Pugin*, London (1971), pp. 90-1.

19 Pugin, *True Principles, op. cit.*, p. 1.

20 A.W.N. Pugin, *An Apology for the Revival of Christian Architecture in England*, London (1843), p. 11.

21 *Ibid., p.* 11.

22 *Ibid.*, p. 21.

23 Biddle, *Victorian Stations, op. cit.*, p. 40; Binney and Pearce, *op. cit.*, p. 72.

24 Gilbert Herbert, *The Pioneers of Prefabrication*, Baltimore (1978), pp. 50, 195; *MG*, 15 October 1881, Obituary.

25 Pugin, *True Principles, op. cit.*, p. 33; *An Apology, op. cit.*, p. 40.

26 Pugin, *True Principles, op. cit.*, p. 33.

27 *Ibid.*, p. 50.

28 *Ibid.*, p. 19.

29 Mark Girouard, *The Victorian Country House*, Yale (1979), pp. 154-63, 441.

30 Price, *op. cit.*, pp. 99, 205.

31 Nancy Ritchie-Noakes, *Jesse Hartley, Dock Engineer to the Port of Liverpool 1824-60*, Liverpool (1980), p. 5; *Liverpool's Historic Waterfront*, London HMSO (1984), pp. 49-51, 146-51.

32 MCA, Proceedings of the Committee of the Trustees of Liverpool Docks, Vol. 2, 1819-1825, 27 April 1824, p. 536; 17 August 1824, p. 576.

33 *Architectural History*, Vol. 4 (1961), J. Quentin Hughes, Supplement II, 'Dock Warehouses at Liverpool', pp. 106, 108-12; *Liverpool's South Docks, An Archaeological and Historical Survey*, Merseyside County Museums (1980), pp. 49-50; *Buildings of Liverpool*, Liverpool (1978), C.R. Hutchinson, 'The Docks', pp. 5, 13.

34 LivRO, 67/2859 South Elevation to West Stack by D.S. Willey; 67/2879 North Elevation.

35 MCA, Proceedings of the Dock Committee, Vol. 7, 1840-1842, 21 May 1841, pp. 407-8; Ritchie-Noakes, *op. cit.*, p. 6.

36 MCL, S&A 120 Tracts, *Report of William Fairbairn Esq C.E., on the Construction of Fireproof Buildings*, Liverpool (1844), p. 11.

37 MCA, Proceedings of the Dock Committee, Vol. 8, 1842-1844, 18 May 1843, pp. 213-14.

38 *Ibid.*, p. 215.

39 *Ibid.*, pp. 228-9.

40 LivRO, Royal Insurance Co.'s *Goad's Plans, Liverpool*, Vol. II, July 1890, No. 233; MCA, Mersey Docks & Harbour Board, Worked Up Papers No. 3, Albert Dock Warehouses, Vol. I, 1882-1905, replacement of broken iron beams, 10 March 1886.

41 LivRO, Acc 1804, Detail of Cast-iron Column, Stanley Dock; 67/2861, 67/2864, 67/2865 Elevations of Stanley Dock Warehouses.

42 LivRO, *Goad's Plans, Liverpool, op. cit.*, No. 230.

43 *B*, Vol. VI, No. CCCVII, 23 December 1848, p. 613.
44 Ritchie-Noakes, *op. cit.*, p. 7.
45 *MPICE*, Vol. XXII (1871–2), Memoir of Jesse Hartley, p. 219; Colvin, *op. cit.*, p. 270.
46 Dixon and Muthesius, *op. cit.*, p. 124.
47 *B*, Vol. XVII, No. 849, 14 May 1859, p. 321.
48 *B*, Vol. XVIII, No. 921, 29 September 1860, p. 623.
49 *MPICE*, Vol. XXXIII (1871–2), Memoir of John Bernard Hartley, pp. 216–18.
50 N. Pevsner and E. Hubbard, *BoE, Cheshire*, Harmondsworth (1971), p. 87.
51 Rees, *Industrial Archaeology of Wales*, *op. cit.*, p. 175; *Historic Industrial Scenes, Wales*, *op. cit.*, plate 91; Hilling, *Historic Architecture of Wales*, *op. cit.*, pp. 142, 143, 157.
52 Brockman, *op. cit.*, pp. 30, 31; Pevsner, *London 2*, *op. cit.*, pp. 429–30; Colvin, *op. cit.*, p. 403.
53 Tann, *Development of the Factory*, *op. cit.*, p. 155.
54 Charles Wilkins, *The History of Merthyr Tydfil*, Merthyr Tydfil (1867), p. 206.
55 *Gentleman's Magazine*, Vol. LXX (1800), p. 87; Colvin, *op. cit.*, p. 608.
56 Robert Lugar, *Villa Architecture, a Collection of Views, with Plans, of Buildings executed in England, Scotland, etc.*, London (1828), Cyfarthfa Castle, plates 41–2; Colvin, *op. cit.*, pp. 369–70.
57 *National Library of Wales Journal*, Vol. VII (1951–2), J.D. Evans, 'The Uncrowned Iron King, the First William Crawshay', pp. 19, 23.
58 Samuel Smiles, *Self-Help*, London (1859), Sphere Books (1968), p. 127.

SIX

The High Victorian movement

1855–80

The key word in the title of this chapter is 'high'. The High Victorian movement represented an apogee of sorts; it witnessed new heights of eclecticism and produced an architecture particularly ornate, colourful and diverse. The Gothic Revival, whose origins lay in the eighteenth century, arrived at its fullest development towards the end of this period as its medieval ideals influenced not only a wide range of buildings but also painting, literature, theology and social attitudes. In addition, this architectural peak coincided with a zenith in Britain's industrial performance. The mid-1870s, when the Empire achieved its greatest commercial and manufacturing might, saw growth reach fresh summits while competition remained manageable, and for many fields the technological initiative was still vested in the United Kingdom. The demand, therefore, for factory and warehouse premises, often of increasingly large dimensions, rose to a new level, whilst the funds to pay for professionally executed designs and good-quality materials did not run short. The third quarter of the nineteenth century produced new heights both in architecture and the economy.

High Victorian Gothic

Just as Pugin and the Ecclesiologists had set the pace for the Gothic Revival earlier in the nineteenth century, so at around 1850, inspired by the published works of John Ruskin (1819–1900) and the example set by the buildings of Butterfield, Street and Scott, this movement passed into an expansive and creative phase. As writers or architects, they did not concern themselves

much, if at all, with industrial structures. But the principles that they devised and practised set the stage for the nation as a whole, and their ideas and influence permeated through to the world of factories and warehouses. So, whilst it might be difficult to detect a direct link between, say, William Butterfield's All Saints Church (1850–9) and R. Stark Wilkinson's Doulton Pottery Works (1876–7), both exhibited a common architectural ancestry.

The two main themes, developed by Ruskin and his contemporaries, that exercised a profound effect on industrial buildings in this period, were the emphasis on eclecticism and a refusal to accept a rigid hierarchy in building. In *The Seven Lamps of Architecture* (1849) and the first volume of *The Stones of Venice* (1851), Ruskin argued, in contrast to the Ecclesiologists, in favour of the massive Italian medieval style and against the more complicated northern Gothic. Similarly Butterfield, Street and Scott all regarded Italian and French examples as important sources for their Gothic structures, often ignoring the patriotic case advocated by Pugin. G.E. Street (1824–81), for example, in his *Brick and Marble in the Middle Ages* (1855), prefaced the 1874 edition to this Italian tour with the remarks that:

> we wished to combine the best architecture, the best painting and the best sculpture in our works. The world seemed to respond to our aspirations, and it is south not north of the Alps that examples of such a combination have been looked for ... These were the special inducements to me in my earliest journey to Italy, and their influence is as strong as ever upon me.[1]

In conjunction with this broadened vision, they argued that Gothic architecture was applicable to much more than churches. In *The Seven Lamps* Ruskin refused, by implication, to support the hierarchy from ecclesiastical down to secular which the Ecclesiologists had so fervently tried to reaffirm in the 1840s.[2] Rather than suggesting that a building's function within a social order should determine its execution, he maintained that 'there is no action so slight, nor so mean, but it may be done to a great purpose, and ennobled'.[3] Ruskin's concern, therefore, was not with the ranking of buildings in a scale of importance, but in seeing that all were constructed with due attention to their operation, the materials employed and the effect that they would create: '... the relative majesty of buildings depends more on the weight and vigour of their masses than any other tribute of their design'.[4] Importing Burke's qualities of the sublime, not then widely associated with Gothic, Ruskin rejected the picturesque principles of the Ecclesiologists in an attempt to improve building across the spectrum.

In a speech in which he criticized the lack of architectural interest shown by Bradford's textile magnates, Ruskin argued, 'You cannot have good architecture merely by asking people's advice on occasion. All good architecture is the expression of national life and character; and it is produced by a prevalent and eager national taste, or desire for beauty.[5] The merchants and mill-owners, he suggested, had selected the Gothic for their new Wool Exchange (1864-7), by Lockwood and Mawson, simply because it was then fashionable, not themselves really caring how it appeared. It is only a short jump from this to say that their own mills and warehouses had been commissioned from a similar standpoint.

Although still arguing that important buildings should be decorated and lesser ones left plain, [Sir] George G. Scott (1811-78) in *Remarks on Secular and Domestic Architecture* (1857) placed emphasis on the proper treatment of warehouses and factories. 'It is customary', he suggested,

among our opponents to speak of a Gothic warehouse as if the idea were a very good joke ... The

medieval builders had no notion of the seats of commerce and manufactures being given up to unsightliness, nor of their buildings, however utilitarian, being allowed to disfigure their cities. We find, accordingly, that their warehouses were as nobly treated as any other buildings.[6]

Referring to 'the great warehouse in the goods station at Nottingham', Scott selected its 'straightforward, massive and natural treatment ... enhanced by the canal passing through it under two massive arches' as being of merit.[7] Equally, he wrote that in the recent past insufficient attention had been devoted to mills. Success in their design could be achieved by:

carrying out the obvious requirements and conditions of the case in the most genuine and natural manner ... giving the whole an obvious air of strength, simplicity and capacity – and reserving the architectural touches for a few special points, as the doorways or the eaves-cornice, and making them rather express severe strength than any refinement of design. The chimneys of factories may be made magnificent objects. They are too frequently very much to the contrary.[8]

Scott still clung to a hierarchical philosophy, stating that 'we must take things in their due order. We have begun with the temple, and must go on into other classes of building; but utilitarian structures ought to be influenced *indirectly* not by effort'.[9] Thus, Scott did not favour over-'Gothicizing' factories. Their design, he believed, should be affected by the general principles of the High Gothic movement, in a subtle and almost unconscious fashion. Scott's own early practice with William Moffatt (1812–87) was dominated by numerous workhouse commissions, buildings that ranked in the architectural hierarchy on a par with industry.[10] Though believing such employment to be 'dirty, disagreeable work', Scott did, nevertheless, argue that architects should never 'pick your subjects but go in for whatever offer whether you like it or not, for if you compete only for the subjects you like you will nearly always fail'.[11] Yet the conclusion to emerge from this brief survey of architectural opinion was that industrial buildings were now a topic of discussion in

60 A Gothic version taken from Rawlinson's *Boiler and Factory Chimneys* (1877).

serious studies; at last they merited the attention of leading architects and thinkers.

Besides these important developments in theory, significant changes that were to influence the construction of industrial plant, had occurred in the organization of the profession. The number of architects had risen and many commissions previously undertaken by builders with pattern-books now fell to qualified men. Standards of conduct rose following the foundation of the Institute of British Architects in 1834 and provincial societies at Liverpool in 1835, Manchester in 1837, Bristol in 1850 and Nottingham in 1858, these being brought together in a general organization in 1862.[12] That associations should have been formed in industrial or commercial centres in part reflected the size of those centres; but another motive may have been a desire to win respect from the capital where so many fashionable architects practised and the most prestigious commissions arose. The old system of patronage had largely given way to a commercial set-up where firms competed on price and the quality of their designs.[13] Hence, not only were warehouses and mills, as building types, considered worthy of an architect's attention, but growing numbers of professional men were actively seeking this form of employment. The rising educational standards of businessmen, some now formally educated at a university, may also have influenced design. As clients, they took an increasing interest in the outward form of their factories. In an age of limited companies and a shareholding public, mills and merchants' warehouses, like banks or insurance offices, served as an advertisement and a symbol of an enterprise's success and probity.

Practical application

That architects considered industrial buildings as lying within the scope of the most fashionable styles may be confirmed by the example in Manchester of Fryer & Binyon's warehouse (1855-6), Chester Street, Chorlton.[14] Although designed by Alfred Waterhouse (1830-1905), this was one of his earliest tasks, and he did not subsequently specialize in such work, which suggested that the emancipation of industry was by no means complete. Further, it seems that Waterhouse, as a newly established architect in Manchester (having recently returned from an extensive tour of the Continent, including Italy, and presumably having read *The Stones of Venice*),[15] needed employment and had gained this commission through Quaker connections of his father, a retired mill-owner of Aigburth, near Liverpool.[16] He selected Venetian Gothic motifs (drawn from the Doge's Palace) to suit the building's function: on the ground floor the entrances were stressed; the round-arched arcaded windows of the first storey served the office and showroom, which demanded plentiful light for inspection, while the upper three floors, forming the store areas, had only very small lights.

In its external detailing and the variety of materials employed, Fryer & Binyon's warehouse, like so many examples that followed, exhibited another important development inspired by Ruskin and his contemporaries – the use of colour. Polychromy sprang in part, from an interest in the inherent qualities of materials themselves, but also from a desire to heighten the potential impact of building. Street, in particular, had been impressed by the polychromy of Italian architecture, writing in 1855 that:

> our buildings are, in nine cases out of ten, cold, colourless, insipid, academic studies, and our people have no conception of the necessity of obtaining rich colour and no sufficient love for it when successfully obtained. The task and the duty of architects at the present day is mainly that of awakening and then satisfying this feeling; and one of the best and most ready vehicles for doing this exists, no doubt, in the rich-coloured brick so easily manufactured in this country.[17]

The demand for different-coloured bricks, together with the wider application of stones, was one that Britain's geology could satisfy with little difficulty, now that the railways existed.

61 Fryer & Binyon's warehouse (1855–6), Manchester, by Waterhouse – based on the Doge's Palace, Venice.

Although the London Printing & Publishing Co.'s premises (1860), Smithfield,[18] by George Somers Clarke (1825–82), resorted to a classical composition (a distinct ground floor forming a plinth, the main order, and a gabled roofline, held together vertically by brick piers),[19] the decorative elements were Gothic, and the use of coloured bricks, Cheesewring granite and Bath stone revealed the appeal of polychromy. The fireproof part of the basement served as a strong-room for plates, books, paper and ink; the ground floor held the counting houses, offices and waiting room. The board room, accommodation for authors and printing facilities were on the first storey, while 'the second floor is reserved for book-binding in its several branches; the third floor to stock and lithographic printing; the fourth to stock and engraving; and the fifth to copper-plate printing'.[20] The existence of so many flammable materials encouraged the adoption of an internal framework of cast-iron beams and columns, with a fire main running from top to bottom supplied by a large cistern in the roof.

Lavers & Barraud's Painted-Glass Manufactory (1859–60), 22 Endell Street, London, designed by Robert J. Withers (1823–94),[21] demonstrated the popularity of the Gothic and a variety in materials: red, black and yellow brick, and Bath stone dressings. Yet cost and practical considerations had not been neglected:

> Internally the whole area is kept as large and simple as possible, the floors being merely united by staircase and lifts, the great object being the employment of a large number of men under careful supervision. Economy in space and materials, and cheapness in execution, have guided the design throughout . . .[22]

Further evidence of the pervasive influence of the High Victorian Gothic was offered by E.W. Godwin's (1833–86) carriage factory (1862) for John Perry at 104 Stokes Croft, Bristol.[23]

Godwin achieved a more delicate polychromy through the use of subtly contrasting stones, which accentuated the three round-arched arcades that lit the warehouse. Based upon medieval Florentine buildings, it possessed a solidity and purpose that Ruskin would have admired.

'There are as yet few warehouses and shops in any purely pointed style', observed the Ecclesiological Society in 1859, adding that 'while the sumptuous character of new constructions in London and other great towns for commercial purposes denotes the growth of public taste, they have as yet unfortunately scarcely travelled out of the beaten track of Italian and Renaissance'.[24] Among the earliest, and possibly the outstanding warehouse in the Gothic style, was one designed by the son of a civil engineer, William Burges (1827–81), an architect better known for country houses and churches.[25] Having already worked on a City warehouse for Messrs Millington and Hatton, stationers at 32 Bridge Row, in 1858,[26] he was commissioned in 1865–6 to remodel Skilbeck's drysalters' warehouse, 46 Upper Thames Street.[27] Burges was to reface the street frontage and add a top storey, while retaining the existing four levels below. The resulting medieval composition was both practical and original. The ground-floor entrance and office windows were supported by an exposed wrought-iron beam; he enlivened the pointed gable by sculptures including two lions to guide the hoists – the cables emerged from their mouths – and a sailing boat to indicate the mercantile character of the business.[28] The corbel which supported the central crane was carved into the bust of an Oriental maid, symbolizing the geographical basis of the drysalters' products. The experiment drew much comment, almost all being favourable. E.W. Godwin thought it 'strikingly clever';[29] Robert W. Edis (1839–1927) produced a faithful adaptation when commissioned in 1873 to design a warehouse in Southwark Street,[30] and other variations soon appearing in the capital's commercial districts.[31] Charles Eastlake in 1872 referred to the warehouse as 'one of the very few instances of the successful adaptation of Gothic for commercial purposes in the east end of London'.[32]

Referring to it as a 'great success', *The Ecclesiologist* came to this judgement because being suited to 'the most severe business purposes' it also displayed 'great solidity and firmness, plenty of light, every accommodation, and very considerable artistic effect'.[33]

Much of the debate settled around the use of exposed iron. *Building News* in 1866 argued that to reveal the beam in its 'full ugliness ... by a judicious amount of gilded rivet heads and paterae' was 'most praiseworthy', though the writer would have preferred that it had been painted black.[34] A later article spoke of the warehouse with 'pleasure' but concluded that the ground storey was 'not proof against criticism'.[35] Godwin pointed out in 1866 that:

> The warehouse in Upper Thames Street is essentially a Medieval warehouse, if we omit the lower storey, which has nothing in common with the rest of the superstructure ... Had a thirteenth century architect used an iron girder he would not have reduced the pier supporting it to less dimensions than the pier immediately above it. It has, to say the least, an awkward look, and will always remind one of a modern insertion in a Medieval front.[36]

The obvious constructional value of iron and the rising popularity of Gothic architecture created a considerable conundrum for Victorian thinkers. Whilst Ruskin had admired the Crystal Palace as an engineering feat and could then argue that 'the time is probably near when a new system of architectural laws will be developed, adapted entirely to metallic construction',[37] he consistently favoured wood, stone and brick as building materials and later hardened against the use of iron mainly because it was no longer hand made. The desire for truthfulness demanded that iron should be treated in accordance with its structural properties and, as Pugin had already shown, this often meant that it did not look solid or that its great strength imposed different proportions. Iron and later steel, in retreat from the glasshouses of the 1840s and 1850s, were increasingly regarded by architects as the province of the engineer and their use confined to structure, concealed behind masonry or brick walls.

Costing £8,170, a vinegar warehouse (1868) at 33–35 Eastcheap, for Messrs Hill, Evans & Co.[38] showed how the 'Gothic of the South of France, with a Venetian impress' could be adapted to a five-storey warehouse with offices. R.L. Roumieu (1814–77),[39] a former pupil of Benjamin Dean Wyatt (1775–1850), achieved a striking composition by deeply profiling a richly ornamented exterior of red and blue bricks and Tisbury stone dressings. Roumieu made something of a speciality of warehouses, designing others for Messrs Crosse & Blackwell, Crown Street; Messrs Petty, Wood & Co., Southwark Bridge Road; and Messrs Woodalls' Carriage Factory, Orchard Street, London, while the Victoria Ironworks on the Isle of Dogs was also by him. In addition he held the post of surveyor to the Chartered Gas Co. and to the Gas Light & Coke Co.'s estate at Beckton. Less ornate but no less medieval was the paint warehouse, Tradeston Street, Glasgow by William F. McGibbon (*c*.1857–1923), a red-brick variation of the Bargello in Florence.[40] Built in 1900, it featured a square corner tower complete with quatrefoils, battlements and machicolations, while columns of lancet windows lit the main body of the building.

Although Gothic never achieved the same popularity as Italianate for mills and warehouses, its general application may, nevertheless, be illustrated by reference to three buildings: Wait & James' Granary, Welsh Back, Bristol, the Abbey Cloth Mills, Bradford-on-Avon, and the Doulton Pottery Works, Lambeth. Each, designed by a professional architect supported by fair resources, resulted in enduring Gothic monuments. The first, a splendidly detailed polychrome warehouse in Florentine castellated style, was designed in 1869[41] by Archibald Ponton (d.?1880) and William Gough (1842–1918).[42] It cost £6,000 and could store 10,000 quarters of grain, the various brick perforations below the window openings being introduced for the thorough ventilation of the building. It obtained contemporary approval and a British Association guide to Bristol remarked that 'this handsome building' could show that 'beauty and roominess are not incomparable even in a

62 The deeply-profiled Venetian Gothic windows that lit the City vinegar warehouse (1868) by Roumieu.

granary'.[43] A military feel was imparted to the Abbey Cloth Mills (1875) by Richard Gane (c.1838/9–77), the London-based architect who had formerly lived in Trowbridge,[44] by the use of masonry blocks and fortress-like fenestration. Narrow columns of pointed windows, a simple dentil cornice and a solid basement combined with its situation on the River Avon to produce an enduring medieval image.[45]

Thirdly, the elaborate elevations of Waring & Nicholson and R. Stark Wilkinson (?1844–1936) for the Lambeth Pottery (1876–7),[46] executed in conjunction with its owner, Sir Henry Doulton, made these ornate premises not simply a workplace, but, in *The Builder*'s words, an advertisement:

> Primarily they are, of course, intended to subserve the business and manufacturing requirements but Messrs Doulton, as manufacturers of terra-cotta

and faience have very wisely ... determined that the buildings shall serve the secondary purpose, if such it can be considered, of showing the adaptability of their products for architectural treatments.[47]

The palatial works were described as Venetian Gothic 'freely treated', while the colourful decorative elements had all been 'specially designed and executed by Messrs Doulton themselves'.[48] A later assessment, remarking on the quality of the blue Staffordshire and Fareham red bricks, together with its red-and-buff dressings of terracotta, noted that the latter material 'is steadily on the increase'.[49] Its chimney was a slim 233-ft version of the Palazzo Vecchio's campanile, an idea said to have originated with Ruskin.

Messrs Doulton also supplied the ornamental tiles and stained glass for the stairwell and entrance hall in the head office at the St Vincent's Works of John Lysaght, manufacturers of galvanized sheet and agricultural metalware in Bristol.[50] Given that Thomas Royse Lysaght

63 A detail from the decorative doorway to the Lambeth Pottery (1876–7). The building was an advertisement as well as a workplace for its owners, Doultons.

latterly had his offices at the St Vincent's Works,[51] it seems likely that he had been responsible for the large galvanizing shop there – 150 ft by 120 ft and 70 ft high.[52] This was supported internally by four massive Bath stone pillars. Inside these were lead pipes to channel the water from the glazed roof to the drains. The use of timber for its framework, rather than iron or steel, and the insertion of the pipes within masonry columns was to guard against the corrosive effect of the sulphuric acid in the atmosphere. The accentuated round-arched windows that decorated the gables were typical of much of Bristol's industrial architecture and were a feature of the style of Gingell, with whom Lysaght had been a pupil and briefly a partner. The retort and engine houses, for example, at Canon's Marsh gasworks were of a similar

design and employed the same deep-grey coursed rubble. Yet Lysaght was not the author of the castellated office building. The plans, dated December 1891, had been effected by 1893.[53] Richard Milverton Drake, a Bristol architect, who in 1889 had designed a factory for Frys in Broadmead, signed the drawings. It appears that Lysaght had died in c.1890–1 and that the commission may have been put to tender. No expense was spared. Battlements and round turrets with arrowloops defended this robust fortress of Pennant stone. The tiling by Doulton was of great variety and intricacy, whilst the offices on the second floor were panelled in walnut. When the western arm was lengthened from two to five bays shortly after completion, the large Romanesque arch of rubble was painstakingly reconstructed further along Silverthorne Lane.[54]

In 1876 Lysaghts began a Constructional Engineering Department, which in time occupied a site nearby at Netham. One reason why T.R. Lysaght might have moved from his office in

Royal Insurance Buildings to St Vincent's Works was that his skills were required in the execution of the company's architectural structures. These included Swansea Market, the Round House at Woolwich Arsenal, Llanelli Market, the concert pavilion on Aberystwyth Pier, and the car sheds for the Bristol Tramway & Carriage Co.[55] Although much concerned with bridges and viaducts, they also designed the machine shops for Vickers, Son & Maxim at Barrow – a steel framework supporting overhead cranes and a glazed roof – and similar sheds for Avonside Engine Co., Portsmouth Dockyard and Llanelli Steel Co.[56] Their expertise in structural ironwork was such that they won the commission to provide the steel frame to the Manchester Royal Jubilee Exhibition Hall of 1887, designed by Maxwell & Tuke.[57]

Mills were not commonly built in the Gothic style but an exception was the Anglo-Scotian Mill (1871), Beeston,[58] which conformed to a rigidly symmetrical plan, while lancet windows, a central stepped gable, turrets and arrowloops enlivened this castellated red-brick factory. Although constructed in 1889, Templeton's carpet factory, Glasgow, designed by William Leiper (1839–1916),[59] owed much to the High Victorian movement.[60] One of the few large-scale mills in the Venetian Gothic style, the extravagance of its façade attracted much comment. 'Built of gaudy coloured bricks [red, light-green and cream] with blue glass mosaic in the heads and spandrels of the windows', remarked *The Builder*, 'the colours are harmonious, if rather louder than one is used to; and we have no hesitation in saying that we think the experiment is a decided success'.[61] This exotic mill, decorated with fanciful towers and battlements, was said to have been based upon the Doge's Palace, though the range of ornament and colouring lifted it clear of any simple adaptation. Leiper was not, however, a specialist factory architect, but had a general practice in Glasgow that embraced churches, insurance offices and mansions. Chance or some personal connection had brought what appears to have been his only major industrial commission.

Gasworks, naturally, were not ignored by the Gothic movement, though two of the most elaborate examples occurred on the Continent. A highly ornate Gothic façade was erected for the gasholder at Tegel Works, Berlin, while in Vienna the application of ornate battlements, buttresses and blind arches produced a building resembling a medieval keep.[62]

The enormous plant laid down by the Gas Light & Coke Co. at Beckton ultimately became the world's largest gas and by-product works. Its design and construction was entrusted to Frederick John Evans (1810–80), the company's chief engineer, assisted by Vitruvius Wyatt. The contractor was Sir John Aird (1833–1911), who had recently built the Millwall Docks.[63] The first four retort-houses (360 ft long and 90 ft wide, each with 270 retorts), erected in 1869–70, were of brick, but the ventilation inlets, placed above blind panels between pilasters, were decorated with terracotta. Lozenge openings alternated with groups of Romanesque arches. The 'regard to architectural effect' detected by *The Engineer* also spread to the offices and purifying plant, whose gabled buildings exhibited a similar range of ornament.[64] 'One ingenious arrangement consists of tanks, 10 ft wide and $1\frac{1}{2}$ ft deep, running the whole length of the retort-houses on each side, just below the edge of the roof, so as to gather the rainfall and affording a capacity for 250,000 gallons of water, which will thus be available for the boilers of the steam engines'.[65] The elliptical-arch iron roofs were supported by cast-iron columns, though some parts of their structure were considered almost superfluous: 'a good deal of taste – much more than is usually displayed in connection with ironwork – has been shown in the girders, but we question the constructive value of some of them'.[66] To facilitate charging, coal entered the retort-houses by wagon along a high-level railway which ran over a wrought-iron viaduct from the pier set in the Thames. The total cost of this massive project was estimated at £600,000 and some 1,500 men had been continuously employed in its execution.

Reference has been made to the cathedral-like qualities of some early glassworks. When Pilkingtons decided to build a plate-glass factory this

64 (*opposite*) The ornate and colourful façade devised by William Leiper for Templeton's carpet factory (1889) in Glasgow.

65 No. 2 Retort House nearing completion at Beckton Gasworks (1869–70), with the railway viaduct to transport coal from the jetty in the Thames.

comparison was not ignored. The site, on a slope at Cowley Hill, offered particular advantages for the storage and disposal of sand without inhibiting layout.[67] The works (1873–6) took about three years to build. The partners had, however, to keep a close eye on costs, as in April 1875 they discovered that George Harris, the builder, had apparently 'put a heavy profit upon the work and other extras'. Henceforth they took such responsibilities into their own hands whenever possible. The principal building (in plan, a cross with two shorter arms) consisted of a large hall with three 30-pot furnaces in the centre and ample space for casting plate glass; the annealing kilns were arranged along the side of each nave in four blocks. Nearby were a matching room, grinding shed, smoothing and polishing rooms and a warehouse. The gabled roof of the

casting hall stood above the surrounding buildings; its 'transepts' were lit by groups of narrow windows placed between buttresses and, from a distance, it resembled a capacious church turned to industrial pursuits. The cost of this development was around £153,000.[68] The Cowley Hill Works appeared in marked contrast to Pilkingtons' sheet and rolled glass works at Grove Street, St Helens, which had grown in an *ad hoc* fashion throughout the century.

Whilst most of the buildings in the warehouse districts of Bradford and Manchester continued

66 The plateworks at Cowley Hill, a glassworks belonging to Pilkingtons, illustrated as completed in 1876.

to be constructed in a *palazzo* or classical manner, a few Gothic versions were erected. This, in part, resulted from the southward migration of Scottish architects. George Corson (1829–1910) was born in Dumfries where with his elder brother, William Reid Corson (b.1821), he trained with Walter Newall. Moving to Leeds in 1849,[69] he designed a number of warehouses there and in Bradford. Having a particular liking for the Scotch baronial style, modified to provide extra light, he was responsible for a five-storey stone warehouse in Peckover Street, Bradford for Messrs Haugh, Dunlop & Co. in 1870.[70] Although externally distinct from its *palazzo* neighbours, its internal arrangements appear to have been similar:

> The boilers and engine are placed in a vaulted sub-basement. The packing room and blanket room occupy all the basement floor ... the ground floor is occupied by stock rooms for grey goods &c. The first floor is counting houses and grey room. The remaining floors are used as stock and making-up rooms.[71]

The style, with its circular pointed turrets and gable roof, was also exhibited by Central House (1880),[72] Princess Street, Manchester, a five-storey brick warehouse designed by W.R. Corson in partnership with Robert W. Aitkin, who had also received a Scottish training but with

67 Beside the Rochdale Canal, Central House (1880), Princess Street, Manchester, appeared slightly incongruous as a rare example of the Scottish Baronial style in the city's warehouse district.

Peddie & Kinnear of Edinburgh.[73] After his articles, W.R. Corson worked in London and, following a period in Leeds, moved to Manchester in 1854 to take over the practice of J.E. Gregan who had also been a pupil of Newall.[74]

A far more elaborate and extensive factory-warehouse was erected in St Paul's Street, Leeds in 1878. This lavish building in a Moorish style, designed by Thomas Ambler (1838–1920) of Leeds, housed Messrs Barran & Sons' garment business.[75] The basement contained the cutting rooms where power-driven knives helped to shape the cloth; the ground floor served as offices, packing and receiving rooms; the first floor the stock room for made-up garments; the second was in part dining facilities and part workrooms; while the third floor contained the sewing machines. The whole was fireproof, having cast-iron columns and joists with stone stairs.[76] Its façade was divided into three principal sections; the degree of decoration increased with height as the windows became smaller, the whole being topped by Moorish battlements. Each of the corners had an octagonal tower capped by a terracotta minaret. The materials were no less fanciful. Glazed tiles and intricate terracotta mouldings (supplied by Doulton of London) made Barran's warehouse one of the most extravagant in Britain. That such a building could be treated in such a manner showed how far the dictates of the hierarchy of decorum had been eroded and the extent to which both architects and clients considered it important to pay serious attention to the appearance of workplaces, though because of its central situation in Leeds, this factory, like Doulton's Pottery, served as an advertisement as well.

Summary

Whilst the following chapter will seek to demonstrate that the majority of industrial buildings erected in the second half of the nineteenth century retained an adherence to Italianate or neo-classical models, the advance of the Gothic Revival had nevertheless exerted a significant influence on this field of architecture. First, a number of warehouses and factories were constructed in various Continental Gothic styles. Secondly, and possibly most important, the Gothic movement had been accompanied by a major reappraisal of architectural principles. Professional architects now accepted that industrial buildings were worthy of their serious consideration and that the most elevated treatment could be adapted to their purpose. Neither the emphasis on polychromy, massive interpretations, nor the desire for eclectic sources presented any special problems in the design of warehouses or factories. The new richness and strength to be observed in the Gothic works of Street or Scott had repercussions for those still committed to the Italianate, as their buildings often took on a greater massiveness, were more highly ornamented and sought variety from the use of coloured stones and bricks. The major area of stagnation, if not retreat, occurred in the application of advancing construction techniques. Iron, and increasingly steel, which were recognized as invaluable in the erection of fireproof structures, remained concealed behind masonry. Such strides as had been made in the use of exposed iron and glass were not pursued.

Notes

1 George Edmund Street, *Brick and Marble in the Middle Ages, Notes of a Tour in the North of Italy*, London (1874), p. ix.

2 Stefan Muthesius, *The High Victorian Movement in Architecture 1850–1870*, London (1972), p. 38.

3 John Ruskin, *The Seven Lamps of Architecture*, London (1849), Everyman Edition (1925), p. 8.

4 *Ibid.*, p. 181.

5 Quoted from Pevsner, *Building Types, op. cit.*, p. 210.

6 George Gilbert Scott, *Remarks on the Secular and Domestic Architecture*, London (1857), p. 209.

7 *Ibid.*, p. 211.

8 *Ibid.*, p. 212.

9 *Ibid.*, p. 213.

10 Clark, *Gothic Revival, op. cit.*, p. 175.

11 Quoted from T.G. Jackson, *Recollections*, Oxford (1950), p. 51.

12 Barrington Kaye, *The Development of the*

Architectural Profession in Britain, London (1960), pp. 88–90.

13 Muthesius, *op. cit.*, p. 160.

14 *Ibid.*, pp. 190–1; Papworth, *op. cit.*, said that Waterhouse designed 'Grafton's block of five' (1869) in Manchester, Vol. V, 'M', p. 23.

15 Fawcett, *Seven Victorian Architects*, *op. cit.*, Stuart Allen Smith, 'Alfred Waterhouse: Civic Grandeur', p. 104.

16 Sally Maltby *et al.*, *Alfred Waterhouse 1830–1905*, London RIBA (1983), pp. 6–7, 11.

17 Street, *Brick and Marble*, *op. cit.*, p. 400.

18 *BN*, Vol. 6, 23 November 1860, pp. 894–5.

19 Muthesius, *op. cit.*, p. 191; Brockman, *op. cit.*, pp. 30–1.

20 *BN*, Vol. 6, 24 August 1860, p. 663.

21 *B*, Vol. XVII, No. 849, 14 May 1859, pp. 360–1.

22 *Ibid.*, p. 360.

23 Hitchcock, *Nineteenth and Twentieth Centuries*, *op. cit.*, p. 262; Burrough, *Bristol*, *op. cit.*, p. 61; Gomme, *Bristol*, *op. cit.*, p. 370.

24 *20th Annual Report of the Ecclesiological Society* (1859), p. 9.

25 J. Mordaunt Crook, *William Burges and the High Victorian Dream*, London (1981), p. 238, plate 71.

26 *Ibid.*, p. 392; RIBA Drawing Collection, W. Burges, 'Abstract of Diaries', 1858.

27 RIBA Drawing Collection, W. Burges, 'Small Note Books' xxxii (1865), p. 64.

28 *BN*, Vol. XIII, 23 November 1866, p. 783; *B*, Vol. XXIV, No. 1241, 17 November 1866, pp. 850–1.

29 *BN*, Vol. XIV, 17 May 1867, p. 335.

30 *BN*, Vol. XXVI, 21 February 1873, pp. 212, 220.

31 *Victorian City*, Vol. 1, *op. cit.*, John Summerson, 'London, the Artifact', p. 316.

32 Charles L. Eastlake, *A History of the Gothic Revival*, London (1872), p. 127.

33 *The Ecclesiologist*, XXVII, N.S. XXV (1866), pp. 310–11.

34 *BN*, *op. cit.*, 23 November 1866, p. 783.

35 *BN*, Vol. XXVI, 9 January 1874, 'Our Streets', p. 30.

36 *BN*, Vol. XIII, 30 November 1866, Edwin W. Godwin, 'Three Modern Architects', p. 800.

37 Ruskin, *Seven Lamps*, *op. cit.*, p. 70; *Architectural History*, Vol. 13 (1970), Stefan Muthesius, 'The "Iron Problem" in the 1850s', pp. 58–63.

38 *B*, Vol. XXVI, No. 1340, 10 October 1868, pp. 748–9; Gavin Stamp and Colin Amery, *Victorian Buildings of London 1837–1887*, London (1980), p. 103.

39 *B*, Vol. XXXV, No. 1796, 7 July 1877, Obituary, p. 691; *The Architect's ... Directory* (1868), *op. cit.*, p. 134.

40 Gomme and Walker, *Glasgow*, *op. cit.*, p. 228; Hume, *The Lowlands*, *op. cit.*, p. 171.

41 *B*, Vol. XXIX, No. 1478, 3 June 1871, pp. 426–7.

42 *The Architect*, Vol. X, 22 November 1873, pp. 270 ff; Gomme, *Bristol*, *op. cit.*, pp. 436, 440.

43 British Association, *Bristol and its Environs*, London (1875), p. 209.

44 *TM*, Vol. II, 15 September 1876, p. 251.

45 *BN*, Vol. 28, 28 May 1875, pp. 600, 604; RIBA Biography File, Richard Gane; Brockman, *op cit.*, pp. 65, 66.

46 *B*, Vol. XXXV, No. 1786, 28 April 1877, p. 422.

47 *Ibid.*

48 *Ibid.*

49 *B*, Vol. XXXVII, No. 1904, 2 August 1879, pp. 856, 859.

50 *The Lysaght Century 1857–1957*, Bristol (1957), pp. 22–3.

51 *J. Wright & Co.'s Bristol Directory* (1890), p. 403.

52 BCL, *Work in Bristol, A Series of Sketches ... reprinted from the Bristol Times & Mirror*, Bristol (1883), p. 5.

53 New Offices for John Lysaght Ltd, Plans and Elevations, Nos 1–3, 31 December 1891, signed by R. Milverton Drake, 24 College Green.

54 Information from Rheemco Ltd.

55 *John Lysaght Ltd, Bristol, Constructional Engineering Department* (*c.*1900), pp. 2, 44, 48, 49, 50, 55.

56 *Ibid.*, pp. 27–8. 30–1, 37, 52–4.

57 *Royal Jubilee Exhibition Manchester, 1887, Official Catalogue*, the contractors were Robert Neill & Sons, p. 19.

58 N. Pevsner, *BoE, Nottinghamshire*, Harmondsworth (1979), p. 69.

59 *B*, Vol. CX, No. 3826, 2 June 1916, Obituary, p. 409.

60 Andor Gomme and David Walker, *Architecture of Glasgow*, London (1968), p. 226.

61 *B*, Vol. LXXV, No. 2892, 9 July 1898, p. 29.

62 Alwyne Meade, *Modern Gasworks Practice*, London (1921), pp. 652, 654.

63 *The Story of Beckton*, reprinted from *Gas Times*, pp. 1, 3; *Beckton 1868-1968* (North Thames Gas).

64 *The Engineer*, Vol. XXVIII, 2 July 1869, p. 1.

65 *Ibid*.

66 *Ibid*., 10 September 1869, p. 178.

67 T.C. Barker, *The Glassmakers, Pilkingtons: The rise of an International Company 1826-1976*, London (1977), p. 146.

68 *Ibid*., p. 147.

69 *BN*, Vol. 59, 1 August 1890, p. 166; Linstrum, *West Yorkshire*, *op. cit.*, p. 375.

70 *BN*, Vol. 29, 3 September 1875, p. 252.

71 *Ibid*.

72 Philip Atkins, *Guide across Manchester*, Manchester (1976), pp. 100-1.

73 *The Architect's ... Directory* (1868), *op. cit.*, pp. 97, 106-7.

74 JRL, 1/1/14 W.R. Corson, President 1867-9.

75 *BN*, Vol. 36, 17 January 1879, p. 62; Linstrum, *West Yorkshire*, *op. cit.*, pp. 306, 370.

76 LivRO, *Goad's Plans of Leeds*, Vol. I, No. 2, February 1927.

SEVEN

The Italianate tradition continued

1855–1900

Whilst Gothic achieved new heights in popularity and variety, Italianate architecture, which in the earlier decades of the century had established a powerful hold over the minds of mill and factory designers, retained its following in most industrial regions. If anything, it became more ornate and richly expressed than before, under the influence of the High Victorian movement. Some of the thoughts expounded by Ruskin and his fellows – such as the importance of all forms of building and the desirability that architects should not rigidly discriminate between them – had a general application and indirectly encouraged this trend. For example, when called upon to expand its output, the Royal Gunpowder Factory at Waltham Abbey

68 'E' Mills at the Royal Gunpowder Factory, Waltham Abbey; the central brick tower contained the beam engine which drove the grinding stones in each of the six self-contained mills.

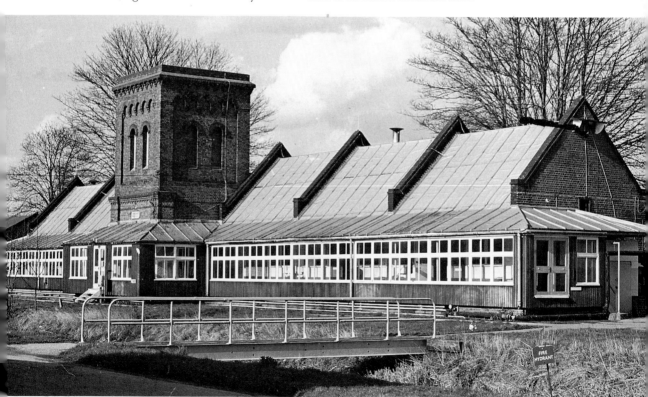

in 1877–8 erected a number of steam-powered incorporating mills for mixing and grinding the basic ingredients.[1] The beam engine which drove the machinery and the single-storey mills themselves, fronted by a cast-iron verandah, were not executed in the Gothic but in an Italianate style. It seems that Captain H. Tovey, RE, designed the symmetrical brick structure under the supervision of Lt. Col. W.H. Noble, RE, Inspector of Works, Woolwich.[2] Thus, a government establishment commissioning new works at the height of the Gothic movement retained an allegiance to an established style of building, which had earlier included the Royal Small Arms Factory (1854), nearby on the Lea at Enfield, the architects having been Lockwood and Mawson.[3]

Mills and chimneys

Sufficiently large numbers of Italianate mills survive to make a demonstration of their appeal a question of selection rather than painstaking discovery. In Bradford, for instance, James Drummond, having chosen a suitable site for a new enterprise, instructed Lockwood and Mawson in 1856 to prepare plans for a mill,

warehouse and small weaving shed. As the excavations turned up a good deal of fine clay, Drummond used this to make bricks to line the 'inner walls so as to make the buildings fire-proof',[4] though this was by then not a novel technique; in the early period of mill construction quarry rubble had been used for the interior linings of load-bearing walls. Lumb Lane Mills were completed in 1858. However, in 1869 a larger mill was added (seven storeys, 237 ft long and 55 ft wide), distinguished by two Italianate staircase towers. The designs were prepared by William and Richard Mawson, the latter being responsible for the elevations. This extension was also of Yorkshire stone with an inner lining of brick, and had cast-iron columns and beams.

More impressive still was India Mill (1859–67), designed by Ernest Bates (d.1877) of Manchester, for Eccles, Shorrock, Brothers & Co., whose six-storey building (333 ft by 99 ft and holding 67,968 spindles) at Darwen was dwarfed by a magnificent 310-ft campanile chimney.[5]

69 Lumb Lane Mills (1858–9) in Bradford for James Drummond & Sons; the 1869 addition is on the right.

.Shepherd.

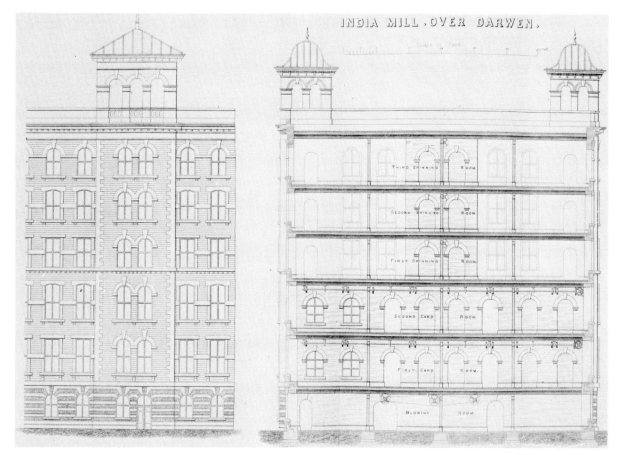

INDIA MILL, OVER DARWEN,

THIRD SPINNING ROOM

SECOND SPINNING ROOM

FIRST SPINNING ROOM

SECOND CARD ROOM

FIRST CARD ROOM

BLOWING ROOM

70 A cross-section through India Mill (1859–67) and the elevation of a staircase tower with its decorative loggia from Leigh's *Science of Modern Cotton Spinning* (1873).

Before illustrating the building in a section entitled 'Cotton Mill Architecture', Evan Leigh in 1873 asserted that:

> a modest amount of architectural display is not condemned; it distinguishes the educated man from the vulgar, civilization from barbarism; but what is contended for is economy with equal efficiency, having due regard for practical and *known* science.[6]

The chimney, constructed of red, white and black bricks with gritstone dressings, provided a further example of polychromy and the advance of Italianate architecture under the impetus of the High Victorian movement. Each of the mill's four corners and the two staircase towers rose to

a decorative loggia mimicking the topmost part of the chimney, while the several window forms that it exhibited contrasted with simpler factories constructed earlier in the century.

Another equally ornate chimney, based on a Renaissance campanile, rose at the Camperdown Linen Works, Lochee, Dundee in 1865–6.[7] Designed by James MacLaren (1843–90),[8] 'Cox's Stalk', 282 ft in height, consisted of two principal sections: a square tower of bands of red and white brick supporting an upper octagon. An ornamental iron balcony was placed at their meeting point.[9] Consuming over a million bricks and costing £6,000, it attracted considerable contemporary comment.[10]

Chimneys, described disparagingly by Dickens as 'sick black towers',[11] had been an object of attention from the earliest days of factory construction. They were visible and obvious landmarks and, like the buildings themselves, they reflected changes in popular taste. Just as a steeple marked the site of a church, they could contribute to a dramatic scene; Cooke Taylor remarked in 1842:

> I well remember the effect produced on me by my earliest view of Manchester ... and saw the forest of chimneys pouring forth volumes of steam and smoke, forming an inky canopy which seemed to embrace and involve the entire place.[12]

Generally, chimneys had remained short during the eighteenth century, and were often square in plan, with an external batter. As they became higher to increase the draught, the flat surfaces generated greater levels of wind resistance. The solution was to make the chimney of circular cross-section, though the need for suitably shaped stones or bricks increased costs. The problem could be partially circumvented by the adoption of an octagonal cross-section, whereby specials were only required for the quoins, and flat, regular stones preponderated. At Dean Clough Mills an octagonal stone chimney of 381 ft was erected, though the topmost 60 ft had to be removed because of the immense weight.[13] Tallest of them all was at Messrs Townsend's Alkali Works, Port Dundas, where a brick chimney (1857–9), circular in section, designed by Duncan Macfarlane, a Glasgow engineer and architect, rose 454 ft.[14] The need to disperse their noxious gases meant that alkali works used particularly lofty stacks to increase the draught – the higher the chimney the greater the column of light, hot air.[15]

Decrying the fact that most factory chimneys visually offered few pleasing qualities, *Building News* observed in July 1864 that:

> it does not fall to the lot of every architect to find himself called upon to supply designs for a palace, a club house or a first-class metropolitan hotel, still more rarely is there a demand for his services in the erection of a great bridge or memorial column. But it does happen that a young architect is called upon to undertake the construction of a large factory or engineering establishment and such being the case ... the stack which he will have to build is at once quite as conspicuous and quite as suitable for the exercise of his talent as any column which he could possibly erect by his country's desire in memory of

a hero. It is quite true that there may not be so much room for mere decoration, but ... the much despised factory chimney affords an ample opportunity for the display, not alone of talent, but of genius.[16]

Although readily acknowledging the value of industrial architecture as a training ground for young men, the journal opposed any attempt to conceal the chimney's character 'after the fashion of a Grecian column' or a 'Corinthian capital'.

When a new mill was added at Saltaire in 1868 its chimney (unlike the simpler Italianate version already standing) took the form of a campanile, a copy of the Venetian bell tower of Santa Maria Gloriosa[17] – no isolated example, for in 1859 [Sir] Robert Rawlinson (1810–98) had produced a pattern book of chimney designs based upon campaniles, watch towers and minarets.[18] As well as recommending these structures, Rawlinson also urged the use of colour through the selection of varied materials.[19] In an earlier paper, delivered to the Liverpool Architectural Society, he asked why so many chimneys then offered little interest:

> If the question 'Who is to blame?' is fully sifted, expect the great mischief worker 'nobody' designs all the tall chimneys; for I presume it rarely enters into the mind of a cotton lord to employ an architect of known reputation to design a chimney. There are, however, exceptions.[20]

The Builder subsequently published a full-page illustration of seven chimney adaptations.[21] The son of a Lancashire builder and millwright, Rawlinson entered the office of Jesse Hartley as a draughtsman and measurer of masonry. Largely self-educated, and primarily an engineer with a thorough knowledge of the North-west, a personal passion for architecture drove him to argue that the buildings of industry offered scope for improvement. His engineering experience, however, drew him into the public health question and he rose to prominence by designing sewers rather than factories or warehouses.[22]

As an example of the architectural lengths that some industrial patrons were prepared to

71 Further examples from Rawlinson's treatise designed to promote the execution of ornate chimneys.

go, the Wainhouse Tower (1871–5) may be cited. It was initially designed by Isaac Booth (1823–91), a Halifax architect and surveyor, as a conventional chimney to serve the Washer Lane Dyeworks of John Wainhouse, though never functioning as such. In 1873, on Booth's departure, Richard Swarbrick Dugdale, a former pupil of his and later Borough Engineer

for Huddersfield, was commissioned to enliven the upper section of the chimney.[23] Incorporating balustraded balconies, surmounted by a lantern dome and finial, it became an altogether grander object, and on its completion in 1875 served as a viewing tower, the dyeworks having been sold in the previous year. Some 253 ft high, it had cost £14,000 to build, an extravagance that few factory owners could afford.

The chimney to Dalton Mills, Keighley, also had a staircase that wound around the shaft to a balcony near the top of the column. The buildings, in the 'Roman-Italian style' by the Leek

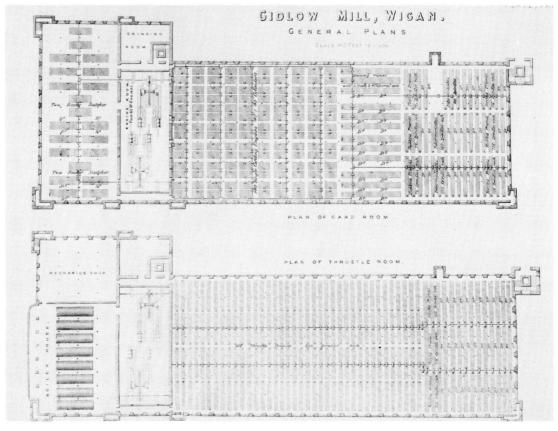

72 Plans of Gidlow Mill showing how the size and number of machines ultimately determined the precise dimensions of the buildings.

architect, Sugden, demonstrated in the words of *The Builder* that:

> mills need not necessarily be hideous, shapeless and dingy apparitions ... The blue slated roofs contrast with the colour of the stone walls. The walling itself is pitch-faced throughout, with ashlar-moulded strings, rusticated quoins, arches & etc.[24]

The lasting appeal of Italianate architecture for designers was demonstrated in Leeds at Harding's Tower Works, where in 1899 William Bakewell (1839-1925), a local architect, devised a chimney shaft based upon Giotto's campanile in Florence. Although built of red brick, the bell louvres, which formed part of the dust extraction plant, were decorated with gilded panels, while the base was adorned with portrait medallions by Alfred Drury as a tribute to famous textile engineers.[25] The campanile stood beside an earlier adaptation: Thomas Shaw's version of 1864 based on the Lamberti tower in Verona.

No mere caprice dictated the incorporation of fanciful additions to the shaft, it has been argued, for ornament toward the cap is said to have assisted the chimney's draught.[26] Yet this was by no means proved, and the erosive effects of the smoke and escaping gases concentrated there. This prompted the use of cast iron for some coronets as at Dean Clough. Recently many caps, becoming unsafe, have been removed. The problem was that engineers could protect the lower portions of the shaft with an inner skin of firebricks, but the load factor prevented them from extending it to the very top without constructing chimneys of immense dimensions; the caustic chemicals and warm gases could thus attack the upper portions at will.[27]

In addition, as boilers fell out of use, less heat passed up the shaft. This allowed damp to penetrate, which, with frost, caused further damage.

By virtue of their very size, T. Houldsworth & Co.'s Reddish Mills (1865) and Messrs Rylands & Sons' Gidlow Works (1865), Wigan, deserve a mention. The first, apparently the work of A.H. Stott, was a massive symmetrical brick structure divided into three sections by twin Italianate staircase towers, its central nine-bay block being surmounted by a clock pediment. Each of the bays were linked vertically by pilasters, the fourth-storey windows uniting them in a round-arched arcade.[28] The Gidlow Works, by George Woodhouse, a three-storey red-, blue- and cream-brick mill, 392 ft in length and 108 ft wide, with Italianate towers, was described at the time as being 'not surpassed and, we believe ... not equalled by any other mill in the world'.[29]

73 A Victorian photograph of Ryland & Son's Gidlow Mills (1865) when the Mesnes district of Wigan appeared rural. In the 1880s its workforce of 1,300 equipped with 1,600 looms produced 300,000 to 400,000 yards of calicoes, twills and cloth per week.

As an indication of the way that mill-owners now felt obliged to embellish their factories, the case of Highgate Mills, Clayton Heights, may be quoted. The mill itself was a simple, unadorned stone structure (possibly early nineteenth century, and enlarged in 1851 and 1862), but the dressed-stone entrance, added in 1865, could only be described as grand.[30] Announcing the mill's name and topped by a date pediment supported by scrolls, such an elevated classical gateway would have been considered a sheer waste of capital when the enterprise was founded.

One of the finest, and possibly the largest, British example of a late-nineteenth-century Italianate mill was commissioned by Messrs Lister of Manningham in Bradford.[31] The plans were drawn by Thomas G. Andrews (1838–86), son of William,[32] and Joseph Pepper (1837/8–81),[33] the Bradford architects, and the structure erected between 1871 and 1873. Its dimensions gained it admission to the pages of *The Builder*, which remarked:

The new mill is six storeys high ... of good external appearance – in dressed stone, having a bold cornice, with blocks, and above this an ornamental and panelled parapet. The staircase is in the centre

74 A view along Patent Street of Manningham Mills (1871–3), Bradford, dominated by its 249 ft campanile chimney.

of the front, and stands clear out from the main walls. It is more ornamental than the rest of the building, and, with its staff, makes a feature in the great length of the frontage.[34]

Moreover, special attention had been reserved for its campanile chimney, which rose to 249 ft

in height,[35] helping to establish Listers' as a landmark, the whole factory being built on the crest of a hill. To provide a better vent for the smoke as it ascended and expanded, the internal chimney gradually widened towards the top so that the ornamental outer casing had in addition a practical purpose.[36] Because the former Manningham Mill had been burnt to the ground in 1871, E. Cunliffe Lister determined that its successor should be as fire-resistant as possible.[37] 'Each floor', reported the *Illustrated Weekly Telegraph* in 1885,

> is of Dennett's concrete arching, resting on iron beams supported by massive pillars of the same material. The supporting pillars are fluted and highly ornamented, and, as they are painted with nice regard to decoration ... they form a pleasant sight for the eye to rest upon.[38]

The staircases were of stone, and the window frames all of cast iron. This wool-combing and worsted-spinning mill, given its size, was regarded by contemporaries as 'an unsurpassed piece of industrial architecture, and special praise is due to the loftiness and perfect lighting and ventilation of the rooms, and to the many conveniences and well-considered sanitary arrangements'.[39] The scale of the enterprise appears all the more remarkable because the mill had been constructed without resort to limited liability – such protection not being sought until 1889[40] – and was financed solely by Samuel Lister (1815–1906).

Because the northern industrial towns had grown rapidly from small beginnings, they commonly possessed few established professional services to call upon. The weak coverage provided by the Church of England, for example, encouraged the evangelical drive of the Non-conformists and resulted in the building of so many chapels. Just as the numbers of priests, doctors and lawyers were limited in these manufacturing regions, so too architects remained scarce. 'A Stockport Cotton Spinner' wrote to *The Builder* in January 1864 to reveal this deficiency:

> A few weeks ago a 'Stocktonian' complained in your pages of the great want of an architect. I think, however, the 'Stockportians' feel the want in

a still greater degree. The only representatives of the architectural profession in Stockport, a town of 60,000 inhabitants, are a firm who advertise themselves as 'Builders, Timber-dealers, Surveyors, Valuers and Architects' and their place of business is a saw mill.[41]

It was, however, during the 1860s and 1870s that architects in the industrial towns, men such as George Woodhouse, A.H. Stott, J.J. Bradshaw and Edward Potts, were increasingly attracted by factory commissions. Born and educated in the north, they understood the needs of the textile trade and could see the mushrooming demand for mill architecture. Based upon work completed in their locality, they established reputations that covered whole counties and later even spread overseas.

George Woodhouse (1827-83), the Bolton mill architect,[42] produced a number of unusual designs, including Bliss' tweed mill (1872), Chipping Norton.[43] Built to resemble a great house

75 The tweed mill of Bliss & Sons at Chipping Norton (1872), which appears either as a modified stately home or as part of industrial Lancashire transplanted to rural Oxfordshire.

in a park, this symmetrical four-storey stone mill achieved distinction by the use of a balustraded parapet and square corner towers with urns, but more particularly by the centrally placed Tuscan chimney which rose from a fluted dome. It is possible, in view of the similar plan – a circular staircase around a central chimney and covered by a dome – that Woodhouse also designed the Victoria Mills, Miles Platting, possibly erected in the 1870s for W. Holland & Sons Ltd.[44] A substantial brick structure of six storeys, its symmetrical and regular elevation was dominated by the untypical incorporation of the chimney. In October 1874 *The Builder* reported that probably 'the largest cotton manufactory in Lancashire' had been opened for Messrs Tootal Broadhurst Lee Co. at Daubhill, Bolton. Designed by Woodhouse, the four-storey mill and enormous weaving shed (278 ft long and 235 ft wide) had been over two years in building, the first brick being laid on 14 January 1872. Executed in the 'Italian style of architecture', Sunnyside Mills' prominent feature was a tower and a 165-ft chimney.[45]

That Woodhouse designed Peel No. 3 Mill for Messrs George Knowles & Sons Ltd of Bolton is

76 Victoria Mills, Miles Platting, erected for W. Holland & Sons. The chimney arrangement suggests that Woodhouse could have been the architect.

certain.[46] Built in 1876, this six-storey structure earned the local nickname 'The Glass Factory', as two sides consisted entirely of glass held in place by light iron pillars. Woodhouse was not, however, attempting to devise a new form of architecture, but had resorted to this expedient because its situation (at the corner of Waterloo Street and Slaters Lane),[47] in proximity to the company's other two mills, cut down the level of available daylight.[48] So flimsy did it appear that, it was said, insurance companies hesitated before offering the building cover. In order to make it fire resistant, the floors were constructed of concrete on brick arches, a method never before applied to a British factory, French contractors being employed to perform the work.[49] Whether the mill's demolition followed 'unsatisfactory' reports is unclear.[50]

Woodhouse, a Methodist, died prematurely in 1883, suffering from overwork, having become one of Lancashire's foremost architects. Born at Lindlay, near Huddersfield, he had been articled to James Whittaker, of Skipton Mill, Doffcocker, a leading Bolton architect.[51] When Whittaker joined Messrs Ormrod & Hardcastle as their architect and engineer, Woodhouse transferred to his employer's brother, John W. Whittaker, also an architect. Such was his application that he was admitted to the partnership before the expiry of his articles and several years later set up on his own account. His first major commission came from John Knowles, JP, to design his house, Heaton Grange. From this connection (he married Knowles' half-sister) other projects followed, and though his practice was a general one – including joint authorship with William Hill (1828–89), the Leeds architect, of Bolton Town Hall (1866–73)[52] – it could be argued at his death that his mill work had placed him at the forefront in this 'department of architectural skill'.[53] He had latterly been in partnership with Edward Potts at Oldham, who had assisted Hill on the Bolton project (p. 158),[54]

77 No. 3 Mill (1876) for George Knowles & Son, Bolton – known locally as the 'Glass Factory'; the glass-and-iron wall is on the right.

but the firm had been dissolved in 1872 and to ease his burdens he joined W.J. Morley (1847–1930) of Bradford, also a Non-conformist.[55] Their reputation as designers of mills travelled far and the partnership of Woodhouse and Morley built a number of fireproof factories in Paisley (p. 162). Morley himself also designed part of the Nevski Thread Mill, St Petersburg, which belonged to a syndicate of English owners.[56]

To show that as late as the 1870s mill architects were capable of producing elevations that would have served just as well thirty years before, Richard Kershaw's Woodvale Mills at Brighouse may be quoted.[57] The architects, George Hepworth & Son of Brighouse, produced a 300-ft-long, four-storey stone structure, whose pedimented central three-bay block contained the engine house. The repetition of simple window forms, plain dentil cornice and symmetry revealed the conservatism of certain architects and their clients. The boilers, ware-

houses and packing rooms were housed behind separately. Richard Kershaw, who then occupied Albert Mills, purchased the land at Well Holme Park in 1876 and began construction in the following year. Although a silk spinner, the demands of his business seem to have been comparable to the other textile trades, as the buildings were planned to afford 'the fullest light' and the 40,000-spindle plant operated on the belt-driving principle.[58]

Thus, the High Gothic movement did not find many adherents in the world of mills. As the following discussion seeks to demonstrate, there appear to have been no Gothic mills in Oldham, while the spinning district of Paisley similarly retained a loyalty to Renaissance or classical models. Henry Lockwood, for example, the designer of so many Italianate mills and warehouses, had in 1834 written a *History of the Antiquities of the Fortifications to the City of York*[59] (whose subscribers included the architects G.T. Andrews, J. Baird, W. Burn, L. Cubitt and J. Dobson), in which the development of medieval towers, gateways and walls were described in detail. His knowledge of the Gothic based on the restoration of York Castle was, therefore, precise, but so far as is known he did not import the style into any of his industrial commissions. Why, then, given the strength of the Gothic Revival elsewhere – it predominated in the field of churches, country houses and public buildings – did designers of textile mills remain comparatively unimpressed by its qualities? It is a difficult question to answer, for to reply that an established tradition of mill design in the Italianate manner determined future choices ignores the fact that in the 1840s this was also true of public buildings and stately homes, and that they succeeded in switching allegiance. However, some reasons may be advanced to show why the hold of the Italianate over factories was stronger than elsewhere. First, as has been seen, and will be shown more clearly in the case of Oldham and Bolton districts, specialist mill architects, who lived locally, increasingly came to dominate the market. A small number of like-minded men could, therefore, control patterns of taste. The Italianate movement, with its commercial and business associations, had been considered particularly appropriate for industrial buildings and possibly it was the power or conservatism of regional customs that maintained its popularity. This appears to have been true of the Potteries and large areas of Lancashire and Yorkshire where, despite the influence of the railways, local building materials were still preferred, and clients would rather that their new mills, though often larger and technically superior to their old ones, be constructed, in appearance at least, according to the old rules. The contrast between the various red bricks of Oldham and the millstone grits of Halifax and Huddersfield, for example, each consistently employed in these towns, remained striking even in the twentieth century. Whilst the High Victorian movement had an important impact upon these industrial regions, it manifested itself more in the development of established styles than the promotion of new ones.

The pattern of lavish treatment and greater scale was also evident in the field of warehouse-building. In Bradford, for instance, the restraint of the mid-nineteenth century disappeared as a number of warehouses with particularly ornate

façades were erected during the 1870s. Lockwood and Mawson were responsible for the richest designs in Little Germany: De Vere House (1871), 62 Vicar Lane; and Law, Russell & Co.'s warehouse (1874), 63 Vicar Lane.[60] Whilst the overall plan and internal arrangement of rooms scarcely differed from their plainer neighbours, the degree of ornament applied to their lower floors and entrances was far greater. Beneath the pedimented doorway to De Vere House an aggressive eagle hinted at the American business connection of the original owners, Thornton, Homan & Co.; a theme reiterated in the stars-and-stripes medallions of the first-floor windowheads. Grander still, resembling the many ornate tiers of a wedding cake, was the canted entrance corner of Law, Russell & Co.'s warehouse. This was treated as a pavilion, with coupled Corinthian columns to frame each of the superimposed stages surrounding progressively shorter windows, and the crowning pediment forming a light for the attic. Skilfully executed in ashlar, it housed the building's decorative spiral staircase. Hence, when surveying Bradford in 1898, *The Builder* could conclude:

> large mills and warehouses, which form a very important feature in the street architecture of the city . . . are built of hewn stone in a somewhat dignified style, and would impart an air of distinction to the city but for two drawbacks – the sombre hue which they assume from weather and smoke stain, and the insufficient width of the streets.[61]

Indeed, one classical warehouse in Leeds Road so much resembled a 'public building' that the journal suggested it had probably been constructed as such and subsequently converted for use in trade. In fact, this building, designed by William Andrews for Rennie Tetley and dating from the mid-1840s, had always been a warehouse, though one for which the desire to impress wholesale drapers overrode some practical

78 Lockwood and Mawson designed this palatial warehouse in 1874 for Law, Russell & Co., and the contractor was Archibald Neill, also based in Bradford.

LAW RUSSELL & C°

79 This warehouse (1897), on the corner of Barker Gate in Nottingham's Lace Market, was by the local architect, Watson Fothergill (1841–1928). His buildings (including Milbie House, Pilcher Gate, executed in 1882–3) had a distinctive character. The oriel windows on the first and second storeys illuminated the sales offices.

considerations,[62] for the Ionic portico restricted daylight to the lower floors, and there was no back yard or rear entry, limited provision for deliveries being made by the narrow doorway in the main frontage.[63]

The internal arrangement and structure of these warehouses was in the main determined by the various functions that they performed. The top, or fifth, floor, in the case of Law & Russell's building, served as a making-up room where under plentiful natural light the cloth received from the dyer could be inspected and measured before being rolled on boards or folded.[64] Illumination from the closely-spaced windows was supplemented by a central well lined throughout with glazed bricks.[65] The fourth floor was used to lay out incomplete orders, the third served as a sample room and store for woollen goods, the second for cotton, worsted and silk cloth, and the first for plain goods, whilst the ground floor contained the offices and a dining room for directors and clients. The engines (to drive the hoists and rolling machines) were in the basement, together with the workers' dining facilities, a blanket store and auxiliary grey room.[66]

Despite their vulnerability to fire, most Bradford warehouses continued to be constructed with cast-iron columns and timber floors, with load-bearing walls of local sandstone. In part this was because beams, subject to compound stress as distinct from the simple compression forces that occurred in vertical columns, required metal free from flaws, a condition impossible to guarantee with the imperfections of the casting process.[67] On the other hand, lengthy structural members could be rolled satisfactorily from wrought iron, yet these were only slowly adopted in the mid-nineteenth century, presumably through reasons of cost. Hence cross-beams

were commonly of Baltic or pitch pine. Improvements in structure came not with the introduction of wrought-iron substitutes, but in the 1880s, with 'jointless construction' techniques. These reduced the quantity of timber required, and lowered labour costs by eliminating the need for beam-notching for the closely set joists on which the floors were supported. Under the new system longitudinal beams of $13\frac{1}{2}$–15 ft in length and $15\frac{1}{2}$ in square section were attached to the main beams by cast-iron socket plates. The number of vertical supports was reduced, thereby increasing the available area for storage. In addition, the heavy plank floors were capable of a greater intensity of loading.[68]

The Oldham limiteds

The preceding survey of the Italianate in part revealed a continuing growth in the size of factories. This expansion did not simply reflect the continued advance of industrialization but was encouraged by improved methods of finance, which, in the field of textiles, were pioneered in Oldham, when the passing of the 1856 and 1862 Companies Acts opened the floodgates of equity finance.[69] An example of the town's industry prior to this important legislation may be provided by Phoenix Mill (1856).[70] The modest dimensions (four storeys and 20 bays in length) accorded with the simple brick structure and lack of architectural adornment, and revealed an affinity with an earlier period of mill-building. When occupied jointly by Taylor & Buckley and James Wild it contained no more than 11,664 spindles in the two buildings on each side of Cromwell Street. By the mid-1850s some cotton-spinning enterprises had become frustrated by the capital restraints imposed upon them by partnership arrangements.[71] Expanding markets, the continued development of steam-powered machinery and a desire to exploit further economies of scale meant that larger mills could generate high profits; the problem was raising the funds to build and equip these factories. The grant of limited liability in 1856 for companies selling shares to the public created

80 Sun Mill (1858–63), Watts Street, Oldham. The round-arched window, decorated with a sun motif, lit the engine house. Although subsequently surrounded by larger mills, it was, when built, of outstanding size.

the mechanism by which savings could be channelled into industry. As William Marcroft related:

> The Sun Mill [1858–63], the oldest of the now many flourishing limited liability mills of Oldham, was the first company enrolled in this district under the Joint Stock Companies Act. The date of its enrollment was the 30 January 1858 and the capital was £5,000 in 5,000 shares of £1 each.[72]

Because of its dimensions ($97\frac{1}{2}$ yds long by $35\frac{1}{2}$ yds and five storeys) it was, when only one storey high, one of the largest mills ever erected in Oldham.[73] Its size had, in fact, partially determined the site, for the land round about contained sufficient clay to make its bricks.

Although the initial plan had been drawn by William Marcroft (1822–94), then a foreman at Platt Brothers works,[74] and some of the directors 'declared that they could do without an architect', there being 'talent enough in their body to construct and complete a cotton mill', the fact that shares to the value of £2,000 then remained unsold prompted them to take no risks and to 'make enquiries as to the commission charged by architects'.[75] Whilst considering his fee to be substantial, they concluded that:

> there was no alternative if they built a mill, but to engage an architect. After much debate, Mr James Howard was consulted, and ... said, 'If the mill premises are to cost about £25,000, the architect's duties should be done at one per cent commission ...' It was further agreed that the architect's commission should be chargeable on all the work done and the cost of the material used in preparing the land and mill premises including boilers, engines, shafting and other requisites.[76]

James Howard (1822–79), a local architect,[77] designed a mill that was to form the model for so many of the Oldham limiteds. Construction started early in 1861[78] and Sun Mill began work towards the end of January 1863,[79] the building having been structurally complete by December 1861. Howard, the son of an Oldham furniture dealer and joiner, had some experience of the textile industry. As a youth he had devoted much of his spare time to the study of building methods and encouraged his father to enter the construction trade, the young Howard preparing the plans and specifications. At the age of twenty-one he designed and superintended the construction of Highfield Mill, Featherstall Road. Having attracted the attention of Mr Schunck, of Schunck, Souchay & Co., the Manchester textile firm, he was commissioned to build Bank Top Mill, Oldham, for them, being employed as the clerk of the works. During the three years that he worked for the company he saved enough capital to set up as an architect on his own account in George Street, Oldham. Howard's involvement in the Sun Mill venture established him in the district. He became a principal promoter of the Oldham Twist Co. and served as a director of the Swan Spinning Co. This followed an accident in 1861 whilst engaged on the erection of a mill in Middleton Road for J. Walton & Sons (later the Lansdowne Spinning Co.), which occasioned his partial retirement from architectural practice. When his brother-in-law, the Revd S. Firth, was invested at the Salem Independent Church, Middleton, in 1870, James Howard moved with him, and there designed the Liberal Club, opened in 1876, and J. & L. Thorpe's silk works, Spring Gardens.[80]

While the desire of directors not to waste shareholders' money probably determined that Sun Mill be restrained in its ornament, the architect's touch may be detected in the Italianate staircase tower and sun motif which decorated the huge round-arched windows to the engine house. Indeed, the modern store[81] added by Ernest S. England (1882–1948)[82] could scarcely be regarded as architecturally superior. Presumably for reasons of cost, only the first two floors were fireproof, the upper storeys having timber beams supported by cast-iron columns.[83] The *Oldham*

Chronicle remarked in 1877 that most mills in the district were no wider than 80 ft but that the Sun and Melbourne Mills (the latter in Middleton Road, Chadderton and built c.1860)[84] had achieved widths of 100 ft and constituted 'models of a class of mill architecture which although somewhat improved has not been superseded. These two mills may be said to have inaugurated a new era in mill building'.[85] At a time when a factory holding 20,000 spindles was considered large, Sun Mill assumed almost inconceivable dimensions, being planned to accommodate 60,000 spindles.[86]

The 1870s, observed Middleton, 'witnessed what was called the "floating mania". The landowner, the architect, the contractor, the machinist and the mill manager formed combinations and floated companies in almost every street'.[87] Between 1866 and 1884 Oldham's spindleage grew by 6.6 million, which represented 81% of the total increment made by the British cotton industry, and by 1890 there were 10.5 million spindles at work in the town.[88] As the number of limited companies multiplied in the district, so specialist architects cornered the market in mill design. Of particular importance for Oldham was the Stott family. Their supremacy started with Abraham Henthorn Stott (1822–1904), father of Jesse Ainsworth Stott (1853–1917), Abraham Henthorn Stott Junior (1857–1931) and Philip Sidney Stott (1858–1937). A.H. Stott had established his architect's firm at 37a King Street, Oldham, in 1847,[89] earning his reputation by designing mills for Callender in Manchester during the 1850s and for Houldsworth at Reddish in the 1860s.[90] One of the earliest mills by A.H. Stott to draw contemporary comment was for the Abbey Mill Spinning Co. Ltd at Oldham Edge in 1875–6. Externally it conformed to the building tradition that had evolved in South Lancashire (a symmetrical five-storey brick block with twin staircase towers balancing a central entrance). 'Our readers', noted *The Textile Manufacturer* in 1891, 'will observe the mill does not make such a picture as some structures we have seen erected by individual mill-owners, the reason for this, of course, being that ornamentation does not assist in paying dividends'.[91] Their interest arose from the adoption of a novel form of fireproof floor which Stott had patented in 1871. Consisting of rolled-iron girders and an unusual arch construction supported by brackets attached to the pillars, the system permitted broader windows and so indirectly encouraged the erection of wider mills.[92]

In time the Stott family divided itself into a number of separate architect partnerships. A.H. Stott's firm, Messrs Stott & Sons, consisted of the founder together with his two eldest sons, Jesse Ainsworth and Abraham Junior.[93] 'The immense reputation enjoyed by this firm in mill architecture and consulting engineering', suggested a survey of 1888, 'shows itself by the erection of some twenty or thirty of the largest mills of modern date during a period of the last three or four years'.[94] It is possible that Jesse Stott took greatest responsibility for designing the terracotta clock tower, 142 ft in height, that kept time for Messrs Strutt's mills in Belper.[95] Sidney Stott (later known as Sir Philip), his younger brother, briefly joined the partnership, but during the mill-building boom of 1883-4, at the age of 25 he set up on his own account.[96] He was joined by Alfred J. Howcroft (1862-1946), who had recently completed articles in his native Wakefield, and who continued to assist Sidney Stott until 1898, when he too established a firm in Oldham which derived much work from nearby spinning companies.[97] Joseph Stott (1837-94),[98] the younger brother of Abraham Senior, who had been engaged in 'the erection of a large percentage of the local cotton mills',[99] was in turn followed in the architectural profession by his son, George Stott (1876-1936),[100] and he, too, specialized in the design of mills (p. 187). James Stott (1854-1934), the younger brother of A.H. and Joseph, started his working life as an architect, but later founded a firm of ventilating and canteen engineers, at the Vernon Works, Lee Street, Oldham.[101]

The specialist architects' dominance of the mill market was, in part, a function of the system by which these buildings were financed.[102] A.H. Stott, with his eldest two sons as partners, held 7,363 five-pound shares in 19 companies promoted between 1863 and 1892, at an average of 388 shares per company, though he had only been responsible for the promotion of two of these, including the Abbey Mill Spinning Co. Yet after a final subscription to the Granville Mill Co. for ten £100 shares in 1884, Stott seems to have abandoned Oldham financially to his brother Joseph, who took up a total of 6,619 shares, or the equivalent, in 21 companies established in Oldham between 1863 and 1892, building the mills for all of them, and being specially favoured in the Shaw district. He subsequently became a director of five spinning companies – the Coldhurst (erected in 1866), Anchor (1881), Olive (1884), Crown (1885) and Pine (1890)[103] – and apparently extended his activities outside Oldham on only one occasion, and then merely as far as the Vernon Cotton Spinning Co.'s mill at Stockport.[104]

This pattern of behaviour seems to have been typical throughout much of Lancashire. Architects and contractors, whether builders or suppliers of engines and machinery, took shares in new schemes (sometimes as a part-payment) in order to secure contracts.[105] Architects commonly bought an initial shareholding, only to dispose of their interest once the mill went into production. This enabled them to hold a financial interest in a number of mill companies at moderate cost and to be able to invest in fresh ventures as they arose.[106] In fact, on occasion, the architect was the principal promoter. Messrs Stott & Sons, for example, held the first company meeting in January 1904 to plan a mill on land that they owned. The ornate and relatively expensive building, and the decision to erect a second mill to use the existing chimney and engine house before the first was in full operation, pointed to the power of the architect to influence the board.[107] Similarly J.B. Gass, senior partner of Bradshaw Gass & Hope, speculated widely in many of the cotton mills that his firm designed for South Lancashire.

United Mill (1874), Suffolk Street, Chadderton, designed by Thomas Mitchell (d.1883), an Oldham architect,[108] may serve as a superior example of the period. Although Mitchell, a former pupil of Thomas Prosser, the North Eastern

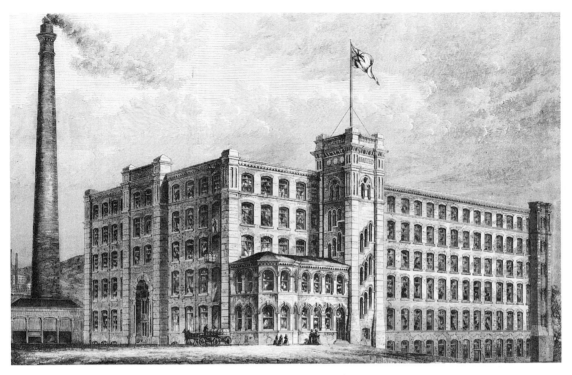

81 United Mill (1874), Chadderton, as illustrated in *The Builder*.

Railway's architect from 1854 to 1874, built up a general practice, his work embraced a number of local spinning companies, including Oak, Glodwick and Hey Mills, together with Bangor Mills, Waterhead, Holyrood Mills, Higginshaw, and Park Lane Mills, Royton.[109] Another limited, the six-storey United Mill, 80 yds by 43 yds, typified those of the district, for such Italianate detailing as it possessed concentrated on the tower, offices and principal windows of the engine house. The large areas of glass (closely spaced and regular fenestration) were needed to illuminate the broad interior, while the simple corner pilasters were already an enduring feature of Lancashire mill architecture. Internally it was fireproof, with cast-iron columns and transverse beams, wrought-iron joists and segmental brick arches filled with concrete to form the floors. The contractors were Robert Neill & Sons of Manchester, who performed much mill work in Lancashire, including that at

Daubhill for Tootal Broadhurst Lee.[110] It was estimated that the mill would cost £50,000 and that the machinery would raise this figure to £130,000. Mitchell's career may have been brought to a premature end by the wrangles over the completion of Oldham's Free Library and Museum.[111] Winning the competition in 1881, Mitchell's designs were effected in the following year but an acrimonious dispute arose over costs which persisted until his death in 1883.[112] He remained, nevertheless, one of the district's few qualified architects and performed a variety of important work there.

The Stotts and Mitchell were not the only architects designing mills in Oldham during the 1870s and 1880s, as Edward Potts (1839–1909) obtained a substantial share of this market. Born in Bury and later to become a senior partner of Potts, Son & Hennings, architects of Manchester, Bolton and Oldham,[113] this 'great expert in cotton mill buildings' was accounted on his death as being 'the architect of more spinning mills in this and other countries than perhaps any other firm'.[114] Potts set up on his own account around 1860 at 18 Clegg Street,

Oldham. Although he formed a partnership with George Woodhouse of Bolton, they seem to have remained based in their respective towns.[115] Whilst the arrangement was formally dissolved in 1872, they subsequently produced plans for a major extension to Oldham Town Hall (1879–80);[116] Potts in the meantime had concentrated on winning commissions from the booming cotton industry and in 1875 was responsible for the erection of a number of mills, including the Equitable, Green Acres, Westwood, Industry, Swan and Prince of Wales, together with a 70,000-spindle mill for the Hathershaw Spinning Co. (1877).[117] Joined in the partnership by George Pickup (d.1891), then a sole practitioner in Manchester,[118] and Frederick W. Dixon (1854–1935),[119] who had been employed by Woodhouse & Potts, his firm proceeded to win considerable respect from industrial clients; they designed Belgrave No. 1 (1881) and Textile Mill (1882). As Potts, Pickup & Dixon, they produced plans for the district's first ring-spinning mill, which, containing 80,000 spindles, attracted contemporary comment – Palm Mill (1885), Chadderton. In its supplement to commemorate the opening in June, *The Textile Manufacturer* remarked that the firm had earned much praise in creating 'an exceedingly handsome specimen of mill architecture'.[120] In 1884 Potts, Pickup & Dixon erected the Mutual Mill at Heywood.[121] Others for which Edward Potts, who on his death was credited with the design of 200 mills,[122] was the architect, included Copster (his first in Oldham), Northmoor, Borough, Tongue, Vale, Townley (Middleton) and Grimshaw Lane. Thus the partnership dominated much of the Oldham area in the period before the Stott family rose to prominence (pp. 155, 185).

When, probably in 1889, Frederick Dixon decided to leave the partnership to establish his own practice, he initially occupied the same building as Potts, 18 Clegg Street, but in 1895 moved to 52 Union Street and also opened an office in Manchester.[123] Chadderton, which developed later than the other villages around Oldham, produced rapid growth in the first decade of the twentieth century, eight mills being

raised between 1904 and 1908.[124] Dixon won a considerable portion of this market, designing the following mills there: Lark (1902), Magnet (1902), Wren (1903), Malta (1905), Ramsey (1906), Rugby (1907) and Belgrave No. 4 (1914).[125] He and his partner (Dixon, Hill & Co.) were also responsible for Werneth Ring No. 2 (1891), Majestic (1895), Gem (1901), Mona (1902), Monarch (1903), Glen Rutland (1907); and Argyll, Fox, Mersey, Orme, Rugby and Trent, all in 1908.[126]

Meanwhile, Edward Potts had admitted his son, William Edward, to the partnership and his firm continued to practise as Potts, Son & Pickup, and ultimately as Potts, Son & Hennings. Under the last style, they designed Bell (1904) and Iris Mills (1907), both in Oldham, together with Times No. 2, a mammoth 174,104-spindle mill.[127] In addition, Edward Potts planned and superintended the construction of works in France (including a mill at Rouen erected on the Oldham model),[128] Germany, China and Mexico.[129] Nevertheless, he was not exclusively a mill and chapel architect, and had been responsible for part of the Manchester Corn Exchange, Blackpool Town Hall (1895–1900) and other public buildings. A Fellow of the RIBA and the Manchester Society of Architects, he was a Liberal and an ardent Wesleyan Methodist.

The other firm of architects in Oldham to attract a clientele from the spinning companies was Wild, Collins & Wild at 15 Clegg Street. The senior partner, John Wild (1836–1901), had set up the practice in his home town, taking his long-serving assistant, Joe Collins (1848/9–1929), into the partnership in 1876;[130] the admission of his son, Frederick Wild, in c.1890 completed the style. Before 1870 John Wild designed Crown, Clarence, Glebe and Rushbank Mills in Oldham, followed by Royton Spinning No. 1 (1872) and Shaw Spinning (1874), together with Ridgefield, Londfield and Hathershaw & Smallbrook in 1875. Further commissions followed: High Compton (1878), Hopkin (1882), Ash (1883), Oldham Albion (1884), Lion (1890), Royton (1890), King (1899), Vine (1899), Bee (1900) and Shiloh No. 2 (1900).[131]

Almost without exception, these mill architects also undertook the design of churches and, more especially, chapels. This was in part because many of them were ardent Non-conformists – Dixon followed Methodism, and Potts, who lived in Eccles, was a fervent Wesleyan. In addition the rapidly growing manufacturing districts in which they worked often lacked a well-established ecclesiastical network; a vacuum usually filled by Non-conformist sects. Potts designed a great number of chapels in the Oldham area (including King Street Methodist, Waterhead Congregational and Greenacres Wesleyan), as did Dixon and Wild.

Something of the technical advances achieved in cotton mill architecture may be discerned from the works of Potts. For Palm Mill (280 ft by 126 ft) steel joists and concrete had been employed in the construction of the fireproof and watertight floors, while brick window arches had been rejected in favour of iron lintels bolted between the brick piers and flush with the level of the ceiling to admit the maximum amount of daylight. Indeed, the limited application of ornament (concentrated on the corner and staircase towers) in part resulted from the provision of generous areas of glass.[132] In the case of the Castle Spinning Co.'s mill, erected in 1891 at Stalybridge, Potts, Son & Pickup adopted an improved fenestration – broader windows supported by a cast-iron mullion – and the corner towers were enlivened by mock battlements and turrets inspired by the name of the business.[133]

The importance of the architect in all this should not, however, be overstressed, for as a rule cotton mills were ordered by owners or boards of directors on a cost per spindle basis. The proprietors calculated how many spindles were needed to make a reasonable return on their capital investment, and the architect had to produce designs to a specific price. 'The first duty of an architect instructed to prepare plans for a mill', argued Sington,

> must necessarily be to ascertain the number, lengths, breadths, weights and spacing of the machines for which accommodation is required, and to plan the rooms and spaces so as to permit them being worked with the greatest economy of labour

to keep down the cost of the building. The processes through which the article manufactured has to pass ought to follow ... without overlapping or reversal of direction ... so as to reduce to a minimum ... handling and transference.[134]

In this way established tradition exercised a powerful hold on the appearance of these buildings, as little latitude was allowed in the costings for adornment or the extravagant use of materials. Any expenditure on 'fancy' towers, good-quality Accrington brick or decorative additions was often prompted by a desire to outshine a neighbouring rival – names such as Ace, Majestic or Export indicated an owner's pretension. In the case of a mill promoted in June 1907, the directors, having decided on the number of spindles they wanted, appointed an architect, George Stott, to be paid on a commission of 4% on the cost of the freehold. He then submitted three alternative block plans for their consideration. After they had examined these and visited a number of mills the directors concluded 'that the mill tower be similar to the Regent, that the height of the rooms be the same as those at the Manor Mill, and that the general style of the offices be left with the architect'.[135] They later agreed that the engine house should be similar to that at Lily Mill and the rope drum as that at Kent Mill. In the case of another mill company established in 1875, the directors, wishing to build an extension, interviewed three architects, selecting Arthur Turner (p. 188) at a fee of £800; he was to pay for a clerk of works. In November 1911, having studied the initial plans, the board chose to have 'four concrete floors, ceiling and roof, that the mill be sufficiently strong and that at any future date another storey can be added'.[136] In this way the size of the mill was roughly fixed and the machinery plans devised to fit within these overall dimensions.[137] Where an architect held a financial stake in the enterprise his influence was correspondingly greater, particularly if he had been a promoter of the scheme.

Hard economics were also at the root of the simple rectangular shapes formed by mill blocks. Because the cost of the perimeter walls and their foundations accounted for half or three-fifths of the total structure (the floors and roof being responsible for the remainder) it was vital to obtain the maximum area for the length of walling that could be afforded. A building 10 ft by 10 ft and one 50 ft by 2 ft both encompass an area of 100 square feet, but the former will require only 40 ft of wall and the latter 104 ft. Thus a square was the most efficient shape; yet for various reasons mill designers found it necessary to build oblongs, keeping as close as possible to an equilateral rectangle. Among these was the need for plentiful natural light at tabletop level across the entire width of the mill. Fig. 82 reveals that with a height of 15 ft between floors, and light entering a building at an angle of 20°, the maximum width that a mill could be constructed with adequate natural illumination was around 90 ft. To increase this breadth it would have been necessary to raise the ceilings, which, in turn, would have increased the costs of building materials disproportionately.

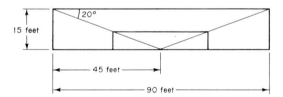

82 A cross-section through a Lancashire cotton mill.

The other factor that exercised a major influence on the design of mills was, of course, the type of machinery that they were to hold. In the early days their width had been dictated by:

> the length of a frame, and the length of a frame was to some extent governed by the quality of light thrown upon the middle of the frames ... In process of time, as mule yarn came more into request, the form of factory building was altered to enable the new class of machinery to be placed across the mill, and the breadth of building has increased with the length of mule carriage.[138]

In general, improvements meant that the mule became wider to accommodate a greater number of spindles.[139] In 1896, for example, there were 5,142 pairs of mules in Oldham, each with an average of 1,040 spindles per mule. By 1914 these figures had risen to 7,909 and 1,087 respectively.[140] A mule of 120 ft across could contain 1,200–1,300 spindles.[141] Wider mules meant wider mills, and more spindles in total meant that buildings became longer or had additional storeys. In Burnley, where they produced much narrow cloth for the Chinese market, mills tended to be smaller than in Blackburn, where the broader cloths sold predominantly to India required wider mules. The importance of the machinery in determining the final design can be seen in a directors' minute concerning a mill erected in 1905 by Sidney Stott. It was resolved that 'we accept the machinery plans formulated by Messrs Platt Bros. & Co., and that the secretary write to the architect to that effect'.[142] This was not always the case, especially in those schemes where the architect took a leading role, his plans produced at early stage often dictating the outcome of events.

One general observation is true of Lancashire's textile mills, whosoever had been responsible for their design. Their owners, whether families or boards of directors, were intensely cost-conscious, and their construction methods had been trimmed and refined by long experience to give value for money. With the adoption of the hard-pressed brick from Accrington and Withnell – the 'Nori' (iron reversed) brick manufactured by the Accrington Brick & Tile Co. – it was possible to do without pointing. By filling the frogs between each brick (which had been sized and sorted before purchase) with blue lime mortar and placing them firmly together, the joints could be reduced to the narrowest dimensions.[143] 'Thus the office block', remarked Sington:

> may be faced with stock bricks of a special sort brought from a distance, and the main block of a mill faced with local stock to keep down cost. The best seconds facing bricks are occasionally specified, and if the building is not in a prominent position the cost may be further reduced by the use of selected common bricks, with stock bricks for the arches and string courses. Occasionally a combination of white and red bricks is specified, and a very effective elevation is obtained.[144]

The use of string courses, like projecting heads over windows or sills under them, had a practical rationale, although their precise positioning and shapes were, of course, determined by aesthetic considerations. In Lancashire's heavy rainfall, they were designed to throw water away from the building so that the lower floors were not deluged by falling torrents. Window frames in most cases were timber – of the oldest well-seasoned woods – to survive the rigours of the climate without distorting or splitting. Floors that needed to be flagged to take the wear of metal wheels were often finished in York stone for its hard, smooth qualities, while spinning rooms were covered with maple boards; being a tough, smooth timber this could do no harm to the spinners' feet, as they worked barefoot in the high temperatures.

Where a mill had a series of pitched roofs, the water that collected in the internal valleys was channelled to the drains through the hollow cast-iron columns that supported each storey, thereby minimizing the need to have pipes on the outside of the building. During snowfalls slatted wooden boards were placed over the gutters. The snow, settling on these, melted from below by the heat of the mill, and the melt-

83 Failsworth, near Oldham, on the Rochdale Canal: Failsworth Mill stands nearest to the camera, and from left to right are Bank and Hope Mills. Regent Mill (1906), designed by Joseph Stott, is distinguished by the flat asphalt roof. The absence of water in this reservoir may have been because of hot weather or closure from want of orders, the photograph having been taken in September 1927.

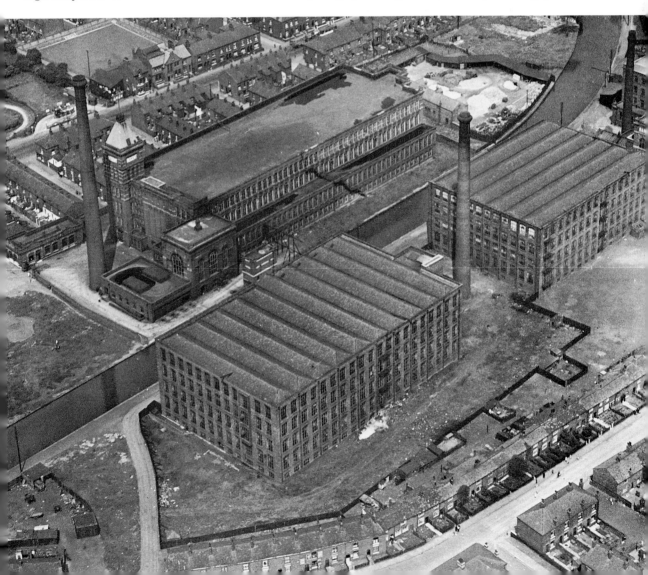

water was drained as usual. Flat-roofed mills, popular from the 1880s, were coated with two layers of asphalt, which, when covered with water to serve as a tank for the sprinkler systems, was virtually indestructible. They also had the added advantage of allowing vertical extensions to take place with the minimum disruption. An early example of a concrete roof covered with asphalt to form a reservoir was provided by Stott's Abbey Mill of 1875–6. That so many mills could be regarded as successful and pleasing architectural compositions as well as serving as practical manufacturing units was a tribute to the skill of their designers and the accumulated experience of their builders and owners.

Fireproofing remained a perennial concern, but the advance of engineering science and the provision of new materials produced new methods. By the 1880s a common solution was to have hollow cast-iron columns, spaced about 21 ft apart, supporting cast-iron beams. These were held together laterally by wrought-iron tie rods and cast-iron arched ribs. The ceiling was formed of brick arches covered by concrete to form a flat surface for the floor boards. The arch of the brick ceiling, which was coated with plaster and whitewashed to reflect daylight down to the machines, corresponded with the top of the segment-headed windows.[145] The architect's intention was to provide the greatest possible area of uninterrupted floorspace (so as not to restrict the installation of larger machines) without

weakening the building's structure or making it less resistant to fire. There were variations on the theme. Stott & Sons often adopted the method (devised pre-1865) by which the lateral distance between pillars could be widened by the insertion of transverse beams at seven-foot intervals, so that the brick arches ran along the length of the mill rather than across it. This meant that the supporting columns could be placed 21 ft apart in both directions.[146]

However, by the 1890s it became increasingly common to substitute concrete floors for brick arches, and to replace cast-iron beams by wrought-iron or steel.[147] One of the earliest examples had been designed by W.J. Morley of Bradford for J. & P. Coates in 1886[148] – No. 1 Mill, Ferguslie Mills, of five storeys and executed in French Renaissance style.[149] Cast-iron columns placed in orthodox fashion (21 ft apart longitudinally and 10 ft 6 in transversely) supported rolled steel beams between which were fixed steel joists, encased in concrete to the level of the timber floor. Morley argued that:

> the advantages of the concrete are: it is more compact, and more quickly done. The combination of the iron members is more perfect. The steel girders are much lighter than cast iron and much more reliable. With the concrete floor there is an absence of thrust on the walls.[150]

To protect the columns against fire, since they were liable to crack in great heat, they were given three coats of plaster over galvanized wire netting. The timber doors and their frames were covered in tinplate to resist flames, rather than fit iron doors which warped under fierce temperatures.[151]

Potts, Son & Pickup invented a different system for their Lancashire mills. Columns 20 ft 6 in and 14 ft 9 in apart held steel girders linked together by steel joists. The space between the joists was filled with concrete 6 in thick, on top of which a layer of 1-in waterproof concrete was placed.[152] Curiously, 'no architect', Nasmith recorded in 1894, 'has been bold enough to use in mill construction the built steel columns which have been employed in other forms of constructive work'.[153] Given the material's resistance to

84 An example of fireproof floor construction common in the 1870s.

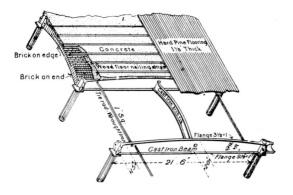

fire and greater strength, it seems that conservatism or considerations of cost ruled. In 1890 the surveyor of a leading insurance company estimated that 40% of British textile mills had a fireproof structure and that almost all of those erected in the previous ten years had fireproof floors.[154]

Whilst the growing demand for yarn, both cotton and wool, was effectively satisfied by the construction of multi-storey buildings of greater dimensions for spinning, this was not true of the weaving trade. Firms that combined both activities, such as Rylands' Gidlow Mill, Wigan,[155] or Lister's Manningham Mills, Bradford, attached single-storey sheds with gabled roofs to house their looms. From the early days of power-weaving, they were simply constructed buildings with rooms attached for warping, reeling, dressing and storage,[156] the drive being transmitted by overhead shafting. The weight of the machinery and the heavy vibrations caused by their operation, together with the need for ample overhead light to thread the shuttles and inspect the cloth (but not bright sunlight, which would affect the length of the material), meant that weaving sheds remained single storey and eventually adopted north-facing saw-tooth roofs. The glass face was arranged at an angle of about 30° from the vertical, and the slated portion was at 60°. The valleys between the ridge contained cast-iron gutters which ran transversely across the shed and were supported by columns. The

device for controlling the pattern woven by the Jacquard loom could be compactly accommodated within the extra space created by the gable. During the 1840s and 1850s the attempt to eliminate the use of timber in the construction of weaving sheds resulted in the elegant cast-iron roof structure erected c.1856 at Hunslet Mill, Leeds.

Innovation in the design of weaving sheds had the intention of increasing the area of clear floor space without sacrificing the quality of natural light. Potts, Son & Pickup devised a shed for Horrocks, Crewdson & Co. in which the columns ran in lines 22 ft apart. On them were placed longitudinal 'I' beams across which lighter girders of the Warren pattern were arranged to form a frame for the roof. The windows were, however, aligned almost vertically, and the underside of the slate roof was plastered and whitened so that light entered the building indirectly by reflection thereby reducing the glare produced by glass set at a lesser angle. The other advantage of this plan was the transverse distance between columns, giving an unobstructed floor space of 968 sq. ft.[157]

Among the reasons for Oldham's success as a cotton town was the close connection it

85 The scale of Platt Bros & Co.'s plant at Oldham Werneth may be appreciated from this artist's view of the Hartford New Works.

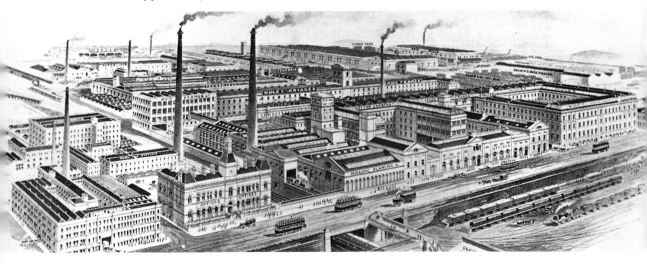

maintained with the manufacturers of spinning machinery, in particular the Soho Iron Works of Asa Lees & Co. and Platt Brothers, whose Hartford Works (providing jobs for 6,000 in 1870 and 12,000 in 1890) became the largest employer there.[158] Makers of power looms, carding and roving machines together with self-acting mules, Platt Brothers gradually expanded the Hartford New Works, Werneth, where they had moved in 1844.[159] By 1891 it comprised five foundries which were unusually situated on the first floor so that castings could then be lowered into trucks for transport to other parts of the works. A vast four-storey block of workshops was devoted to the finishing of iron and steel components, while the loom department, in a building 363 ft long, housed 'some hundreds of special boring, sawing, planing and other machine tools, being also provided with lifts and other appurtenances'.[160] Externally, Hartford New Works bore considerable resemblance in its architecture to the neighbouring cotton mills. This was scarcely surprising, as the designer responsible for much of the late nineteenth-century development at Werneth was Theodore Sington (1848–1926),[161] who had been educated at Owen's College and Heidelberg, practised in Manchester and was the author of a series of articles on the construction of cotton mills.[162] The materials were the same (Platts had their own brick kilns at Moston and Oldham) and those structural techniques devised for the textile industry could be reapplied to machine and assembly shops.

When the established manufacturers of textile machinery, Mather & Platt, decided to extend their operations, they selected a new site at Newton Heath, Manchester. The first building was erected in 1900.[163] This had originally stood at Vincennes for the Paris Exposition of that year to house machinery exhibits from the United States, and had been designed by the Berlin Iron Bridge Co., engineers and architects of Connecticut.[164] Mather & Platt purchased the structure and had it dismantled and shipped to Manchester. Subsequently Fred Mitchell & Son, constructional engineers and specialists in reinforced-concrete and steel work (established

in 1893), were responsible for completing new pattern and machine shops. These had a steel framework infilled with brick to form the outside walls and reinforced-concrete floors.[165] In 1909 two additional machine shops were constructed at the Park Works, and a further seven added in the following year. By 1912 all the main departments (only the heavy-iron foundry and boiler yards remaining at the Salford Iron Works) had moved to Park. With the exception of the two-storey offices, marked from a distance by the water tower with its mansard roof and mock turrets, the manufacturing shops were single storey. In total there were 17 of these, each 40 ft wide and some extending 600 ft in length.[166] The need to shift heavy materials and the forging and founding processes rendered multi-storey buildings unpractical.

A similar case of importation, borrowing expertise from the United States, had occurred in 1891 when the American Screw Co. decided to transfer an entire mill to Leeds. Acquiring a bankrupt forge in Kirkstall Road, they engaged Wm. Irwin & Co., a local builder, to put up a brick shell to receive the interior of their factory, then situated in Providence, Rhode Island. The original building had been designed by one of the owners, Charles D. Rogers, a mechanical engineer, but Thomas Ambler, the Leeds architect, was commissioned to adapt it to conform with the existing by-laws. Unusually for a screw factory, there were two storeys, the ground floor containing the offices, shipping room and the heavy heading machines; and the first floor the screw-cutting lathes and packaging departments. Brick piers only 2 ft wide between windows and the provision of a clerestory roof provided generous levels of natural light (supplemented by 50 arc and 500 incandescent lamps) by which to inspect finished screws. Yet the structure was timber framed, and this ultimately led to its destruction by fire in 1948. The heating system, by Sturtevant of Boston, had its novelties: fresh air was drawn through heating coils before being forced through longitudinal ducts; in hot weather the system operated as an early, if crude, form of air conditioning. For safety, as in other screw works, working

86 Nearing completion, the new works in Kirkstall Road, Leeds for the British Screw Co. in 1892. Note the timber clerestory roof; the two projecting blocks contained the lavatories.

wheels and belts were placed at floor level. In all it took about six months to reassemble the mill (360 ft by 100 ft), which had been shipped from America in 204 freight cars, a track being specially laid from the main line to the site. The gravel roof was provided by a contractor from Providence because this was found to be cheaper, even with transport costs, than employing a local firm.[167]

Bolton and district

In much the same way that the Stott family dominated Oldham's mill building, so Bradshaw Gass & Hope exercised a powerful hold over Bolton and its environs during the late Victorian period. The firm had been founded in 1862 by Jonas James Bradshaw (1837–1912),[168] who had apparently started life as a master craftsman before setting up as an architect. His earliest commissions included the Union Workhouse, Chorley (1869–72); Clitheroe Union Workhouse (1874–5);[169] Todmorden Workhouse (1876–9)[170] and the Eden Orphanage, Bolton (1877–9).[171] The Howe Bridge Spinning Co. Ltd at Atherton provided Bradshaw with his first industrial project, and was to prove a valuable client, as a number of additional mills were ordered. Bradshaw designed and superintended the construction of their No. 2 Mill between 1875 and 1878.[172] For this five-storey brick mill he devised a number of the details that later distinguished the industrial work of his practice. A particular feature was a square Italianate tower topped by a pitched roof and overhanging eaves.[173] This device he and his firm subsequently adapted to cover water tanks and dust flues,[174] and it was applied on occasion almost as pure decoration.[175] This first industrial commission demonstrated not only the strength of

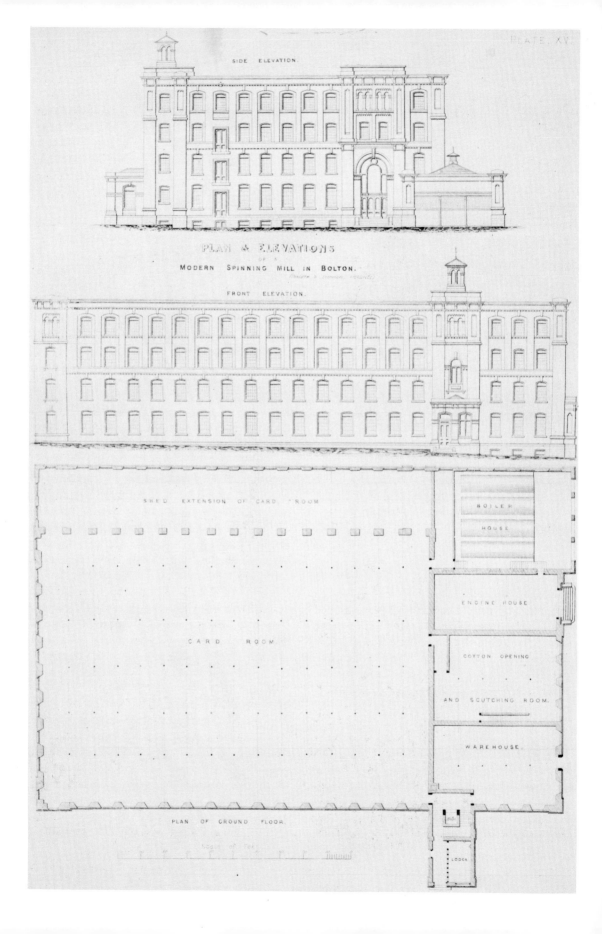

PLATE XV

SIDE ELEVATION.

PLAN & ELEVATIONS
OF A
MODERN SPINNING MILL IN BOLTON.

FRONT ELEVATION.

SHED EXTENSION OF CARD ROOM

BOILER
HOUSE

ENGINE HOUSE

COTTON OPENING

CARD ROOM

AND SCUTCHING ROOM.

WAREHOUSE.

PLAN OF GROUND FLOOR.

LODGE

87 The plan and elevations of a mill in Bolton (containing 32,400 mule spindles) by the local architects George Cunliffe and Richard Knill Freeman.

the Italianate tradition, but also Bradshaw's scrupulous care and skill in creating an imaginative composition. The bands between the projecting blocks and voussoirs in the rusticated ground floor were of black brick, while the corner towers exhibited a range of ornament and window forms in keeping with those of a public building.[176] The segment-headed windows that lit the mill proper were ordered so that the ground and first-floor openings were 9 ft 6 in in height, those on the second and third floors 8 ft 6 in and the top storey only 8 ft high.[177] In 1876 Bradshaw was appointed to design a factory for the Mather Lane Mill Co., Leigh,[178] and its completion in 1878 seems to have established the firm in the town, as other commissions followed

from the same company and other rival cotton spinners.

The founder's nephew, John Bradshaw Gass (1855–1939),[179] was admitted to the partnership in 1880,[180] having been articled to the firm; he had studied at the Bolton School of Art; Owen's College; Victoria University, Manchester and the Royal Academy Schools, and travelled extensively in Europe and America. As Bradshaw & Gass, the firm established a powerful hold on the mill world. In 1882–4 a second mill (an almost rectangular block of six storeys) was erected for the Mather Lane Co.,[181] and two more for the Howe Bridge Co. (fig. 88) – a new No. 1 Mill in 1883–6,[182] and No. 3 in 1889–91.[183] With the completion of No. 4 Mill in 1900, Bradshaw & Gass had designed a major

88 A plan of the Howe Bridge Spinning Co.'s mills at Atherton; No. 1 Mill (1883–6) and No. 2 Mill (1875–8). The architects were Bradshaw & Gass.

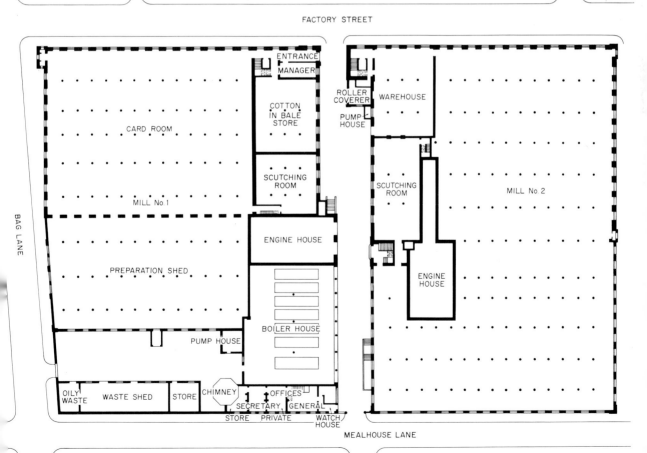

FACTORY STREET

ENTRANCE
MANAGER
COTTON IN BALE STORE
SCUTCHING ROOM
CARD ROOM
MILL No.1
ENGINE HOUSE
PREPARATION SHED
BOILER HOUSE
PUMP HOUSE
OILY WASTE
WASTE SHED
STORE
CHIMNEY
OFFICES
SECRETARY
STORE
PRIVATE
GENERAL
WATCH HOUSE
BAG LANE

ROLLER COVERER
WAREHOUSE
PUMP HOUSE
SCUTCHING ROOM
MILL No.2
ENGINE HOUSE
MEALHOUSE LANE

0   22   44   66   88

SCALE IN FEET

spinning complex in Atherton. The site, nearly a square, circumscribed by Bag Lane, Mealhouse Lane and Fletcher Street, was divided into halves by Factory Street.[184] In each case the warehouse was contained within the main mill block, as was the scutching room (with the exception of No. 4). The engine house was situated within the body of the mill in Nos. 2 and 3, but attached to Nos. 1 and 4. Each pair of mills shared a boiler house and chimney, though they possessed their own reservoirs.

Summary

The cotton-manufacturing districts of Lancashire and the woollen and worsted industry in Yorkshire were not deeply affected by Gothic architecture, if their mills and warehouses alone are considered. The strength of the Italianate tradition was not weakened as larger and more ornate buildings were commissioned. The reliance on architects who practised in these regions rather than nationally-known designers, the continued use of locally manufactured materials and the conservatism of clients, whether boards of directors or family businesses, lay at the root of this continuity. In general, and for factories in particular, the dictates of prevailing architectural theory took second place to the practical requirements of the plant. Developments were not stylistic so much as technical and concerned with considerations of construction. Following the grant of limited liability, promoters demanded mills of greater lengths and widths and with more storeys than before. They used part of the capital so gained to engage the services of an architect, whose employment resulted in the adornment of the water tower and the addition of a decorative cornice or a flourish to the offices and entrance. The tight financial controls and rigorous business outlook of the directors meant, however, that any embellishment was subject to restraints and that the building's form was critically determined by its ability to earn dividends.

Notes

1 M. McLaren, *Journal of Naval Science*, Vol. I (1975), 'The Explosives Research and Development Establishment', pp. 179–80; James Thorne, *Handbook to the Environs of London*, London (1876), p. 655.

2 Information from the Propellants, Explosives and Rocket Motor Establishment (Waltham Abbey): Drawings signed by H. Tovey, Capt. RE, 10 March 1877 and countersigned by Lt. Col. W.H. Noble on 15 March 1877.

3 J. Tuff, *Historical, Topographical and Statistical Notes of Enfield*, Enfield (1858), pp. 195–9; *VCHM*, Vol. V, London (1976), p. 238.

4 BL, 'Bradford Weekly Telegraph', Vol. II, 1883–9, *The Illustrated Weekly Telegraph*, Vol. XL, No. 4140, 5 December 1885, p. 101.

5 *BN*, Vol. 15, 27 November 1868, pp. 806, 809; Joseph Nasmith, *Recent Cotton Mill Construction and Engineering*, Manchester [c.1895], p. 14.

6 Evan Leigh, *The Science of Modern Cotton Spinning*, Vol. I, Manchester (1873), pp. 24, 26–7.

7 Walter Pickles, *Our Grimy Heritage*, Fontwell (1971), pp. 40–1.

8 *B*, Vol. LIX, No. 2491, 1 November 1890, Obituary, p. 348.

9 Robert Wilson, *Boiler and Factory Chimneys, Their Draught-Power and Stability*, London (1877), p. 49; Bancroft, *Tall Chimney Shafts, op. cit.*, p. 55, Fig. 17.

10 *B*, Vol. XXIV, No. 1233, 22 September 1866, p. 709.

11 Charles Dickens, *The Lazy Tour of Two Idle Apprentices*, Chapter 1, *Household Words*, Vol. XVI, 3 October 1857.

12 W. Cooke Taylor, *Notes of a Tour in the Manufacturing Districts of Lancashire*, London (1842), pp. 1–2.

13 Robert Wilson, *Boiler and Factory Chimneys*, London (1877), pp. 46, 47; Bancroft, *op. cit.*, p. 51.

14 *B*, Vol. XVIII, No. 893, 17 March 1860, p. 174; Bancroft, *op. cit.*, pp. 33–5.

15 *Skinner's Cotton Trade Directory for 1923*, London (1923), p. lxxxi.

16 *BN*, Vol. 11, 15 July 1864, p. 535.

17 Reynolds, *Saltaire, op. cit.*, p. 18.

18 R. Rawlinson, *Designs for Factory, Furnace and other Tall Chimney Shafts*, London (1859).

19 *Ibid.*, pp. 5, 7.

20 *B*, Vol. XV, No. 734, 28 February 1857, R. Rawlinson, 'Chimney Construction', p. 120.

21 *B*, Vol. XV, No. 742, 25 April 1857, p. 231.

22 *MPICE*, Vol. CXXXIV (1898), Obituary, pp. 386-8.

23 John B. Dunn, *Wainhouse Tower: The Remarkable Tower*, Halifax (1979), pp. 2-5; Linstrum, *West Yorkshire, op. cit.*, p. 372.

24 *B*, Vol. XXIX, No. 1504, 2 December 1871, p. 946.

25 Linstrum, *Historic Architecture of Leeds, op. cit.*, p. 53; *West Yorkshire, op. cit.*, pp. 306, 371, 384.

26 Wilson, *op. cit.*, p. 51.

27 *TM*, Vol. XXIII, 15 April 1897, T. Sington, 'Cotton Mill Planning and Construction', pp. 129-31.

28 *Manchester of Today*, London (1888), p. 80; *The Fine Cotton Spinners' and Doublers' Association Limited*, Manchester (1909), p. 26.

29 *Manchester City News*, 15 April 1866, quoted from H.R. Fox Bourne, *English Merchants: Memoirs of the Progress of British Commerce*, Vol. II, London (1866), p. 400; Leigh, *op. cit.*, Vol. II, p. 196.

30 Linstrum, *West Yorkshire, op cit.*, pp. 293-4.

31 William Cudworth, *Manningham, Heaton and Allerton*, Bradford (1896), pp. 115, 118.

32 *BO*, Vol. LIII, No. 7316, 11 June 1886, Obituary, p. 7.

33 *BO*, Vol. XLVIII, No. 5635, 19 January 1881, Obituary, p. 4.

34 *B*, Vol. XXXI, No. 1610, 13 December 1873, p. 990.

35 *B*, Vol. XXXIV, No. 1723, 15 April 1876, p. 369.

36 *B*, No. 1610, *op. cit.*, p. 990.

37 *BO*, 6 February 1889, 'Manningham Mills and their Founder', p. 6.

38 BL, *The Illustrated Weekly Telegraph*, Vol. XL, No. 4131, 26 September 1885, p. 77.

39 *The Century's Progress, Yorkshire*, London (1893), p. 62.

40 W. English, *The Textile Industry*, London (1969), p. 206.

41 *B*, Vol. XXII, No. 1092, 9 January 1864, p. 35.

42 *Whellan & Co.'s Directory for 1853*, Bolton (1853), Architects, Woodhouse, George, Silverwell Yard, Bradshawgate; *Drake's Commercial Directory of Bolton*, Sheffield (1861), Woodhouse, George, St George's Road, p. 54; *Axon's Commercial & General Directory of Bolton*, Bolton (1881), p. 105.

43 N. Pevsner, *BoE, Oxfordshire*, Harmondsworth (1974), pp. 540-1.

44 *Fine Cotton Spinners', op. cit.*, pp. 19, 25.

45 *B*, Vol. XXXII, No. 1652, 3 October 1874, p. 834; *TM*, Vol. XVII, 15 May 1891, p. 230.

46 W.P. Crankshaw and Alfred Blackburn, *A Century and a half of Cotton Spinning 1797-1947*, *The History of Knowles Limited of Bolton* [c.1947], pp. 26-7.

47 BA, B901[B] BOL, Plan of the Borough of Bolton, 1882, Sheet 15; ZZ/258/1 Plan of Peel Mills, 1940; 2, 1943; 3, 1950.

48 *Bolton Weekly Journal*, 29 November 1879, p. 8.

49 Crankshaw, *op. cit.*, p. 27.

50 BA, B725.4[B] Bradley, 'Evolution of the Cotton Mill', *op. cit.*, p. 23.

51 *The Bolton Evening News*, Vol. XXXV, No. 5045, 4 September 1883, p. 3.

52 James Clegg, *Annals of Bolton, History, Chronology and Politics*, Bolton (1888), p. 205; James C. Scholes, *History of Bolton*, Bolton (1892), p. 505.

53 *Bolton Weekly Journal*, 8 September 1883, p. 3.

54 *The Architect's Directory* (1868), *op. cit.*, pp. 131, 145; Colin Cunningham, *Victorian and Edwardian Town Halls*, London (1981), pp. 43, 206.

55 *B*, Vol. CXXXVIII, No. 4547, 28 March 1930, Morley's Obituary, p. 608.

56 Nasmith, *Recent Cotton Mill Construction, op. cit.*, p. 133.

57 *BN*, Vol. 42, 21 April 1882, p. 476.

58 W.T. Pike, *An Illustrated Account of Halifax, Brighouse and District*, Brighton [c.1890], p. 106.

59 Henry F. Lockwood and Adolphus H. Cates, *The History and Antiquities of the Fortifications to the City of York*, London (1834).

60 Roberts, *Little Germany, op. cit.*, pp. 26-8; BL, *Illustrated Weekly Telegraph*, Vol. XL, No. 4165, 22 May 1886, p. 149.

61 *B*, Vol. LXXIV, No. 2872, 19 February 1898, p. 170.

62 Roberts, 'Bradford Textile Warehouse', *op. cit.*, pp. 160-1.

63 *B*, No. 2872, *op. cit.*, Fig. 2, p. 171.

64 Roberts, *op. cit.*, pp. 107-8.

65 LivRO, *Goad's Plans, Bradford*, Vol. I, No. 7, 1929.

66 Roberts, *op. cit.*, pp. 109, 115.

67 Fairbairn, *Application of Cast and Wrought Iron*, *op. cit.*, pp. 53-6.

68 Roberts, *op. cit.*, pp. 125-6, 180-1.

69 19 & 20 Victoriae *c.*47, 1856 *Joint Stock Companies Act*; and 25 & 26 Victoriae *c.*89, 1862.

70 Located in Phoenix Street, Oldham, it is one of the town's few mid-nineteenth-century mills still in good condition, most of the pre-1860 factories having been demolished.

71 P.L. Cottrell, *Industrial Finance 1830-1914*, London (1980), p. 107.

72 William Marcroft, *Sun Mill Company Limited: Its Commercial and Social History from 1858 to 1877*, Oldham (1877), p. 5.

73 *Ibid.*, pp. 34, 77.

74 *TLCAS*, Vol. 80 for 1979, Manchester (1980), R.E. Tyson, 'William Marcroft (1822-94) and the Limited Liability Movement in Oldham', p. 60.

75 Marcroft, *op. cit.*, pp. 17-18.

76 *Ibid.*

77 *Worrall's Oldham and District Directory* (1871), p. 49.

78 Marcroft, *op. cit.*, pp. 33, 87.

79 R.E. Tyson, 'The Sun Mill Company Limited – A Study in Democratic Investment 1858-1959' (MA Thesis, Manchester University, 1962), p. 129.

80 *OC*, 18 January 1879, Obituary.

81 *Sun Mill Co. Ltd, Oldham, The Story of a Great Enterprise 1858-1958*, p. 2.

82 *Oldham Evening Chronicle*, Obituary, 29 January 1948. E.S. England, ARIBA, a native of Wakefield, served his articles in Blackpool, coming to Oldham in 1903 and after working for Joseph Stott & Son set up his own practice in Clegg Street: *E.F. Cope & Co., Directories of Oldham 1932-2*, E. England, 12 Clegg Street, p. 50.

83 Marcroft, *op. cit.*, p. 87.

84 *Cotton Mills of Oldham*, *op. cit.*, p. 22.

85 *OC*, 18 August 1877.

86 Tyson, 'Democratic Investment', *op. cit.*, pp. 116, 123.

87 James Middleton, *Oldham, Past and Present*, Rochdale (1904), p. 186.

88 D.A. Farnie, *Saddleworth Historical Society Bulletin*, Vol. 12, No. 3 (1982), 'The Emergence of Victorian Oldham as the Centre of the Cotton Spinning Industry', pp. 41-2.

89 *Manchester of Today* (1888), p. 81.

90 *TM*, Vol. II, 15 June 1876, p. 156; see p. 145.

91 *TM*, Vol. XVII, 15 May 1891, p. 229.

92 *TM*, 1876, *op. cit.*, pp. 156-7; D.A. Farnie, 'The English Cotton Industry 1850-1896' (MA Thesis, Manchester University, 1953), p. 541.

93 *Kelly's Directory of Lancashire with Liverpool and Manchester*, London (1887), pp. 485, 529. They were then based at 60 Haworth's Buildings, 50 Cross Street, Manchester with an office at 12 Clegg Street, Oldham.

94 *Manchester of Today*, London (1888), p. 81.

95 *B*, Vol. CXII, No. 3876, 18 May 1917, Obituary, p. 321.

96 *B*, Vol. CLII, No. 4915, 16 April 1937, Obituary, p. 843; Ernest Gaskell, *Lancashire Leaders: Social and Political*, London [n.d.], 'Philip Sidney Stott, Esq.'.

97 *OC*, 11 July 1946, Obituary.

98 *OC*, Obituary, 22 January 1894.

99 *B*, Vol. LXVI, No. 2662, 10 February 1894, Obituary, p. 121.

100 *OC*, Obituary, 19 December 1936.

101 *Oldham Evening Standard*, Obituary, 1 June 1934.

102 Farnie, *op. cit.*, p. 541.

103 *Ibid.*

104 *TM*, Vol. VII, 15 November, p. 424.

105 Jones, 'Cotton Spinning Industry', *op. cit.*, p. 27.

106 *Ibid.*, p. 32.

107 *Ibid.*, pp. 126-7; from the dates and description it would seem that these were Bay Tree and Laurel Mills.

108 *B*, Vol. XXXIII, No. 1713, 4 December 1875, pp. 1083-5; *The Cotton Mills of Oldham*, Oldham and District Historical & Antiquarian Society (1979), pp. 32-3.

109 RIBA Biography File: Handwritten List

'Works already executed and in progress by Thomas Mitchell, Architect, Oldham, 21 February 1876'.

110 *B*, No. 1713, *op. cit.*, p. 1083; *ibid.*, No. 1652, p. 834.

111 OLIC, PX:M1 *Description of the Oldham Free Library & Museum; Worrall's Commercial ... Directory of Oldham* (1888), pp. 4-5.

112 OLIC, CBO/20 1/1/1 'Oldham Corporation, Free Library & Museum Committee Minute Book', No. 1 (1882-5), pp. 1, 3, 126-7.

113 *Oldham Standard*, 17 April 1909, Obituary; *The Architect & Contract Reporter*, Vol. LXXXI, 23 April 1909, p. 280; *Slater's Trades Directory of Manchester and Salford* (1896), p. 1120.

114 MCL F942 7389 M119, Manchester Newspaper Cuttings 1903-1909, Vol. 7, p. 161.

115 *The Architect's Directory* (1868), pp. 131, 145.

116 Cunningham, *op cit.*, pp. 88, 119, 280-1.

117 *TM*, Vol. III, 15 May 1877, pp. 143-4.

118 *Slater's Directory of Manchester* (1874), pp. 13, 547.

119 Farnie, 'Emergence of Victorian Oldham', *op. cit.* p. 52.

120 *TM*, Vol. XI, 15 August 1885, p. 397; *Oldham Standard*, 3 May 1884.

121 *TM*, Vol. X, 15 July 1884, p. 312.

122 *OC*, 17 April 1909, Obituary.

123 *Slater's Directory of Manchester* (1896), p. 1119.

124 Farnie, 'Emergence of Victorian Oldham', *op. cit.*, p. 47.

125 OLIC, Card Index of Mills; *Cotton Mills of Oldham, op. cit.*

126 *OC*, 16 November 1935, Obituary, F.W. Dixon. His firm was also credited with the design of Butterworth Hall, Castle, Derwent, Majestic and Mons Mills.

127 OLIC Card Index; *OC*, 17 April 1909.

128 *TM*, 1885, *op. cit.*, p. 397.

129 W. Burnett Tracy, *Manchester and Salford at the close of the Nineteenth Century* [1899], p. 218.

130 *Oldham Standard*, 8 August 1901, Obituary, John Wild; *OC*, 2 March 1929, Obituary, J. Collins.

131 OLIC Card Index of Mills.

132 *TM*, 1885, *op. cit.*, p. 397.

133 *TM*, Vol. XVII, 15 October 1891, p. 484.

134 Theodore Sington, *Cotton Mill Planning and Construction*, Manchester (1897), 1.

135 Jones, 'Cotton Spinning Industry', *op. cit.*, pp. 84, 171.

136 *Ibid.*, pp. 85, 202.

137 From the description, this appears to have been Park No. 2 Mill, Royton.

138 *TM*, Vol. XI, 15 October 1885, p. 466.

139 Joseph Nasmith, *The Students' Cotton Spinning*, Manchester (1896), pp. 392-3.

140 L. S. Wood and A. Wilmore, *The Romance of the Cotton Industry in England*, Oxford (1927), p. 190.

141 Jones, *op. cit.*, p. 67.

142 Quoted from *ibid.*, p. 154.

143 Walter R. Jaggard, *Brickwork and its Construction*, Oxford (1931), pp. 2-4, 12.

144 *TM*, Vol. XXII, 15 June 1896, pp. 209-12.

145 Nasmith, *Recent Cotton Mill Construction, op. cit.*, pp. 22-3; *TM*, Vol. XVII, 15 April 1891, J.R. Freeman, 'Comparison of English and American Types of Factory Constructions', p. 178.

146 *Ibid.*, pp. 25-6.

147 *TM*, Vol. XVII, 15 May 1891, p. 229.

148 Nasmith, *op. cit.*, p. 27.

149 Hume, *Industrial Archaeology of Scotland Vol. I, op. cit.*, pp. 218-20.

150 Quoted from *TM*, Vol. XVII, 15 May 1891, p. 230.

151 Nasmith, *op cit.*, p. 57.

152 *Ibid.*, pp. 29-30.

153 *Ibid.*, p. 56.

154 *TM*, Vol. XVII, 15 April 1891, p. 177.

155 Leigh, *Modern Cotton Spinning, op. cit.*, Vol. II, p. 197.

156 George White, *A Practical Treatise on Weaving, by Hand and Power Looms*, Glasgow (1846), p. 336, plate I.

157 Nasmith, *op cit.*, pp. 40-1.

158 James Middleton, *Oldham Past and Present*, Rochdale (1904), p. 178; Farnie 'Emergence of Victorian Oldham', *op. cit.*, p. 48.

159 Platt Brothers & Co Ltd, *Progress in the Cotton Industry and Textile Machinery Making*, Oldham (1929), p. 26.

160 *TM*, Vol. XVII, 15 December 1891, p. 552.

161 Burnett Tracy, *op. cit.*, p. 221.

162 Published in *TM* and later as *Planning and Construction of Cotton Mills*, Manchester (1898).

163 MCL, Q338.47621 Sa 2, 'Salient dates in Mather & Platt's History' (typescript).

164 Information from Mather & Platt Ltd, Park Works; Plan No. 198, Main Cross Section, Berlin Iron Bridge Co., 1900.

165 GMRO, D/Butterworth, *Reinforced Concrete Construction and Engineering Works*, F. Mitchell & Son Ltd, Manchester [*c*.1930], pp. 21–3.

166 *The Iron, Steel & Engineering Industries of Manchester*, Visit of the Iron & Steel Institute (1935), p. 71.

167 *The News* [Providence], 12 August 1892, W.I. Lansing, 'An American Innovation'; *The Illustrated Carpenter & Builder*, 21 October 1892, p. 293; *Practical Engineer*, 10 July 1891, 'A New Industry for Leeds'.

168 *Journal of the Royal Institute of British Architects*, Vol. 19, 11 May 1912, Obituary, p. 492; *Axon's Commercial and General Directory of Bolton*, Bolton (1881), p. 105.

169 J.J. Bradshaw's Certificate Register 'A' 1875–76, p. 12.

170 *Ibid.*, pp. 37–8.

171 *Ibid.*, pp. 45–6, 83–4.

172 *Ibid.*, pp. 27–8, 41–2, 47–8, 51–2.

173 BGH Folder No. 115, Howe Bridge Spinning Co, Plans for No. 2 Mill, Drawing No.6, April 1875, Signed J.J. Bradshaw.

174 BGH Folder No. 116, Howe Bridge Spinning Co., No. 1A Mill, Details of dust flue cover, [*c*.1898].

175 BGH Folder No. 117, Drawing No. 4, Elevations to Factory Street, April 1875.

176 *Ibid.*

177 BGH Folder No. 115, Drawing No. 6, *op. cit.*, Elevation to Bag Lane.

178 Certificate Register 'A', *op. cit.*, pp. 30, 59.

179 B, Vol. CLVII, No. 5031, 7 July 1939, Obituary, p. 5.

180 RIBA Biography File, J.B. Gass; *Who's Who in Architecture*, London (1914), p. 87; Frederick Chatterton (Editor), *Who's Who in Architecture*, London (1926), p. 118.

181 Bradshaw & Gass Certificate Register 'B' 1881–1891, pp. 24, 32.

182 *Ibid.*, pp. 35–44.

183 *Ibid.*, pp. 97–8, 101–2, 99–100.

184 The Howe Bridge Cotton Spinning Co. Ltd, Plan of Mills, shewing Pipes, etc., Bradshaw & Gass, FRIBA, Bolton, December 1899.

EIGHT

Edwardian industrial architecture

1900–1914

In contrast to the dominance of the Gothic over the late Victorian period, and the two-cornered fight with the Italianate that had preceded this, it is difficult to isolate any one style which could be said to characterize the Edwardian era. Indeed, one of the period's features was the search for an original interpretation of established styles, while a return to classicism and the baroque, together with the flowering of the arts-and-crafts tradition, meant that this was a time of particular diversity. In addition, if it is accepted that the seeds of the modern movement germinated in these early years of the twentieth century, then the picture is further complicated. When this architectural mix is placed in the context of continued growth and development in Britain's manufacturing sector (involving an expansion in the range of activities pursued, combined with an increase in the scale of the older industries), the Edwardian period becomes one of considerable interest and importance.

Rationalism

Defined as the expression of a steel or concrete structure in a building's outward form (rather than its concealment beneath masonry reflecting historical styles), rationalism had a slow gestation in British architecture – the field of industry being no exception. There had, of course, been a precedent, if the glasshouses of the 1840s could be regarded as architecture. More obviously a building in the traditional sense, though no less unacceptable to the theorists, was the factory erected in 1848–50 by James Bogardus (1800–74) in Center Street, New York.[1] Prefabricated cast-iron sections not only formed the internal framework of this four-storey works, but also determined its external appearance. Bogardus had previously visited England to study the work of Hodgkinson and Fairbairn (who in 1839 had prefabricated a three-storey iron house, 50 ft by 25 ft, to serve as a corn mill, assembled in Istanbul during the following year).[2] As a manufacturer of iron-grinding machinery, Bogardus decided to apply his technical knowledge to a multi-storey block, the skeleton of which formed an integral part of the street elevations. Yet the design did not win universal approval, and though scattered examples of iron-and-glass façades followed, the development of such a building system was delayed until the last two decades of the nineteenth century. (Masonry buildings that featured metal skeleton façades included the warehouse and shop for A. Gardner & Son (1855), Jamaica Street, Glasgow, by John Baird (1798–1880), known as the 'Iron Building'; the Gothic warehouse (1873) in Basinghall Street, Leeds, by Thomas Ambler (1838–1920), that exhibited much cast-iron decorative work; and Arighi Bianchi's furniture store (1882–3) in Macclesfield.) The cheap production of steel did not immediately inspire such innovation as William Menelaus (1818–82),[3] President of the Iron and Steel Institute, complained in 1875:

> There is now ... amongst manufacturers a perfect knowledge of what is wanted for various engineering purposes. There is also the power to produce steel of almost any shape or quality at moderate cost, and it only requires the hearty co-operation of the engineering profession to induce manufacturers everywhere to erect suitable machinery for

converting steel into the necessary forms for constructive purposes.[4]

Architects exhibited a reluctance to specify the material, despite the fact that the 1882 Hanover Architectural and Engineering Congress had concluded that 'the use of steel ... being on the whole preferable to that of iron, was not likely to cause any difficulties of a serious character to such manufacturers as took up the matter seriously'.[5]

Even after the publicity generated by the Crystal Palace, buildings with exposed iron frameworks remained rare during the 1850s. However, the four-storey foundry, ship-fitting shop and boatstore (1858–60), designed by Col. Godfrey Greene (1807–86) for the Royal Navy at Sheerness, relied on an innovative structure.[6] Two aisles, 210 ft in length, flanked a central single-storey nave served by travelling girders. Cast-iron 'H'-section columns supported transverse 'I'-section beams, also of cast iron, and wrought-iron longitudinal plate girders of 29 ft 6 in in span. Curiously, the joists between the transverse beams were timber. Nevertheless, the spaces beneath the long bands of windows were filled with corrugated iron, which helped to create an appearance of refined simplicity. The contractor, Henry Grissell (1817–83), of the Regent's Canal Iron Works, Hoxton, had considerable experience of civil engineering, having erected the iron roof over London Bridge Station in 1844. The Sheerness Boat Store may have represented the first use of simple 'H'-section columns and beams. Chatham, another naval dockyard, saw the assembly of a second iron-framed building in 1867.

The St Ouen Docks, Paris, provided the engineer, Hippolyte Fontaine, with a chance to design a warehouse with iron columns and beams in c.1864–5.[7] The first factory to adopt an unconcealed iron skeleton was apparently also in France and was erected for Chocolat Menier in 1871–2 at Noisel-sur-Marne by Jules Saulnier (1817–81).[8] Situated upon masonry piles driven into the River Marne its foundations were, in effect, those of a bridge, demanding in turn a structure that was both light and strong. Box-girders attached to the piers supported a lozenge-shaped braced framework whose spaces were infilled with brick and covered by tiles. It earned the praise of E.-E. Viollet-le-Duc (1814–79) whose favourable comments in the *Entretiens* reflected his arguments in favour of mixed construction. He suggested that iron and masonry, if used together, could produce great advances in medieval styles of architecture.[9] The factory had been erected over the Marne to enable the hydraulic machinery to be powered by turbines driven by the flow of the river. In addition, its owners, the Menier family, exhibited a concern for the workforce (how often were imaginative and forward-looking plants constructed by entrepreneurs who also took an interest in the well-being of their employees?), building at a cost of almost £40,000 60 double houses, a school, market hall, baths and a dispensary nearby.[10]

However, at this point the initiative moved to the United States. Steel beams had been used in the upper four floors of a nine-storey Chicago office block in 1883–5 – the Home Insurance Building, by William Le Baron Jenney (1832–1907).[11] The structural design was credited to Jenney's engineering assistant, George B. Whitney, a graduate from the University of Michigan. Cast-iron columns were employed for the interior and exterior walls, and though the beams were to have been of wrought iron, permission was granted to substitute some with Bessemer steel rolled by the Carnegie-Phipps Co.[12] The first entire steel frame followed in that city in 1889–90, when Jenney and W.B. Mundie (1863–1939) completed Sears, Roebuck & Co.'s (Leiter) Building. The 21-storey Masonic Building of 1892, by Burnham & Root, described as the tallest in the world, also in Chicago, continued to set the pace.[13] Skyscrapers were erected in New York two years later, demonstrating how new structural techniques, making determined use of the latest materials, could alter the shape of things to come.[14] Yet European rivals remained much closer to the ground. Whilst the Great Northern Railway's five-storey Goods Warehouse (c.1895–8), Watson Street, Manchester, had an internal frame of steel box-pillars and beams,[15] its solid brick outer walls revealed a reluctance to trust entirely to a metal skeleton. A furniture warehouse at West Hartlepool, Robinson's Emporium, built in 1896 by Basil Scott of Redpath, Brown & Co., was, he believed, Britain's first example of a complete steel frame.[16] But more than a decade passed before the London County Council (General Powers) Act of 1909 acknowledged that the thickness of external walls might be safely reduced should a steel skeleton be introduced.[17] Hence, the Ritz Hotel (1903-6), by Mewès and Davis (S. Bylander, who had studied American techniques, being responsible for its engineering), the capital's first major steel-framed building, was also required to have load-bearing walls, though they were for the most part structurally superfluous.

A rarity for the capital in permitting a steel skeleton to determine its external appearance was the Kodak Building (1910-11), Kingsway.[18] J.J. Burnett (1857-1938), in collaboration with his young London partner, the Scotsman Thomas Tait (1882-1954),[19] took advantage of the 1909 Act to design a six-storey building, whose frame found expression in an impressive classical composition stripped of decoration and infilled with tiers of dark metal windows. 'Erected by the Allen Construction Company in little over a year', remarked *The British Architect*, 'with the idea of making a structure suitable in every way for the purpose of a modern office

and warehouse without attempting to copy any style of architecture', it accommodated around 400 employees engaged in all aspects of Kodak's trade, including the developing and testing of films for England and the Continent.[20]

Occurring in conjunction with these advances in the use of steel skeletons, much experimentation took place in the use of reinforced concrete. The major developments initially took place in France, where the specialists in this field concentrated.[21] The first reinforced-concrete factory was by François Hennébique (1842-1921) at Tourcoing, the Charles Six Spinning Mill (1895),[22] built on the post-and-beam or trabeated system; he had, in 1894-5, already erected a reinforced-concrete sugar refinery at St Ouen. These had been made possible because five years earlier Hennébique had devised a system of vertical hoop-iron stirrups embedded in the heads of concrete beams to resist shearing.[23] Significantly, Britain's first multi-storey reinforced-concrete building was designed by Hennébique with Napoleon Le Brun (1821-1901) in 1897-8 when the two were commissioned to produce a large flour mill for Weaver & Co. in Swansea.[24] It was shortly followed by the

89 Britain's first reinforced-concrete building, a flour mill in Swansea (1897-8) by Hennébique and Le Brun.

90 'A' Bond (1905-6) alongside the New Cut at Bristol. A tobacco warehouse, it possesses all the robust strength of a fortress.

country's first massed-concrete bridge of any substance – the Glenfinnan Viaduct (1897–1901), erected by McAlpines for the West Highland Extension Railway[25] – while Rose, Downs & Thompson's Factory (1900) at Hull was said to have been the first industrial works built of reinforced concrete.[26] A simple, box-like structure, it too had been constructed on the Hennébique system.

The progressive adoption of advanced building techniques, though not their influence on external design, may be illustrated by reference to three nine-storey tobacco bond warehouses situated on the River Avon at Bristol.[27] The contractors were William Cowlin & Son, then under the control of [Sir] Francis Cowlin (1868–1945) and his younger brother, Charles (d.1928). The first, 'A' Bond (1905-6) – the further east of the two on the north side of the New Cut – was based on a combined steel and cast-iron frame. Steel stanchions were employed on the first two floors, with iron above, each supporting rolled-steel joists and concrete arches.[28] The height of the warehouse and its basement demanded foundations of 55 ft, these being entirely of mass concrete. The roof

consisted of north lights running the length of each bay to provide ample light by which to examine the samples of leaf tobacco.[29] Although externally its two neighbours – 'B' Bond (1908), and 'C' Bond (1919) in Clift House Road[30] looked identical, they were the result of the successful application of François Coignet's system of reinforced-concrete beams. For Cowlins, the builders of all three, secured a licence to use his patent in 1907. In contrast to Hennébique's 'U'-shaped stirrups, Coignet linked together the tension and compression bars within the beams by a lattice of diagonally braced steel wires. A blue-brick plinth supported unrelieved walls of red brick pierced in a regular manner by narrow unadorned windows. The virtual absence of external ornament helped to create a fortress-like appearance scarcely hinting at the internal structure. In 1922 Cowlins, who had by this time developed an international reputation for ferro-concrete work in power houses, factories and public buildings, were employed to erect two seven-storey tobacco bonds at Canon's Marsh.[31] Using the Mouchel–Hennébique system of construction, S.S. Reay, the architect, produced ranges of austere appearance finished in concrete. Narrow windows, grouped in threes, were arranged between simple pilasters, the only obvious ornament being applied above the footbridges communicating with the fire-escape galleries of the eastern bond.[32]

A notable concrete-framed factory, which significantly had no single architect, being designed in 1914 by the Trussed Concrete Steel Co. Ltd (p. 213), was for the Birmingham Small Arms Co., Small Heath.[33] Yet the regularity of its three 600-ft blocks (each of four storeys and appearing as a chequerboard of concrete piers and rectangular windows) had probably been determined by the need to build a weapons factory cheaply and quickly, rather than by a profound commitment to rationalism.

The reinforced-concrete frame of the Wallace Scott Tailoring Institute (1913–16), Cathcart, Glasgow (a garment factory of substantial size), by J.J. Burnett, resulted externally in a brick grid where (as in the Kodak Building and McGeoch's (1905), a Glasgow store), simple piers enclosed tiers of large rectangular windows.[34] Detailing, kept to a minimum, stressed the factory's structural elements, while the landscaped grounds that surrounded the block and the provision of rest and education facilities revealed the owners' concern for the welfare of their employees. Writing in 1896, George Bibby had claimed:

'show me the back windows of a man's dwelling and I will tell you his character' is a remark capable of extension to some factories and factory owners, and it is to be regretted that some of the finest factories (erected without regard to expense in many respects) not infrequently exhibit in their plans and detailed arrangements a terrible disregard or ignorance of what is due to their workpeople as regards their safety, health and comfort.[35]

In the light-industrial developments of the inter-war years (p. 214) this concern was often translated into action, and recreation, education and medical rooms were provided as integral parts of the factory.

In revealing similar structural techniques and a regard for the workforce, the Garston Match Factory (1919), built for Maguire, Paterson & Palmer Ltd (subsequently Bryant & May), had much in common with the Wallace Scott Institute. Designed by the Mewès and Davis partnership, the long, grid-like two-storey block of reinforced concrete that contained the machinery,

packing and dispatching processes, was fronted by a central 'Welfare Building' (containing canteens, wash- and cloak-rooms) flanked on each side by an assembly hall and office block. *The Builder* suggested that the emancipating influence of the First World War could be detected in its plan: '... the enormous manufacturing output which resulted has brought forth a more comprehensive vision of how a huge factory site should be dealt with'.[36] The architecture of the main façade, they continued,

has been considered. For the sake of economy, all superfluous motif and ornamentation has been eliminated, and a treatment of tile decoration in the bare spaces between the constructional elements gives brightness and colour to the composition. The whole composition represents the needs of factory life as now interpreted and sooner or later every establishment in the country will have to conform to these requirements.

That many of these innovative structures had their origin overseas or were the work of foreign designers was significant for the evolution of British architecture in the Edwardian period, and it mirrored a growing industrial lead held by America and Germany. Although *The British Architect* in 1901 could record that 'important new developments in construction and materials' had taken place during the latter part of the nineteenth century and that 'architects have now a practically unlimited range of materials to choose from',[37] Martin Briggs (1882–1977), then a young architect, claimed only six years later that the profession

exhibits absolute unpreparedness for anything in the nature of change. We ought to study ... iron just as we study the influence of Garden Cities. It is an economical force in the country, as is electric traction, and girders should receive as much attention from thinking architects as any other practical question.[38]

In other words, whilst new materials – steel for beams and reinforcement rods, together with concrete – were being made readily available to British architects by industrial advance, many were slow, not so much to utilize them (as the following examples will show), but to follow the logic of novel structural possibilities through to outward forms. The reason for this, suggested Briggs, was one of knowledge and organization:

> In almost all cases where elaborate steelwork enters into an architect's design he has to employ an engineer, who is responsible not only for the calculation of sizes of members, but also for their arrangement and details. Therefore unless the architect himself has some considerable knowledge of the subject, the engineer is presented with a drawing which takes little account of the all-important steel frame ... And if the position be reversed, and the architect follows the engineer's skeleton plan in designing his elevations, the elevations are bound to suffer ... In America every large architect's office has a staff of steelwork experts, but even this method is not quite satisfactory if the principal himself is unacquainted with the subject.[39]

Free design

The architectural characteristics of many novel industrial buildings of the Edwardian period, though influenced by rationalism, may be more accurately defined by the term 'free design'. The search for a new architecture did not take the form of a complete rejection of historic tradition (as the modern movement abandoned the past) but developed in an attempt to experiment with a variety of established styles.

One industrial building in the 'free style' was by an architect not normally associated with this field of work; indeed, it was his sole industrial commission, accepted presumably because he had produced wallpaper designs for its owners. Sandersons' factory (1902–3), Turnham Green, by C.F.A. Voysey (1857–1941), combined an exceptional expression of structure with function.[40] A contrasting rectangular four-storey block, its apparently simple layout was enlivened by an exciting use of materials and decorative elements: white-glazed brick piers linked together by wavy horizontals at parapet level, and string courses of stone and black brick creating a grid of movement and variety. The capped buttresses and the gracefully curving roofline between have been described as resembling an Arts and Crafts bedstead.[41] The factory's awkward location and the several manufacturing processes (the fenestration is far from being symmetrical) must have increased the architect's problems.

Willens & Robinson's Ferry Works (1901), Queensferry, by H. Bulkeley Creswell (1869–1960), who had been articled to Sir Aston Webb, offered a more austere version of the Edwardian free style, but was none the less impressive and became the architect's best-remembered building.[42] A boiler factory of some size, the simple brick design attempted, in Creswell's own words,

> to give candid architectural expression to engineering workshops ... The building on the left hand ... is the packing and forwarding shops, the next combines the erecting and machine shops, the building with the tower [the centrepiece] is to contain the machinery for providing hydraulic and electric power for the works, and the large block on the extreme right is where the tube drawing and drum making processes will be carried out.[43]

Executed in 'Buckley purple brindled bricks', with strings and copings of 'hard vitrified purple brickware, made also in the Buckley district', it exhibited a coherence based on the consistent use of these materials and the repetition of bold forms – tapered buttresses and simple rectangular windows. The factory represented, as *The Builder* added, 'a highly creditable attempt to give a certain amount of character ... in a manner naturally arising out of structure, and without any introduction of superfluous and unmeaning ornament'.[44] Although he subsequently designed engineering shops at Rugby (1902) and, in collaboration with William A. Forsyth, built the offices for Vauxhall Motors (1915) at Luton, Creswell ran a general practice; he was in no sense an industrial specialist.[45]

Another building which made consistent use of subdued brick was the Tram Transformer Station (c.1906) at Islington, by W.E. Riley (1852–1937), the LCC's Chief Architect from 1899 to 1919.[46] Containing the switch gear, the interior of the machine room was lined with ivory-glazed bricks with a galt-glazed brick dado, the floor being of steel and coke-breeze concrete covered with terrazzo. Its sublime

91 Sanderson's wallpaper factory (1902–3) at Turnham Green – Voysey's unusual design for an awkward site.

exterior had been achieved by use of stock brick, with limited Portland stone dressings, in an effective adaptation of George Dance's (1741–1825) detailing for Newgate Gaol (1769–78). The rusticated piers and recessed arches filled with pedimented blind windows were a simplified copy of the grim decoration that adorned the high walls of Newgate, only recently demolished in 1903. That these prison motifs could be so successfully applied to an industrial building underlined the particular appropriateness of the sublime for them both.

On a much larger scale were the designs by Edwin O. Sachs (1870–1919) for Shannon Ltd's Cabinet Works (1901–2), Dalston.[47] *Building News* praised Sachs for his attempt to give 'this factory an architectural character, using the simplest materials – i.e. ordinary stock bricks with plain red facings'.[48] The heavily modelled frieze of windows beneath the eaves, conical turrets to each of the staircases and absence of detailing on the lower floors imparted a continental castellated feel. It was not, however, a Romantic fancy, as the irregular 'U'-shaped plan reflected an efficient arrangement of workrooms. Attention to safety regulations, recently revised by the London Building Act of 1894, was precise in a factory containing so much inflammable material. 'The constructional steelwork is entirely encased in concrete two inches thick to ... protect them against heat ... Ample staircases afford an easy means of exit for the workmen.'[49] This emphasis on safety was no mere coincidence, for Sachs founded the British Fire Prevention Committee, a voluntary body formed in 1897 and composed largely of architects, that sought to test and publicize methods of fire protection.[50]

James Henry Sellers (1861–1954), then in partnership with Edgar Wood (1860–1935), erected an office building (1906–7) for Dronsfield Brothers, the engineers, in King Street, Oldham.[51] Apart from the subtle use of materials (the entrance, ground floor and window surrounds in grey Cornish granite, upper floors in dark-green glazed brick, the whole fronted by suitably refined railings from Coalbrookdale), the building represented the innovative use of reinforced concrete in its flat roofs, an application in which Sellers specialized. Although born in Middleton, the son of a mill-owner, and in practice in Manchester, Wood, a leading member of the Arts and Crafts movement in the north, did not undertake many industrial commissions and, like his partner (who had been born in Oldham), never made an impact on the Lancashire mill market.[52]

A disinfectant factory of ingenuity and interest was erected for the Sanitas Co. at Limehouse in 1909 by the London architect Arthur T. Bolton (1864–1945), whose design followed 'the special requirements of the internal use of the different parts'[53] Increasingly architects were called upon to devise elevations and plans to suit the growing complexities of a business's operations, whereas in earlier periods, when enterprises were smaller and the technology less advanced, architects or builders could successfully encompass their activities in regular, rectangular blocks without too many modifications. As for the Dronsfield example, glazed bricks were employed, not simply for decoration, but for their self-washing properties in a polluted district, while internally the floors and roof had been constructed of steel and concrete. The clever arrangement of the windows and positioning of the corner staircase revealed a careful free-style composition of deceptive simplicity. The Sanitas commission had been something of a departure for Bolton who, having trained with Sir Robert Edis in 1884–7, had a rather limited period as

a practising architect.[54] This appears to have been his only industrial project and he was probably best known for the Hamburg–America Line Building (1911–13), Cockspur Street, and the P&O Offices. Bolton's consuming interest was architectural history and in 1917 he became Curator of Sir John Soane's Museum.[55] Like so many young architects, he had presumably accepted the Sanitas commission for experience and because he could not yet pick and choose his subjects.

Something of the Edwardian period's Baroque Revival may be detected in Thomas Hubbuck & Son's paint factory and warehouse (1910),[56] Ratcliff, by Ernest J. Gosling (1865–1932).[57] Although particularly reserved for prestigious public buildings, the grandiose classical manner, if suitably diluted, could reappear in an industrial context. The reticulated stone ground floor and the symmetrical arrangement of windows and hoists rose to a dentil cornice and central angled pediment. Its vigour, confidently stated forms and imaginative use of materials (Cornish grey granite, Ham Hill stone and red-brick facings with concrete floors and staircase) did not prevent this from being a practical working building.

Even more positively stated and grandly executed Baroque buildings were erected in Manchester's mercantile districts during this period by the local architect, Harry S. Fairhurst (1869–1945).[58] Born in Blackburn, Fairhurst came to Manchester aged nineteen to enter the offices of Maxwell & Tuke, and after several visits to Italy and experience with William Fame, Lord Bute's architect, he began to practise on his own account in his home town. Possibly attracted by the major commissions that the city could offer, he returned to Manchester in 1901 to earn his first important job four years later: India House (1905–6), Whitworth Street, for Lloyds Packing Warehouses Ltd. This was a magnificent seven-storey structure whose vigorous Baroque

92 India House (1905–6), Whitworth Street, Manchester. One of the city's grandest warehouses, based on a steel framework.

93 Orient House (1914), Manchester, by Goldsmith, another ornate textile warehouse.

ornate storey above the cornice completed matters. Executed in good red brick with glazed sienna tiles and mouldings, it could withstand the dulling Manchester atmosphere. Internally, the warehouse consisted of a framework of rolled-steel joists encased in concrete.[60] Fairhurst was also responsible for Lancaster House (1907-9), Princess Street, to which India House was linked. More ornate still, this packing house and offices occupied an awkward corner site, which gave Fairhurst the opportunity to erect an elaborate tower.[61] Its bright sienna terracotta dressings were self-washing, making it, in sunlight after a shower, a sparkling pinnacle of golden hues.

Nearby Orient House (1914), 65-66 Granby Row, by the Manchester architect George H. Goldsmith,[62] offered an equally elaborate, though contrasting, example of an Edwardian warehouse. Baroque in interpretation, its white glazed façade was dominated by a row of fluted Greek Ionic columns, the classical image being reiterated in the key frieze, palmettes and cast-iron lamp stands at its central entrance. Like India House, whose rear elevation consisted of large metal windows set in an unadorned wall of glazed white brick,[63] Orient House exhibited the greatest imaginable contrast between its elaborate Baroque street façade and the modern side and rear elevations, which, corresponding with its concrete and steel-framed structure, formed a simple grid pattern of large metal windows. The distinction drawn by Fairhurst and Goldsmith between the public face and the unseen working areas was one that architects were soon to reject, as the notion that buildings should uniformly reflect their internal structure caught hold.[64] Thus these formal exteriors of the early twentieth century in Manchester represented a final stage in traditional warehouse design, whilst the rear elevations, whose treatment had been dictated by the need for plentiful natural light and a desire to reduce costs in fact served as harbingers of future trends.

Although possessing elements of traditional warehouse design, Fairhurst's York House (1911), Major Street, Manchester, had a striking stepped rear elevation rising up to the roof-

detailing and size, in streets of limited width, concealed its symmetry.[59] Two entrance bays topped by ornate gables balanced a composition in which the basement and first two storeys formed a rusticated base, the main order comprised the next four storeys, and a higher more line to provide maximum natural light in a limited space.[65] The bold use of glass compared well with many modern structures and offered a contrast with Fairhurst's earlier Baroque buildings.

The search for a free style took many forms in the Edwardian period, including a number of buildings in the manner of New Scotland Yard (1887-90), by Norman Shaw, which combined elements of the Baroque with Scottish baronial. In 1898 a large five-storey warehouse was constructed in Manchester for Horrockses, Crewdson & Co., designed by Charles Heathcote (p. 209).[66] In its use of bold gables, rusticated columns and a variety of windows, circular corner towers and horizontal bands of colour, this manifested the two styles. Similar in treatment was the station (1900) and Moorgate Station Chambers of the City & South London Railway, by T. Phillips Figgis (1858-1948).[67] In red brick and Portland stone, its Scottish corner tower and gables were enlivened at the entrance by the company's arms, which displayed tube trains passing through tunnels under the Thames.

Oldham and Lancashire

The rationale for treating the Oldham district as a separate entity, when this history has concentrated on styles and types of buildings rather than regions, is that, like the Potteries and the Lace Market in Nottingham, a local tradition or continuity of expression developed. In Oldham, where a family of architects dominated, resisting the temptation to import new styles or interpretations, owners could generally satisfy the rising level of demand produced by the cotton boom of the 1880s only by building ever more mills, in which greater capacity was achieved by doubling up plant in a repetitive fashion. Wider carding machines and longer mules meant that their dimensions advanced progressively (longer, wider and higher buildings), though the essential design and appearance was not subject to dramatic change. The comparative size of Lancashire mills may be indicated by the number of spindles that they contained; the new mills erected in Oldham during the 1874-5 boom had

on average 50,000 spindles, double the capacity of the average mill in the county. Those of 1883-4 had an average spindleage of 75,000, and those built in 1889-90 one of 90,000.[68] By 1908 the most common size of mill being constructed had risen to 90,000-100,000 spindles, and by 1914 some had attained 120,000 spindles.[69] As a result, the record for the largest mill was constantly being broken – a contest that culminated with the erection of Sidney Stott's mammoth Dunlop Cotton Mills (1914-19), Rochdale, whose twin linked blocks held some 221,520 spindles.[70]

Although ring spinning replaced the slower, less efficient mules, it was not suitable for the quality grades of yarn. In addition, it was expensive to convert mills specifically erected for mules so that they could withstand the heavier weights imposed by ring spinning. The mass of the mule (the headstock and the gate) rested on the beams between the columns, the space at the side being used for the lateral motion of the light frame. By contrast, the compact shape of the ring machine, with its vertical operation, meant that three of these could be accommodated within the area needed by one mule; but to support the extra weight it was necessary to insert steel girders and reinforce the cast-iron columns, an expenditure that some mill-owners felt was prohibitive.

The main developments in spinning-mill design principally occurred in the use of new materials and construction methods rather than the adoption of novel architectural styles. The Centenary Mill (1891), Preston, erected for Horrockses, Crewdson & Co.,[71] was among the first factories to incorporate rolled-steel beams and concrete floors.[72] The Preston architect, Frederick Mallot, was responsible for various alterations to this building and the nearby Yard Works in the early twentieth century,[73] but is unlikely to have drafted the original design. The open loggia on the main staircase tower followed in the well-established Italianate tradition. Also cast in this Lancashire mould, Falcon Mill (1904-8), Handel Street, Bolton, designed by George Temperley (d.1909), was one of the first cotton mills to possess concrete joist floors.

Externally, however, the six-storey red-brick Falcon Mill could not be distinguished from its earlier iron-framed predecessors. It was planned to hold 90,000 spindles, and the contractor Jonathan Partington of Middleton had also been responsible for erecting the Swan Lane Mills (p. 185). As the *Bolton Journal* reported, it as to be electrically driven, and the

> consequent steadiness and speed of the spindles will be a great advantage in production. Messrs Musgrave and Sons Ltd, of Bolton, will supply the steam turbine engines, and the motors and remaining parts of the electrical driving are in the hands . . . of Siemens Bros Ltd, electrical engineers.[74]

Falcon Mill was completed in 1908.[75] Apart from their vast dimensions, the Dunlop Cotton Mills were unusual in being among the first buildings to be roofed with asbestos-cement tiles – known as 'Trafford tiles' as their makers, Turner Brothers, had in 1913 opened their factory at Trafford Park, Manchester.[76]

With 95,720 spindles, the Imperial Mill (1900–1), Gorse Street, Blackburn, by Sidney Stott, was said when opened to have been the world's largest ring-spinning mill. That it was executed in a traditional manner, the modern machinery being incorporated in a building of great length, indicated the hold of established architectural styles. It remained, nevertheless, a mill of striking impact, its twin mansard towers balancing a symmetrical arrangement of regular-sized windows and a central name pediment.[77]

94 Revealed more clearly by the demolition of some of the surrounding terraced houses, Falcon Mill (1908), Bolton, by Temperley, relied on concrete joist floors which permitted the insertion of wide groups of windows.

Sidney Stott produced a hundred or so cotton mills and their extensions, presumably the greatest number ever executed by one architect. Among his better-known works may be included: Pearl Mill (1893), Netherhay Street, Oldham, which when built contained 136,892 spindles and was the largest spinning mill in the world; Mona Mill (1893); Nile (1898); Marlborough No. 1 (1903) and No. 2 (1906); Dale (1904); Heron and Roy (both 1905); Dee, Gorse, Orb and Raven (all in 1906); and Ace and Lilac (both 1914).

A large commission for the Swan Lane Spinning Co. Ltd, Bolton, was executed by Stott & Sons – No. 1 Mill (1902), No. 2 (1905) and No. 3 (1915). Although appearing as a single six-storey block with symmetrical staircase towers, No. 1 and No. 2 Mills (announced in 1904 as the largest of the kind in the world, containing 210,000 mule spindles)[78] were, in fact, constructed separately. The first was completed in December 1902,[79] its engines being started in the following June,[80] and No. 2 was finished in 1905. Such progressive expansion revealed the caution of the directors. Rather than raise finance for one enormous speculative project, they preferred to build a 90,000-spindle mill and, when it became clear that rising demand would justify an extension, planned for a further 120,000 spindles in an adjacent building able to use the same engine house, boilers (suitably duplicated) and chimney. In this period mills were commonly constructed in such a manner as to allow for the later doubling of the premises. The first block would be erected with the offices and engine house at one end so that a second could be attached. Now situated in the middle, the engine house and chimney formed the focal point of the composition, while the twin staircase towers, sometimes placed two-thirds of the distance from the centre, balanced the whole. At the time, spinning companies offered a sound investment yielding 6% and more, higher than consols, 'and if not quite so sure as government stock, a loan to a big mill company [was] ... as safe as the proverbial houses'.[81]

Of the three mills in the Swan Lane complex, No. 3, containing 120,000 spindles, created the

greatest architectural interest.[82] Occupying an awkward corner site, this eight-storey red-brick building offered a variety of window forms, and stone swans decorated the eaves and name blocks lower down. Structurally it was innovative, for the cast-iron columns supported steel 'H' girders, the hipped slate roof having trussed steel principals.[83] The chimney had a green band on which a swan in white brick rested, the whole being topped by a yellow terracotta cap. They were mills, therefore, on which more than the usual amount of attention had been lavished.

Another fine design was by Sidney Stott for the Maple Co., Cardwell Street, Oldham, where No. 1 Mill, containing 89,928 spindles, was erected in 1903–4, and No. 2 Mill followed alongside in 1912–14 with 96,880 spindles,[84] though it was not apparent from their exteriors that a decade had separated their construction. Stott's signature – the incorporation of two corbelled rings towards the top of the chimney shaft, beneath the cap – at once marked his authorship, whilst the excellent red Accrington 'Nori' brick has not been darkened by years of pollution. The corner towers revealed the region's architectural preoccupation with the recessed pilaster, but their refinement and simplicity were discernably features of the Edwardian age. The large metal-framed windows, set between narrow brick piers, contrasted with the rows of smaller, segment-headed windows that characterized late-nineteenth-century mills. The strength of steel beams allowed architects to space columns more generously, so that the outer walls, still load-bearing, became almost a series of pillars interspersed by broad windows above brick panels. This enabled designers to insert longer openings, which often took the form of double windows supported by a central cast-iron mullion.[85] The possibility of inserting broader windows meant that there could be a corresponding reduction in their heights, which, in turn, resulted in lower storeys. These could save as much as 20% on building costs. In addition, the influence of technical innovation had played its part, as Joseph Nasmith, editor of the *Textile Recorder*, observed:

95 Part of No. 3 Mill (1915), Swan Lane, by Stott & Sons. Notice the variety of window forms and the decorative swans at the eaves and on the corner stone. The bright red 'Nori' bricks were from the Accrington district.

Gradually the lengths of the machines increased, and the mill was of necessity correspondingly enlarged. As a sequence to this there came a consideration of the method of providing light, so that a room 130 ft wide should not suffer in that respect. Gradually the ceilings became loftier, and the window area of greater importance. Thus, at the present day [1894], in England, the cotton mill is distinguished by the enormous ratio of the window area to that of wall.[86]

The impact of steel on textile mill construction, not yet fully assessed, appears, however, to have been muted. The introduction of rolled section steel beams, noticeable from the 1890s, had been prejudiced by a period of cold, short failures. The material was treated with conservatism by architects who employed it as a substitute for cast iron rather than exploiting the engineering possibilities of the steel framework. The Britannia Mills (1912), Huddersfield, for example, had steel beams simply to support wooden floors.

Architecturally speaking, some of the finest mills in Oldham were not the work of Sidney Stott, but his cousin George, a member of the Joseph Stott & Son partnership.[87] In particular, he was responsible for Manor (1906) and Kent Mills (1908-9), both in Victoria Street, Chadderton.[88] Although their elegant five-storey brick blocks appeared to be identical, the corner staircase towers exhibited an interesting contrast: at Manor Mill a dome capped a restrained Baroque tower, while Kent Mill featured a crested mansard roof beneath which more traditional fenestration and corner pilasters adorned the square tower. Other equally pleasing mills for which George Stott can take credit included Rome Mill (1907-9), Devon Mill (1908-10), Soudan No. 1 Mill (1903-4) and No. 2 Mill (1906-8), together with Lily Mill (1907).[89]

Whilst the influence of Edwardian free style

96 By George Stott, Manor Mill (1906) stands as one of Oldham's most distinguished architectural monuments, marked by its copper-covered dome.

could be seen merely to have modified these Stott family designs, other examples revealed the force of its impact more clearly. Both Coppull Mill (1906), Coppull, near Chorley[90] and Broadstone Mill (c.1910), built for the Reddish Spinning Co.,[91] had novel towers where the formality of a dome or mansard roof had been abandoned in favour of a Byzantine minaret in

97 The Byzantine staircase tower of Broadstone Mill (*c.* 1910) Reddish. Yellow glazed brick and terracotta mouldings contrast with the clean red Accrington brick.

alternate bands of red brick and yellow terracotta. The mill blocks, where the need to maximize daylight and accommodate machinery as efficiently as possible were paramount, remained largely untouched by this Eastern interpretation. The Byzantine Revival of the 1890s and 1900s had its adherents among mill architects. The striking similarity between the towers at Coppull and Reddish suggests that they were the work of the same designer. Bay Tree Mill (1904) and Laurel Mill (1905), at Middleton

Junction, which shared a common chimney and engine house, by Stott & Sons,[92] also each had a Byzantine tower, though executed in a more rigid fashion, some of the detailing falling over into the nearby offices, gate lodge and chimney plinth. Their authorship of Alder Mill (1905–7), Leigh, can be confirmed,[93] and its similar Byzantine features executed in light ochre terracotta suggested that the Stott partnership occasionally favoured the style during this period.

Elk Mill, Royton, designed by Arthur Turner & Son for the Shiloh Spinning Co., stood as an example of continuity and the strength of local tradition.[94] Apart from the simplicity of its staircase tower and window forms, it would be difficult to tell that this cotton mill with 107,000 mule spindles, the last to be erected in Lancashire, dated from 1926. The rectangular block framed by recessed pilasters, attached engine house and chimney displaying the name 'Elk' in white brick, and the flat concrete roof, broken only by the stubby turret, marked this unmistakably as an Oldham mill. Arthur Turner (d.1934),[95] who had served as an assistant in the offices of Wild, Collins & Wild before setting up his own firm at 26 Clegg Street, Oldham, practised too late to derive great benefit from the cotton industry, much of his work taking the form of extensions to existing factories as at Fir Mill in 1908 and Thornham Mill in 1920. He did, however, design Park No. 2 (1912), Park and Sandy No. 2 Mill (1913), Hawk (1908) and Wye No. 1 Mill (1914), the last two in Shaw. His son, Percy Robinson Turner (1891–1959), who was also credited with Elk Mill and seems to have been its author, continued the business, producing plans for Wye No. 2 Mill (1925), Shaw, which contained 96,712 ring spindles, and completing extensions to Park Mill in 1940.[96]

Although many mills erected during the Edwardian period had four to six storeys, and remained rectangular in plan to minimize the quantity of bricks consumed, the introduction of ring spinning and new theories of the organization of production led to the design of long, low buildings. Wye No. 1 Mill, containing 67,952 ring spindles, was an example. Only three

98 Wye No. 1 Mill, Napier Street, Shaw, designed by Arthur Turner and photographed c. 1915. It contained 67,952 spindles and typified the long low buildings that ring-spinning encouraged. The lodge in the foreground provided the boilers with an ample supply of water while serving to cool the exhaust steam from the engine room (which can be detected by the large round-arched windows).

storeys in height, it was of considerable length. Whilst mule spinning resulted in buildings of around 140 ft in width in the 1890s, 102 ft would suffice for ring machinery.[97] The compactness of the ring frame meant that far more spindles could be accommodated in a smaller space, though their weight increased the load factor. To overcome this problem and facilitate handling, it was desirable to have fewer storeys of greater length. The case for placing as many machines as possible on one level was forcibly argued by Sington who in 1892 produced plans for a single-storey mill of 200,000 spindles. Its three spinning rooms and card room were arranged symmetrically around a central engine house. The higher cost of land, he suggested, would be offset by the lower cost of construction, 'while the lighting of the building is much improved since, in addition to the side lights, top lights with a north aspect can be obtained to any extent'.[98] Greater efficiencies could be won in a worsted mill, it was argued, if a one-storey plan were adopted (fig. 99). The yarn, from delivery, could thereby be moved through the various processes of manufacture with a minimum of handling and transport until ready to leave as packaged cloth. Bays aligned on an east-west axis would provide steady daylight and keep the rooms as cool as possible.[99]

To continue the story of Bradshaw & Gass in Bolton, the partnership flourished during the Edwardian period as the cotton industry continued to expand. Mill commissions – and villas for the mill directors – followed at Leigh where, with few exceptions, the firm gained all the textile contracts, which included Mather Lane No. 3 Mill (1891–3);[100] Firs New Mill (1902–4) for Tunnicliffe & Hampson Ltd;[101] and mills for the Bedford Spinning Co. (1909–11),[102] Mill Lane Spinning Co. (1912–15),[103] and Leigh Spinners Ltd (1913–15).[104] At Atherton the Howe Bridge Spinning Co. provided two further important contracts – for No. 4 Mill (1898–1900) costing £31,958[105] and what appears to have been the rebuilding of No. 3 Mill (1919–24) for £102,143.[106] The long-standing connection between Bradshaw & Gass and this company must have led to other commissions in the town – such as two mills for the Atherton Cotton Spinning Co. in 1892–3[107] and 1907–9.[108]

99 A plan of a proposed one-storey worsted mill.

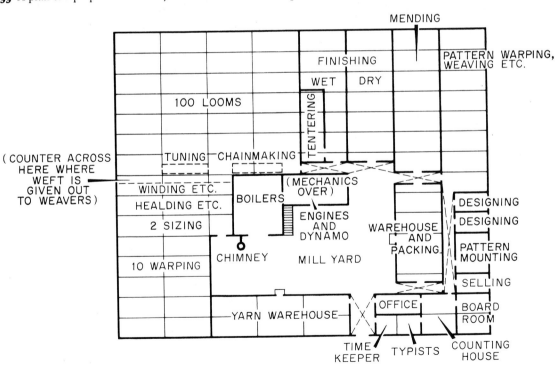

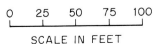

100 Beside the Leeds and Liverpool Canal at Leigh, a typical Bradshaw & Gass factory distinguished by the Italianate dust flue cover and decorative water tower – No. 3 Mill (1891–3), Mather Lane Mill Co.

In Bolton itself the architects designed Croal Mill (1907–8)[109] in Callis Road, a substantial structure 224 ft by 142 ft holding 102,000 spindles, and when Knowles Ltd decided to expand their capacity the firm secured the contract for Mossfield Mill (1914–16)[110] and, more important, their Egyptian Mill (1919–23).[111] Both featured Bradshaw & Gass' distinctive square tower with its pitched roof and overhanging eaves.

As the firm's business grew, so Arthur John Hope (1875–1960) became a partner in 1902.[112] He had been educated at Wigan Grammar School, and it was intended that he should become an engineer, but a chance meeting with J.J. Bradshaw resulted in his entering Bradshaw & Gass' office in 1892 as an architectural pupil. His rise within the firm found outward expression in 1913 when the style changed to Bradshaw Gass & Hope. Although gaining considerably from the cotton industry, the firm developed during this period as a general practice also designing churches, schools, houses and public halls over an increasingly national territory.[113] In 1920 two new partners were created: William Scott (1882–1956),[114] a mill architect who had worked for Sidney Stott before moving to Bolton, and James Robertson Adamson (1883–1943) who had been articled in Sir John

101 Sir John Holden's Mill (1920–6) by Bradshaw Gass & Hope, notable for its size and the absence of a chimney. It was but part of an ambitious plan that never came to fruition.

Burnett's office in Glasgow.[115] The former's skills proved important as this period witnessed the design of an ambitious spinning complex. Sir John Holden's Mill (1920–6)[116] was to have comprised eight blocks, arranged in pairs, the first two (linked by the company's offices) situated on the Blackburn Road at Astley Bridge.[117] Yet because of the unexpected cost of the foundations, caused by the soft nature of the subsoil, and the onset of the slump, only the first mill and the offices were constructed. Nevertheless, this six-storey structure (105 yds by 43 yds), by virtue of its architectural treatment and the incorporation of modern technology, merited serious attention. The variety of its external detailing, much in terracotta, and the copper-domed tower, owed much to the Edwardian neo-classical tradition, while its steel framework and concrete floors, together with the use of electric power, placed it firmly in the twentieth century. The use of electric power meant that there was no need for a chimney, and the adoption of rolled-steel joists as lintels permitted the insertion of large windows. Sir John Holden's Mill was, in fact, the first to take its electricity from a local power station, earlier ones having generated their own. As with most mills, the basement served as a conditioning room, where the regulation of water flowing through brick channels controlled the level of humidity in the spinning rooms (the finer the yarn the warmer the mill needed to be). The ground floor was a warehouse, the first floor a card room, and the four storeys above contained the spinning machinery.[118] Whilst the commission was treated as an office project and the drawings were always signed Bradshaw Gass & Hope, it seems that William Scott took responsibility for the basic mill structure and its engineering requirements and that A.J. Hope produced the elevations, the whole coming under the supervisory attention of J.B. Gass.

Before the arrival of the general building contractor, the mill architect had a role that extended well beyond the production of plans and elevations. In the period up to the 1880s specific tasks such as bricklaying, roofing, joinery, plumbing and so forth were commonly put out to tender and the architect took the responsibility for appointing individual craftsmen and superintending their work on the site. This meant that the mill architect had to be a practical man of business, skilled in the organization of labour: a clerk of works. However, during the 1880s when the mill-building boom made designers and contractors busy beyond recall, methods were rationalized to streamline the process of tender. In May 1887, for example, a 'Standard Mode of Measurement' was 'agreed upon by the architects and builders … as a general statement of the methods proposed to be used in taking quantities and measuring up works'.[119] In this document they specified the terms of reference that excavators, masons, bricksetters, carpenters, joiners, plasterers, painters, plumbers, glaziers, ironfounders, slaters and tilers should observe when tendering for contracts. The bricksetter, for instance, was to:

> 1. Give description of materials, and mortar, and quality of work. The work, unless otherwise mentioned, to be reduced to one brick thick, and called 'Brick-length Walling' in yards super. If sand, gravel, or water on the spot is not intended to be used, state so. If there be much work of half a brick only it is desirable to mention it. Where a building is lofty it is desirable to divide the work into stages vertically.[120]

In addition, the growing volume of mill work accelerated the formation of general contractors, as groups of craftsmen merged or widened their ambit to include other trades. G. & J. Sneddon, for example, originally bricklayers, moved into plumbing and joinery, as did John Dickinson. In 1875–8, for the construction of Howe Bridge No. 2 Mill, only six contractors were employed by J.J. Bradshaw: J. Collin & Son for the mill walls, H. Gregson for the foundations, Homan & Rogers fireproofing, John Green bricks, James Holden reservoir excavation and foundations, and George Bedford for the removal of old flagging.[121] For the new No. 1 Mill, rebuilt in 1883–6, eleven individual contractors were engaged,[122] while in 1897–1900 for the company's No. 4 Mill 15 contractors have been identified.[123] For though groups of craftsmen formed themselves into general units, an expansion in the range of specialist trades produced a growth in overall numbers, as indicated by some of the contractors employed in the construction of Sir John Holden's Mill: E. Taylor & Co. (structure), Widnes Foundry (castings), BRC Engineering Co. Ltd (reinforcements), T. Walmsley & Son (steelwork), Lancashire Dynamo Co. (electric motors), Bolton Corporation Electricity Fittings Dept (switch gear and cables), Slater & Russell (heating), W. Wadsworth (two cage hoists and one transformer lift) and Hall & Kay (plant).[124]

The reputation of specialist mill architects had achieved such heights that by the latter part of the nineteenth century they secured contracts throughout Britain and the world. The case of Woodhouse and Morley in Scotland (p. 162) may be compared with that of Joseph Stott. In 1884–9 this Oldham architect designed two massive red-brick mills (one five- and the other four-storey) for the Glasgow Cotton Spinning Co. Ltd, Carstairs and Swanston Streets, Dalmarnock.[125] The restrained Italianate staircase towers, simple corner pilasters and cornices, and the repetitious arrangement of segment-headed windows, suggested a corner of Lancashire transplanted to Scotland. The same could be said of Sidney Stott's work in Bromford, Birmingham for the Dunlop Rubber Co. Having completed two mills for them in Rochdale, he was approached to design a large warehouse for their Midlands tyre-making plant. The result, Fort Dunlop New Store (1923–6), a seven-storey block of Accrington brick and artificial stone dressings, revealed its northern authorship. The staircase tower (two were planned) in shape and style resembled those that adorned his cotton mills, whilst similarities existed in the fenestration. Based on a steel framework encased in concrete, it had a regularity and solidity which marked the warehouse as a Stott composition.[126]

These northern architects also earned considerable incomes from overseas commissions. In a case during 1907 in which George Temperley unsuccessfully sued the Blackrod Manufacturing Company for the non-payment of his fee, it was declared, to validate his professional standing, that he had:

> done work for the very best people connected with the erection of mills such as Messrs Tootal Broadhurst Lee Co. Ltd. He had also done work in the States, Japan and Brazil and at the present moment was engaged on four large mills in Bolton.[127]

Sidney Stott undertook a number of overseas commissions during the 1890s, building spinning mills at Tannwald, Austria in 1893,[128] two at Calcutta in 1895 and 1899 (20,000 and 30,360 spindles respectively), at Rheine (24,000) and Epe (71,000) in Germany both during 1898, in Syria (20,000) in 1896 and at Boras, Sweden

(23,220) in 1898, together with a 20,000-spindle mill at Haiphong, China also in that year. His practice, in fact, extended to Mexico, Bulgaria, Norway, Denmark, Argentina, Chile and Egypt.[129] Among their export work, Potts, Son & Pickup designed two multi-storey mills for the Société Cotonnière d'Hellemmes, at Lille in the mid-1890s, each with steel-and-concrete floors and flat-headed windows.[130] Britain's expertise (challenged only in America and to a lesser extent Germany) in mill design was thus demonstrated in the latter part of the nineteenth century by the ability of Lancashire architects to obtain work in foreign countries.

102 Tennant's alkali works depicted here probably before the 436 ft chimney had been erected.

Chemical works

So far little has been said on the subject of chemical works, largely because the construction of substantial plant did not occur until the second half of the nineteenth century. Like early gasworks, where the scale and range of processes remained limited and could be contained within a group of moderate-sized buildings of conventional structure, the leading chemical works of the mid-Victorian era commonly exhibited Italianate features. The single-storey buildings of the St Rollox works of Charles Tennant & Co. in Glasgow (considered the largest alkali plant in Europe during the 1840s) possessed tripartite windows, simple pilasters and window aprons.[131] The chimney, 436 ft high, completed in June 1842 after a year in building, was one of the tallest in Britain, having been projected by

St. Rollox Works, Glasgow.
CHARLES TENNANT & CO,
Manufacturers of
Soaps. Soda.
CHLORIDE OF LIME OR BLEACHING POWDER. SULPHURIC, MURIATIC & NITRIC ACIDS.
AGENT for the UNITED STATES, JAMES LEE, NEW YORK.

W.J. Macquorn Rankine (1820–72), Professor of Civil Engineering at Glasgow University, and designed by Messrs L.D.B. Gordon and L. Hill.[132]

In Bristol, the keep-like block of the former Christopher Thomas Brothers' soap works (c.1845), with plain segment-headed windows, was enlivened by Florentine battlements and corner towers, whilst later additions (1860–5) in Old Bread Street and Broad Plain, by the local architect, W.B. Gingell (1819–1900),[133] revealed a continuing interest in that style of architecture though more forcefully expressed with a greater variety of materials and detailing.[134] The theme was subsequently upheld in a chimney said to have been 'an exact copy of the Tower of Palazzo Vecchio ... Near to it and built into the side of the wall, is the carved stone figure of the winged Bull of Nineveh, the familiar trade mark of the firm.'[135] Charles Thomas had paid a visit to Florence in 1881 and had possibly inspired this addition. Gingell was one of Bristol's leading architects and though a general practitioner, he was regularly called upon to undertake industrial commissions, including John Robinson's oil mills, Pilkingtons' glass warehouse, Champion's confectionery works and Glasson's warehouses.[136]

However, with advances in science and the introduction of the Solvay process for the manufacture of soda, the chemical industry underwent a major transformation. Brunner, Mond & Co.'s Winnington Works, an alkali manufactory, illustrated the size and complexity of these plants.[137] Constructed by a local Northwich builder, William Leicester, working to Solvay's plans, the works as they were assembled in 1873–4 comprised five small towers, four stills, a lime kiln, blowing engine and a variety of filtering and pumping equipment.[138] Consisting, after a major expansion programme in 1881–2, of a complex arrangement of corrugated-iron sheds and towers, linked together by conveyor belts and divided by tall brick chimneys devoid of all decoration, the composition and structure had, of course, been determined by the many chemical processes rather than considerations of aesthetic balance. Like contemporary gasworks or ironworks, chemical plants abandoned archi-

tectural pretensions as the increasingly intricate manufacturing processes demanded buildings of irregular or unusual shapes. The emphasis was placed on efficient, practical layouts and simple structures that could be enlarged or modified to suit scientific discoveries and changes in demand.

The soapworks at Port Sunlight, erected from 1888 for Lever Brothers, though a major project undertaken in consultation with the Warrington architect William Owen (d.1910),[139] did not produce a plant of outstanding architectural appearance. This, in part, resulted from William Lever's own philosophy of factory construction. Recalling the character of a neighbouring soapworks at Warrington (Joseph Crosfield & Sons) where his original plant had been located, he observed that:

> buildings [are] piled storey upon storey, departments interlace and overlap, some are badly lighted owing to the impossibility of getting daylight into them, and in the frame room they actually have to have an arrangement by which they can take up the flooring from certain sections as soon as the frames are emptied, in order to let light into the floor below.[140]

To avoid such disadvantages Lever, who had taken the trouble to purchase a spacious area of undeveloped land, insisted that his factory spread horizontally rather than upwards, thereby, he argued, reducing the risk of fire and the cost of handling goods, providing healthy conditions for the workers and giving better ventilation, better natural lighting and greater freedom from dirt and dust. Departments could be marshalled and arranged so as to give a more systematic handling of goods. Hence, the Port Sunlight factory buildings, occupying a substantial acreage, emerged as a series of low, long brick sheds (like so many modern-day light-industrial developments) where the possibilities for architectural embellishment were limited.

Whilst the office buildings – enlarged in 1893 by William Owen and his son, Segar (b.1874),[141] and in 1913–14 by J. Lomax-Simpson – exhibited a certain Edwardian elegance, attention has rightly concentrated on the picturesque model town that Lever built for his workers. In the tradition of New Lanark, Copley, Akroyden, Saltaire and Bournville, the settlement at Port Sunlight stood to the fore architecturally. The houses, generously spaced for gardens, exhibited a variety of styles and building materials. It had all begun in 1888 when William Owen had been instructed to prepare plans for 28 cottages and an entrance lodge.[142] He and his son alone were not, however, responsible for the entire estate, as in 1906-8 Bradshaw & Gass, the Bolton architects, designed 13 cottages for Port Sunlight.[143] Lord Leverhulme, born in that town, had started as a soapmaker not far from their offices in Silverwell Street and may have offered them the commission because of this geographical connection.[144]

The partnership of William and Segar Owen was to Warrington what Bradshaw Gass & Hope was to Bolton. In other words, it comprised a general practice with a strong local base, responsible for the town's Public Hall (1894), St Clement's Chapel (1887) and School of Art (1883-97). The Owens had also assembled a considerable industrial experience which won them contracts beyond the immediate neighbourhood, including the Mersey Chemical Works and Knowles Oxygen Co., both at Bromborough; Messrs Ogston & Tennant's Renfrew Works; and premises for the Cwymfelu Steel Co., Swansea.[145] A comparable example in Scotland was offered by the firm of John Gordon (1835-1912),[146] President of the Glasgow Institute of Architects. *Building News* observed of him in 1890 that in about 28 years:

> he has built a considerable portion of the warehouse and business properties of Glasgow and neighbourhood inclusive of mills, stores, factories, mansions, villas and other country houses. Among his works are ... Baltic Works, Grove Park Mills and Kingston Stores, Glasgow; Regent Mills, Partick; Lace Factory, Newmilns; and additions to the Wool Exchange, London.[147]

The need for new premises enabled George Cadbury (1839-1922), the chocolate manufacturer, to put into practice his belief that a healthy working environment would benefit both employees and the firm.[148] In June 1878, after an extensive search, he and his brother, Richard Cadbury (1835-99), purchased $14\frac{1}{2}$ acres of open country near the Bourn, four miles southwest of Birmingham.[149] Like Lever, George Cadbury was determined that the factory should be purpose-built, and actually drew the initial plans himself as a brief for the Birmingham architect, George H. Gadd, who in turn was assisted by Barrow Cadbury, Richard's eldest son, on vacation from Owen's College, Manchester.[150] The Cadburys, with the aid of a professional foreman, lent by Messrs Tangye, the engineers, supervised the construction, and George moved to a cottage at Lifford to monitor progress. The buildings were complete in the summer of 1879. The factory, a rectangular one-storey block 330 ft by 150 ft with no windows in the long southern elevation, was lit by north-facing roof lights adopted because the direct action of sunlight (as in a weaving shed) could be extremely troublesome for the manufacture of chocolate. Internally it was divided into store and packing rooms, a girls' warehouse, moulding, grinding, roasting and essence rooms.[151]

The rural situation of Bournville created transport problems for the workforce, many of whom travelled from the city centre. Progressive expansion made matters worse – by 1889 there were 1,193 employees and 2,689 in 1899.[152] To ease accommodation difficulties (though the scheme was never restricted to Cadbury workers), George Cadbury had purchased 120 acres of land by 1893 and within several years 200 houses had been erected.[153] All the properties, their layout, size and gardens, as well as the open spaces, were specified by George Cadbury, who in 1905 erected school buildings at a cost of £30,000. Nevertheless, the Bournville Village Trust, like Port Sunlight, remained an isolated example of a paternalistic owner's generosity and concern for the living conditions of his workforce.

The Arts and Crafts movement

Having much of its inspiration in Ruskin's writings, the Arts and Crafts movement, under the leadership of William Morris (1834-96),

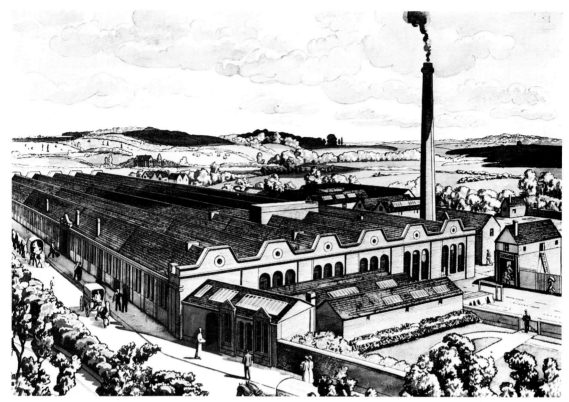

103 Cadburys new purpose-built chocolate factory at Bournville, completed in 1879.

reached a climax in the Edwardian period. In essence Morris and his followers had been attracted by Ruskin's advocacy of the skill of craftsmen as against mass production rendered possible by machinery. In *The Stones of Venice* Ruskin had suggested that buildings and their decorative elements should not only be man-made but should demonstrate such a quality:

> the great cry that rises from all our manufacturing cities, louder than the furnace blast ... this, – that we manufacture everything there except men; we blanch cotton, and strengthen steel, and refine sugar, and shape pottery; but to brighten, strengthen, to refine, or to form a single living spirit, never enters into our estimate of advantages.[154]

Whilst it may seem incongruous to discuss the Arts and Crafts movement in a study concerned with manufacturing industry, whose development Morris, Ruskin and Burne-Jones criticized,

and for which they had no great sympathy, it cannot be denied that some factories and warehouses were influenced by its principles. Morris and Philip Webb (1831-1915), its architectural leader, both argued that architects should forget any preconceived preferences for specific styles and work out each design with regard to the particular site and purpose of a building.[155] They believed that, if an architect possessed an awareness of the materials at his disposal and worked closely with his craftsmen and sculptors, the structures would grow organically and appropriately, as in medieval times.

An early member of the Art Workers' Guild and later William Lethaby's selection as Professor of Architecture at the Royal College of Art,[156] A. Beresford Pite (1861-1934) practised as a leading member of the Arts and Crafts movement. His warehouse (1904) at 21 Little Portland Street, London, illustrated some of its principles. These included the use of a variety of building materials: stocks enlivened by bands of grey-purple brick and moulded engineering bricks for the foundations and entrances, while the arches featured good-quality yellow bricks and Portland stone dressings. The simple but striking expression of window forms, careful internal arrangements and the selection of style to suit a building's purpose all characterized the Arts and Crafts architecture.

In a movement often seen as a rebellion against Gothicism, architects incorporated classical motifs into red-brick architecture, giving rise to the so-called 'Queen Anne' style. When Arthur H. Mackmurdo (1851–1942) was commissioned in 1900 to design a refrigerated warehouse in Smithfield for the Charterhouse Cold Storage Co.,[157] he fronted the four-storey building with a red-brick façade enlivened by white Roman Ionic pilasters and swags of fruit. Mackmurdo had, in fact, been a founder of the first Arts and Crafts' Century Guild.

Summary

For industrial buildings, in common with the architecture of the period, the Edwardian age existed as a turning point. It was time of transition, when the Gothic which had been so popular and widely applied was rejected in favour of a host of styles, including a return to classical models, and when the building materials of a century (wrought and cast iron together with bricks and timber) were gradually replaced by steel and reinforced concrete. Whilst individual factories and warehouses may be selected to illustrate the impact of rationalism, the search for a 'free style', or even the spread of the Arts and Crafts movement, some of Britain's most powerful industrial regions played continuity as their highest architectural card. In part, it was the nature of the game. For example, the projection of a new mill in a district where the construction of such buildings depended on the approval of a committee or board of directors was seldom likely to inspire an adventurous design. Furthermore, a small number of local architects, who had an intimate understanding of the technicalities of these specialized factories and had established a complex network of business contacts, could effectively monopolize the market. Yet such buildings did pioneer constructional techniques and cost-saving materials. The application of rolled-steel girders and the use of reinforced concrete were of particular importance. For the moment, however, they were introduced within an established context of building. Outer walls remained load bearing and the structural possibilities allowed by the steel frame were not so far exploited in Britain.

104 A refrigerated warehouse (1900) by Mackmurdo for the Charterhouse Cold Storage Co. at Smithfield.

Notes

1 *AR*, Vol. CXIV, No. 682, October 1953, W. Knight Sturges, 'Cast Iron in New York',

pp. 234, 236; Hitchcock, *Early Victorian Architecture*, *op. cit.*, p. 526; *AR*, Vol. CIX, February 1951, 'Early Cast-Iron Façades', pp. 113–14.

2 *MPICE*, Vol. II (1843), Fairbairn's description, pp. 125–6; *ibid.*, Vol. XXXIX (1874–5), Obituary, p. 259; Fairbairn, *Mills and Millwork*, *op. cit.*, Vol. II, p. 121; *Journal of the Society of Architectural Historians*, Vol. XV (1956), Turpin C. Bannister, 'Bogardus Revisited, Part One: The Iron Fronts', pp. 12–22; Vol. XVI (1957), 'Part Two', pp. 11–19; Herbert, *op. cit.*, p. 41.

3 *Journal of the Iron & Steel Institute*, part II (1882), Obituary, p. 633.

4 *Journal of the Iron & Steel Institute* (1875), President's Address, p. 34.

5 *B*, Vol. XLIII, No. 2068, 23 September 1882, p. 390.

6 *TNS*, Vol. XXXII (1959–60), A.W. Skempton, 'The Boat Store, Sheerness' (1858–60), pp. 57–66.

7 A.W. Skempton, *The Guild Engineer*, Vol. X (1959), 'The Evolution of the Steel Frame Building', p. 47.

8 Pevsner, *Building Types*, *op. cit*, p. 288; Hitchcock, *Nineteenth and Twentieth Centuries*, *op. cit.*, p. 385.

9 E.-E. Viollet-le-Duc, *Entretiens sur l'architecture*, Vol. II, Paris (1872), translated by B. Bucknall, London (1959), p. 329.

10 *PIME*, Vol. XXIX (1878) 'Excursion to Noisiel Works', p. 554.

11 N. Pevsner, *The Sources of Modern Design in Architecture*, London (1968), p. 38.

12 Henry J. Cowan, *Science and Building*, New York (1978), p. 26.

13 Hamilton, *op. cit.*, p. 479; Derry and Williams, *op. cit.*, p. 416.

14 William H. Birkmire, *The Planning and Construction of High Office-Buildings*, New York (1905), pp. 2, 7.

15 Atkins, *Guide across Manchester*, *op. cit.*, p. 45; Ashmore, *op. cit.*, p. 143.

16 Basil Scott, *Structural Engineer*, Vol. 7 (1929), p. 102; Derry and Williams, *op. cit.*, p. 416.

17 Albert C. Freeman (Editor), *The Architects' and Surveyors' Directory and Referendum*, London (1910), pp. 120B–120E; C.C. Knowles and P.H. Pitt, *The History of Building Regulation in London 1189–1972*, London (1972), p. 98; Charles Singer (*et al.*), *A History of Technology*, Vol. V, Oxford (1958), S.B. Hamilton, 'Building Materials and Techniques', p. 478.

18 *The British Architect*, Vol. 77, 5 January 1912, pp. 3, 29, 34.

19 *B*, Vol. CLXXXVII, No. 5814, 23 July 1954, p. 126.

20 *The British Architect*, *op. cit.*, p. 34.

21 P. Guedes, *Architecture & Technological Change*, London (1979), pp. 255–6.

22 Pevsner, *Building Types*, *op. cit.*, p. 278.

23 Hudson, *Building Materials*, *op. cit.*, p. 56; Derry and Williams, *op. cit.*, pp. 417–18.

24 Hilling, *Historic Architecture*, *op. cit.*, p. 144.

25 Hume, *Industrial Archaeology of Scotland Vol 2*, *op. cit.*, p. 203.

26 Winter, *Industrial Architecture*, *op. cit.*, p. 58.

27 Burrough, *Bristol*, *op. cit.*, pp. 69–70.

28 Gomme, *Bristol*, *op. cit.*, pp. 341–2; LivRO, *Goad's Plans of Bristol*, Vol. II, No. 24, May 1908.

29 Buchanan and Cossons, *op. cit.*, p. 64.

30 *Ibid.*

31 BCL, *Bristol Survey (Part One), 1959 Histories of Famous Firms*, 'William Cowlin & Son Ltd', pp. 24–5; *DBB*, 'Sir Francis Cowlin', pp. 809–11.

32 *B*, Vol. CXXIII, No. 4153, 8 September, 1922, pp. 348–9.

33 Service, *op. cit.*, p. 135.

34 Gomme and Walker, *Architecture of Glasgow*, *op. cit.*, p. 201; Service, *op. cit.*, p. 139.

35 *BN*, Vol. 70, 12 June 1896, p. 852.

36 *B*, Vol. CXVII, No. 3988, 11 July 1919, p. 36.

37 *The British Architect*, Vol. LV, Editorial summarizing the end of the nineteenth century, 4 January 1901, p. 1.

38 *AR*, Vol. XXI, No. 125, April 1907, Martin S. Briggs, 'Iron and Steel in Modern Design', pp. 224–6; Service, *op. cit.*, p. 130.

39 *Ibid.*, p. 226.

40 Frederick Chatterton (Editor), *Who's Who in Architecture*, London (1923), p. 225; Duncan Simpson, *C.F.A. Voysey, an architect of individuality*, London (1979), pp. 89–90; Service, *op. cit.*, pp. 129–30.

41 N. Pevsner, *BoE, Middlesex*, Harmondsworth (1951), p. 37.

42 *B*, Vol. LXXXI, No. 3049, 13 July 1901,

p. 34; Brockman, *op. cit.*, pp. 97–8; Service, *op. cit.*, pp. 108, 201.

43 *Ibid.*, pp. 34–5.

44 *Ibid.*

45 Frederick Chatterton (Editor), *Who's Who in Architecture*, London (1926), p. 78.

46 *The British Architect*, Vol. 71, 30 April 1909, pp. 308–9, 312; *B*, Vol. CLIII, No. 4946, 19 November 1937, Obituary, p. 917; Taylor, *Victorian City, op. cit.*, plate 335, ascribed the Station to E. Vincent Harris (1879–1971) of the LCC's architect's department.

47 *BN*, Vol. 83, 26 September 1902, p. 435; Brockman, *op. cit.*, pp. 104–5.

48 *Ibid.*, p. 435.

49 *Ibid.*

50 Hamilton, *op. cit.*, p. 482; E.O. Sachs (Editor), *Concrete Construction Engineering*, Vol. 1 (1906).

51 *TLCAS*, Vols. 73 and 74 for 1963–64, Manchester (1966), J.H.G. Archer, 'Edgar Wood: A Notable Manchester Architect', p. 160.

52 *Ibid.*, pp. 160–4, 165ff. Sellers may have designed part of Mutual Mills, Heywood, though No. 3 Mill (1914) was by Sidney Stott – *Partnership in Style, Edgar Wood & J.H. Sellers*, Manchester (1975), p. 88.

53 *B*, Vol. XCVI, No. 3448, 6 March 1909, p. 283.

54 RIBA Biography File, A.T. Bolton; *Who's Who in Architecture*, London (1914), p. 31.

55 *B*, Vol. CLXVIII, No. 5321, 26 January 1945, p. 79.

56 *B*, Vol. XCIX, No. 3521, 30 July 1910, p. 128.

57 *B*, Vol. CXLIII, No. 4674, 2 September 1932, Obituary, p. 350.

58 *B*, Vol. CLXVIII, No. 5332, 13 April 1945, Obituary, p. 287; Harry S. Fairhurst, ARIBA was in practice at 54 Church Street, Blackburn and at 21 Spring Gardens, Manchester. A number of his warehouse designs are deposited at the RIBA Drawings Department.

59 RIBA Drawings, RAN 10/K5[1] Foundation Plan, 1905; 5[4] Elevation to Whitworth Street.

60 *Ibid.*, 5[6] Section, 1905.

61 RIBA Drawings, RAN 10/K8[1] Foundation Plan, 1907; 8[8] Cross Section. 1907; 8[9] Elevation to Princess Street, 1907; 8[10] Elevation to Whitworth Street, 1907.

62 Atkins, *op. cit.*, p.100; *Who's Who in Architecture* (1914), p. 90.

63 RIBA Drawings, RAN 10/K/5[9] Back Elevation of India House, 1905.

64 See p. 205.

65 Atkins, *Manchester, op. cit.*, p. 29; the building was demolished in 1974.

66 *BN*, Vol. 75, 1 July 1898, p. 13; for further details of Heathcote, see p. 209.

67 Pevsner, *London Volume One, op. cit.*, p. 271.

68 D.A. Farnie, *The English Cotton Industry and the World Market 1815–1896*, Oxford (1979), p. 270.

69 Fred Jones, 'The Cotton Spinning Industry in the Oldham District from 1896 to 1914' (Manchester University MA(Econ.) thesis, 1959), pp. 6, 63.

70 Sidney Stott, *List of Works and Extensions to Works*, Oldham (*c.*1925).

71 *The Story of Horrockses*, Preston (1950), p. 27.

72 N. Cossons, *The BP Book of Industrial Archaeology*, Newton Abbot (1975), p. 267.

73 LRO, DDHs 56 Plans B100–104; B112, B174; B201–300 *passim*.

74 *Bolton Journal and Guardian*, Vol. XXXVI, No. 1847, 22 March 1907, p. 6.

75 *Ibid.*, Vol. XXXVII, No. 1899, 20 March 1908, p. 2.

76 Hudson, *Building Materials, op. cit.*, p. 85.

77 *The Mills and Organization of the Lancashire Cotton Corporation Limited 1929–1950*, Manchester (1951), p. 22.

78 *Bolton Journal and Guardian*, Vol. XXXIII, No. 1720, 14 October 1904, p. 8.

79 *Ibid.*, Vol. XXXI, No. 1624, 5 December 1902, p. 7.

80 *Ibid.*, Vol. XXXII, No. 1651, 12 June 1903, p. 5.

81 *Ibid.*, Vol. XXXIII, No. 1720, 14 October 1904, p. 8.

82 Jos R. Vose (Editor), *Bolton: Its Trade and Commerce*, Derby (1919), p. 136.

83 BA, ABID (213) Bolton County Borough Industrial Public Relations Dept., 3/26 Swan Lane No. 3 Mill.

84 *Sidney Stott, op. cit.; Mills of Oldham, op. cit.*, p. 22.

85 Bradley, *op. cit.*, pp. 34, 38; *TM*, Vol. XXI, 15 March 1895, Sington, *op. cit.*, pp. 86–8.

86 Joseph Nasmith, *Recent Cotton Mill Construction*, Manchester [*c*.1895], pp. 10–11.

87 See p. 156.

88 OLIC, George Stott's Contract Book (1903–1936), Manor Mill, 1906, pp. 15–16; Kent Mill (1908–09), p. 22; *Mills of Oldham*, *op. cit.*, pp. 20, 22; *Lancashire Cotton Corporation*, *op. cit.*, p. 25.

89 Contract Book, *op. cit.*, pp. 20–4; p. 23; pp. 17–8, 19, 25–6; p. 13.

90 *Lancashire Cotton Corporation*, *op. cit.*, p. 18.

91 *Pennine Mill Trail*, *op. cit.*, p. 26.

92 Pevsner, *South Lancashire*, *op. cit.*, p. 350; *Lancashire Cotton Corporation*, *op. cit.*, p. 24; *Mills of Oldham*, *op. cit.*, p. 20.

93 WRO, Acc. No. 2093 D/DY AL, 3/3 Alder Spinning Co., Leigh, Plan of land showing site of Mill, Stott & Sons, Manchester, 17 July 1905; Cross-section through Card Shed and Mill, July 1905.

94 *OC*, 10 July 1934, Obituary of Arthur Turner; Pevsner, *op. cit.*, p. 382; *Mills of Oldham*, *op. cit.*, pp. 16–7.

95 *OC*, 10 July 1934.

96 *Oldham Weekly Chronicle*, 7 March 1959, Obituary.

97 *TM*, Vol. XX, 15 October 1894, Sington, *op. cit.*, pp. 419–21.

98 *Ibid.*, Vol. XVII, 15 June 1892, 'Plan for a Continental Cotton Mill', T. Sington.

99 D.R.H. Williams, *Textile Factory Organization and Management*, Manchester (1934), pp. 1–3.

100 Bradshaw & Gass Certificate Register 'C' 1891–1909, pp. 1–2, 41–2.

101 *Ibid.*, pp. 276, 285.

102 Bradshaw Gass & Hope Certificate Register 'D' 1905–1920, pp. 105–7.

103 *Ibid.*, pp. 140, 141–2.

104 *Ibid.*, pp. 159–60.

105 *Ibid.*, pp. 163–6, 175–6, 201–2.

106 *Ibid.*, pp. 222–3, 243.

107 Certificate Register 'C', *op. cit.*, pp. 27–8, 71.

108 *Ibid.*, pp. 63–4.

109 *Ibid.*, pp. 57–8; Nasmiths, *Recent Cotton Mill Construction*, (1909), *op. cit.*, p. 163, fig. 83.

110 *Ibid.*, p. 164.

111 *Ibid.*, pp. 221, 271–2.

112 RIBA Biography File, A.J. Hope; *Bolton Journal*, 14 October 1955.

113 *B*, Vol. CII, No. 3613, 3 May 1912, J.J. Bradshaw's Obituary, p. 528.

114 RIBA Biography File, W. Scott.

115 RIBA Biography File, J.R. Adamson; *B*, Vol. CLXV, No. 5251, 24 September 1943, Obituary, p. 246.

116 Certificate Register 'D', *op. cit.*, pp. 269–70; Bradshaw Gass & Hope Certificate Register 'E' 1921–31, pp. 111–12, 123–4, 175–6.

117 *The Empire Mail*, June 1927, pp. 493–4; *The Book of Bolton* (1929), p. 16.

118 *TM*, Vol. XVII, 15 May 1891, John R. Freeman, 'Comparison of English and American Types of Factory Construction', p. 229.

119 'The Standard Mode of Measurement, May 1887' (typescript reproduced by permission of the Bolton Master Builders' Association, and supplied by Mr Frank Smith, partner, Bradshaw Gass & Hope).

120 *Ibid.*

121 Certificate Register 'A', *op. cit.*, p. 30.

122 Certificate Register 'B', *op. cit.*, pp. 35–6.

123 Certificate Register 'C', *op. cit.*, pp. 141–2, 151–2, 163–4, 165–6, 175–6, 201–2.

124 Certificate Register 'E', *op. cit.*, pp. 111–12.

125 OLIC, Glasgow Spinning Co., various plans dated 1883–4, 1885 and 1888, signed Joseph Stott, Architect, 26 Clegg Street, Oldham.

126 Information provided by Dunlop Rubber Co., General Properties Department.

127 *Bolton Journal and Guardian*, Vol. XXXVI, No. 1863, 12 July 1907, p. 2.

128 Robert W. Howard, 'Philip Sidney Stott', *op. cit.*, p. 1.

129 Stott, *List of Works*, *op. cit.*, *passim*.

130 Nasmith, *op. cit.*, pp. 122–4.

131 W.J. Reader, *Imperial Chemical Industries, A History*, Vol. 1, *The Forerunners*, Oxford (1970), p. 8, plate 18.

132 Bancroft, *op. cit.*, p. 37; *B*, Vol. XXI, No. 1561, 4 January 1873, Obituary, W.J.M. Rankine, p. 6.

133 *B*, Vol. LXXVIII, No. 2991, 2 June 1900, Obituary, p. 548.

134 Gomme, *Bristol, op. cit.*, pp. 361–2.

135 BCL, *Work in Bristol, op. cit.*, p. 24.

136 W.T. Pike, *Bristol in 1898–99: Contemporary Biographies*, Vol. 2, Brighton (1899), p. 285.

137 Reader, *op. cit.*, plate 25.

138 John I. Watts, *The First Fifty Years of Brunner, Mond & Co. 1873–1923*, Winnington, Northwich (1923), pp. 26–7.

139 Charles Wilson, *The History of Unilever*, Vol. 1, London (1954), p. 34; *B*, Vol. XCVIII, No. 3508, 30 April 1910, Obituary, p. 500.

140 Wilson, *op. cit.*, p. 36.

141 *Who's Who in Architecture* (1914), p. 169.

142 Wilson, *op. cit.*, p. 36.

143 Bradshaw & Gass Certificate Register 'D' 1905–1910, p. 19.

144 Nigel Nicolson, *Lord of the Isles*, London (1960), pp. 4, 10, plate 2.

145 *Who's Who in Architecture*, London (1914), p. 169; *B*, No. 3508, *op. cit.*, p. 500.

146 The Mitchell Library, Glasgow, Biography Queries Index.

147 *BN*, Vol. LVIII, 7 February 1890, p. 221; RIBA Biography File, John Gordon.

148 *DBB*, Vol. 1, London (1984), Basil G. Murray, 'George Cadbury', pp. 549, 551.

149 I.A. Williams, *The Firm of Cadbury 1831–1931*, London (1931), pp. 54–5; T.B. Rogers, *A Century of Progress 1831–1931*, Cadbury Brothers (1931), pp. 37–8.

150 Williams, *op. cit.*, pp. 56, 73.

151 *Ibid.*, pp. 60, 64.

152 Rogers, *op.cit.*, p. 40.

153 *Cadbury Brothers Ltd, Sixty Years of Planning: The Bournville Experiment*, pp. 10–11.

154 John Ruskin, *The Stones of Venice*, Vol. II, London (1853), 'The Nature of Gothic', p.165.

155 Service, *op. cit.*, pp. 12–13.

156 *Ibid.*, p. 206.

157 *Ibid.*, p. 204.

NINE

The dawn of the modern movement

It has been repeatedly demonstrated for a variety of industries – steel, chemicals, optics and precision engineering among them – how both Germany and America stole the manufacturing initiative from Britain towards the end of the nineteenth century and pushed home their advantage in the inter-war years; so too events occurred in industrial building. Arguably the most innovative factories, executed in the early years of the twentieth century, were by German and American architects. The work of Peter Behrens and that of Walter Gropius revealed that a gap had opened between the Continent and the UK in the field of modern industrial architecture, while Albert Kahn's car factories for Packard, Chevrolet and Ford reiterated the position on the other side of the Atlantic. But to admit that the leading edge of technical advance lay overseas is not to say that Britain failed to generate any exciting modern buildings. Indeed, this chapter argues that, as before, industrial structures were sometimes the proving grounds for new ideas in architecture and constructional engineering.

Prime movers

Among those who advanced the cause of expressionist architecture was Peter Behrens (1868–1940), the German architect, foremost among the founders of the modern movement. For in 1907 he, as an imaginative but middle-aged painter and designer, had been summoned to Berlin by the Allgemeine Elektricitäts-Gesellschaft (or AEG, the German General Electric Company) to serve as their 'artistic advisor' to improve the appearance of their arc lamps and electrical accessories.[1] With the commercial success of his lamps (and later kettles, coffee pots, fans, clocks and radiators), he began to design pavilions and display stands for AEG's products, an activity that drew him, as an unqualified architect, into the world of factories and workshops. One of his best-known and earliest works was the turbine factory (1909) in Moabit, an industrial suburb of the capital.[2] It comprised a voluminous steel-framed hall (initially 402 ft long and 82 ft wide) required to bear the weight of powerful travelling cranes with smaller swivelling cranes along the side walls. Very large turbine engines could thus be constructed and moved about the building until they were finished. It was in essence a steel structure (composed of 22 great girder frames) filled with glass. Yet the tapered concrete corners (non-load-bearing and divided horizontally by steel bands) which appeared to support the gable to the barrel vaulted roof imparted a monumental massiveness not exactly in keeping with Behrens' intentions.[3] This gable, in outline like a single rivet or bolt, contained the only decoration: AEG's badge above the incised lettering 'Turbeninfabrik'.[4] By making use of modern construction techniques and the bold handling of simple elements in steel, glass and concrete, Behrens created a building of profound force and influence.

His subsequent AEG designs – for the High Tension Factory in the Humboldthain[5] and the Small Motors Factory in the Voltastrasse, both in 1910 – though larger, did not achieve the same impact. The former, a double-naved hall

105 A.E.G.'s turbine factory (1909), Moabit; a
seminal industrial building of sublime impact.

surrounded on three sides by a six-storey building accentuated by a pair of towers housing the
lifts and a clever arrangement of window forms,
and the Large Machine Assembly Hall (1911–
12) both exhibited the hallmarks of his style:
modern materials directly expressed, being
governed by structure and operation.

This interpretation was continued in industrial architecture by one of Behrens' pupils, Walter Gropius (1883–1969), who on leaving the
former's office joined forces with Adolf Meyer
(1881–1929) to design a workshop at Alfeld-an-
der-Leine for making shoe-lasts.[6] The Fagus
Factory (1911–13) revealed Behrens' influence
in the direct use of modern materials. The Cubic

three-storey concrete framework was surrounded
by walls of steel-framed glass panels (forming
the corners as well as the sides of the building),
supported by narrow brick piers deprived of all
ornament to create an impression of 'transparent
volume'.[7] Whereas the large windows of Behrens' Turbine Factory had been tied between
pylons of massive masonry, Gropius and Meyer,
by setting back the supporting columns and can-
tilevering the floors, all but created a curtain
wall hanging in front of the structural core.

In this way, therefore, a tradition of expressionist architecture had been able to develop in
Germany before the First World War by virtue
of the generosity and open-mindedness of industrial patrons. Through the work of the Bauhaus
and Le Corbusier, it was to gain adherents during the inter-war period. Their work, together
with that of Behrens and Gropius, was to inspire

a generation of modern architects not only in Germany but in Britain, and also the United States, where a similar expressionist school was already well established.

British developments: towards expressionism

It was really not until the late 1920s that expressionism was accepted in Britain and started to influence the design of new factories and warehouses. Among its leading exponents was Sir E. Owen Williams (1890–1969), the civil engineer and architect, responsible for the Empire Swimming Pool, Wembley (1934); Daily Express buildings (1932–9); and the Pioneer Health Centre, Peckham (1934).[8] Trained as an engineer and employed from 1912 by the Trussed Concrete Steel Co., his first independent job was a gramophone factory at Hayes, whilst the First

World War saw him engaged on the production of concrete lighters and tugs at the Admiralty's auxiliary shipyard in Poole.[9] In 1919 Williams set up his own practice and in that year was commissioned by T. Wall & Sons to execute a meat factory in Friary Road, Acton, which was subsequently converted for the production of ice cream.[10] Various other industrial projects followed (in 1920 for a tannery at Runcorn and an ice-making plant in Hull during the following year) his reputation being established as the principal engineer to the British Empire Exhibition, Wembley, in 1922–4, for which he received a knighthood. In 1927 Williams had been awarded the Telford Gold Medal by the Institution of Civil Engineers for a treatise entitled 'The Philosophy of Masonry Arches'. His best work which set him apart from his contemporaries, followed in the 1930s when having designed the first ramped garage, the Cumberland Car Park, in 1930, he started work on a major undertaking, to create a new plant for Boots, the pharmaceutical manufacturers, at Beeston, Nottingham.[11] The architecture of the first factory (1930–2), for wet processes, principally

106 An aerial view of T. Wall & Son's ice-cream factory, Acton, by Sir Owen Williams, photographed in the 1930s.

107 Boots' factory for wet processes (1930–2)
showing the cantilevered southern elevation with its
covered loading bays.

relied on the characteristics of its reinforced-
concrete structure: concrete mushroom columns
carried four storeys of galleries around a packing
hall, the whole being encased in a glass curtain
wall, while the south front was cantilevered over
the loading dock.[12] Generous steel-framed windows provided natural illumination and the concrete roof was pierced with circular glass lights.[13]
In the rejection of ornament and reliance upon
function and structure to dictate appearance,
this factory followed in the manner devised by
Behrens and developed by Gropius. Williams'
second factory (1937–8), for dry processes,
though less acclaimed, also had a reinforced-
concrete framework. The novelty in Britain, at
least, of this form of architecture was acknowledged in *The Architects' Journal* which in 1932
remarked:

> Sir Owen Williams has discovered a new species of
> factory design. More than this, he has produced,

with his engineering knowledge and experience, a
factory totally new, both in planning and construction: a factory which is bound to influence the design of all similar structures for many moons. It
may be said generally to be erected in two
materials: glass for all walls and roofs and reinforced concrete for the floors and staircases. The
sanity with which these two materials are used and
the simplicity, even nakedness, of the design, immediately arrest and overawe attention by their
dramatic effects.[14]

By temperament Williams was regarded as a
'loner; self-taught, subject to no influences,
member of no group; what he couldn't do himself with a small staff couldn't get done'.[15] As a
master of the practicalities of reinforced concrete, he transcended the role of engineer and
produced a number of buildings that stood to
the fore in inter-war architecture.

Less original was Williams' warehouse for
Sainsbury's at Blackfriars, executed in 1934–5.[16]
The unadorned, trabeated five-storey structure
of reinforced concrete (flat slab-construction
techniques being employed for the first time in
the LCC area) was filled with simple steel-
framed areas of glass in a more conventional

fashion. In the expressionist use of these materials it was, however, in tune with his work at Beeston. Better were his printing offices for the Daily Express, including those in Great Ancoats Street, Manchester (1936–9), where the internal framework supported curtain walls of tinted glass so as to reveal the machinery at work when illuminated during hours of darkness.

Thus by 1934 Reginald Blomfield (1856–1942) could observe of British architecture that:

> since the war, Modernism, or *Modernismus*, as it should be called on the German precedent, has invaded this country like an epidemic and though there are signs of reaction, its attack is insidious and far-reaching.[17]

More favourable, nevertheless, was the young architect Wells Coates (1895–1958), who argued that:

> the new architectural currency is being designed in two materials: first, human needs, and the necessity for a new dimension of Plan and Order in the arrangement and aspect of life; second, the new resources of technology, a multitude of details, processes and conditions of great complexity.[18]

Among the truly novel industrial buildings of the inter-war period was the integrated car factory, and here, too, the world's leaders were not British but lay in America. Outstanding in the field was Albert Kahn (1869–1942), who had spent his early life and training in Detroit where he had started by designing factories before being drawn inevitably into the motorcar industry.[19] With his brother, Julius, in 1905, he produced Packard Plant Number 10, whose two storeys (later enlarged to four) comprised a reinforced concrete framework, executed by the Trussed Concrete Steel Co.[20] In the use of such materials (this was the first automobile plant to be built of reinforced concrete), the creation of open areas of space and the provision of generous windows, it was innovative, though its exterior could scarcely be described as eye-catching. Further industrial commissions followed, including Highland Park (1909–10) for the Ford Motor Co., another concrete-framed structure but finished with greater aplomb and incorporating a powered, moving assembly line.[21] In

1916 Kahn was asked to design what was to become a mammoth car factory, the Ford Rouge Plant, near Detroit. Its expressionist appearance was critically determined by the advanced methods of production introduced by Ford. The assembly line was not particularly suited to a multi-storey building but could be more efficiently operated through a series of single-storey units. This fact encouraged Kahn to use steel rather than reinforced concrete for their structural framework. The Eagle Plant (1917), the first factory in the Ford Rouge site, was an austere shed, lit by vast areas of glass, and its contribution has been summarized as follows:

> it enclosed an immense and complex manufacturing operation within a simple, direct, and economical plan of configuration; it marked a major manufacturer's commitment to one-storey construction; it was therefore framed in steel, marking the turning of industrial architecture toward light, steel-framed, thinly clad enclosures; and finally, as a result of its steel structure, it was built with remarkable speed.[22]

Other factories, a steelworks, and rolling mills followed during the 1920 and 1930s – vertical integration pushed to the limit – so that Fords could produce almost everything that the assembly of their automobiles demanded. Kahn's car factories, not only in their architecture but also in their successful incorporation of a host of productive processes, served as examples for the larger industrial companies of western Europe.

In Britain the first car plants had tended to be built, or extended, in an *ad hoc* fashion as markets dictated. Many companies having their origins in bicycle or motorbike businesses started in small workshops or buildings designed for other purposes. The Daimler Works at Coventry, for example, had been set up in a converted mill in 1896.[23] Herbert Austin's move to Longbridge in 1905 was not to a purpose-built plant but to a derelict printing works. Railway communications, ample space for expansion and an unpolluted atmosphere (for quality paint and varnish finishes) were factors that conditioned his choice of location.[24] More advanced was the Argyll Co.'s new factory at Alexandria-by-

108 Ladbroke Hall (1903), the imposing street façade of the Clément Talbot Automobile Works, the *porte cochère* covering visitors arriving at the main offices.

Glasgow, opened in 1906, though the formal classical entrance and offices which fronted the workshops (executed, as their 1907 catalogue stated, as an advertisement) suggested a lack of flexibility. The plant, which never achieved its full capacity, was immensely costly and this contributed to the firm's bankruptcy in 1914.[25] Ladbroke Hall (1903), Barlby Road, the Clément Talbot Automobile Works, designed by William T. M. Walker (1856–1930),[26] a London architect[27] who had trained with George Sherrin, possessed a similar plan. The assembly shops were fronted by an impressive classical block, which in appearance could have passed for the owner's mansion, being entered through a *porte cochère* – apparently an afterthought.[28] The company's arms (their trademark) in a scroll pediment capped the entrance. Costing about £35,000,[29] the building that contained the offices also housed a large engine room which generated electricity for the plant. The latter offered an early example of the warren roof for a large space uninterrupted by columns, while the use of reinforced concrete for its construction was still novel for London – the silos that Walker designed for Spillers in Bermondsey were another early use of this material. His practice, though embracing houses, consisted mostly of industrial and business premises, including the Lamson Paragon Works, Canning Town; a factory and offices for Ilford at Warley, Essex; the Trafalgar Works, Merton Abbey; and the Imperial Works, Mitcham.[30]

When discussing the construction of the first Rolls-Royce works in Derby, Henry Royce wrote in 1907 that:

> it would be quite unnecessary to employ an architect to prepare drawings, or to supervise the erection of buildings, as Messrs Handyside are engaged, and have for some years been engaged in erecting buildings of a similar nature.[31]

He was here referring to the firm of ironfounders and structural engineers established by Andrew Handyside (1806–87), which had established a reputation for the production of bridges, roofs and prefabricated buildings. But because of the reluctance exhibited in the late nineteenth century to explore the possibilities offered by metal structures, much of their work – such as the 125-ft-span roof to the Agricultural Hall, Islington (1861–2) by the architect H.E. Coe (1825/6–85) – passed comparatively unnoticed.[32] Although responsible for the structural calculations and the design of the ironwork, they remained subordinate to the architect who had commissioned them.

An exception to this pattern of largely traditional architecture was W. Parks' motorworks, completed at Glasgow in 1914 by the local architect, Richard Henderson. Significantly the whole structure, including the external walls, had been executed by the Trussed Concrete Steel Co. on the Kahn system.[33] External ornament was eschewed and the three-storey building lit by simple steel rectangular windows, though a little decoration had been applied to the cornice, corner pilasters and the main entrance. The resort to reinforced-concrete beams, columns and walls meant, suggested *The Builder*,

'that the cost was far less than would have been the case if steel-framed construction and brick walls had been adopted'.[34]

The first integrated car factory in Britain of substantial size and based upon the various manufacturing processes was significantly that of an American enterprise, the Ford Motor Co. Their Dagenham plant, a huge complex incorporating blast furnaces, was designed by Charles Heathcote & Sons and erected by the contractors Redpath, Brown & Co. The commission had been awarded to the former because Charles H. Heathcote (1850–1938), a Manchester architect with a considerable experience of industrial work,[35] had previously been employed by Ford at Trafford Park.[36] About half the factories in that district were by his firm (which had also designed the National Radiator Co.'s plant at Hull, together with factories for Metropolitan-Vickers Electrical Co. and Carborundum Co.). During the First World War he had been appointed by the Ministry of Munitions to build a number of large warehouses throughout South Lancashire for the storage of war material and foodstuffs. This was an area in which Heathcote possessed specialist knowledge, for by 1899 he had built 15 warehouses for the Manchester Ship Canal, together with others for the Liverpool Warehousing Co. and refrigerated stores for the Colonial Co., also in Manchester.[37] Having entered semi-retirement after such a prolific career, in 1928, at the request of Ford,

109 Ford's car works at Dagenham under construction in October 1930.

he returned to practice with his two sons – Ernest G. Heathcote (1877–1947)[38] and Edgar H. Heathcote (1882–1972)[39] – to design their new Dagenham factory, and the offices and showrooms in Regent Street. While the latter exhibited a grand neo-classical façade in Portland stone,[40] the car works offered no concessions to historic styles. The enormous assembly sheds were constructed of a steel framework for lightness and uninterrupted floor space so that the various manufacturing processes could follow one another in a smooth logical order. The advances pioneered in Britain at Dagenham, Beeston and elsewhere could be characterized by Edward Mills' description of 1959:

> The subordination of a factory scheme to the layout of vital and intricate plant and machinery and to production sequence is clearly acknowledged; but the attention has been increasingly focused on the welfare of the occupants, on the amenities of the site and its surroundings and on the necessity for comprehensive treatment and a master plan for orderly development.[41]

This had not been the first factory of this character that Heathcote had helped to design,[42] for he assisted in the planning and construction of the British Westinghouse Electric & Manufacturing Co.'s works (1900–2) at Trafford Park, though the conception and its execution was primarily in the hands of Americans. Unlike so many English engineering enterprises, which had modest beginnings and grew by virtue of extensions, this works was conceived on a colossal scale from the outset, using experience gained in the United States.[43] Having selected a green-field site, George Westinghouse (1846–1914) called in the designer of his Pittsburg Works. Initially a Manchester contractor was engaged to lay the foundations and a London builder to erect the steelwork, but both believed that it would take five years to bring the plant to operation. Against an accumulation of orders, Westinghouse approached James C. Stewart, a Canadian-born contractor with a record of rapid work in the United States. Stewart estimated that he could reduce the five years to fifteen months and in January 1901 sailed for Manchester. Having brought with him a team of assistants, he dramatically expanded the workforce, which rose from less than 250 when he arrived to 4,000. Tracks were laid to all parts of the site to speed the delivery of materials, and riveters were provided with automatic tools, thereby quadrupling their output.[44] Steam hoists replaced human hod carriers and bricklayers were shown how to lay 1,500–2,000 bricks daily instead of their customary 4–500. Within ten months, eight of the ten buildings were in use.

The huge sheds which covered the main manufacturing processes each had a steel structure incorporating travelling cranes. The brick side walls and gabled ends were infilled with brick pierced with large timber-framed windows. The largest was the machine shop (900 ft by 440 ft) which was divided into five aisles, the outside and central ones having galleries to make a second floor. The two main aisles had a span of 90 ft and rose 80 ft to the ridge of the

110 The Trafford Park works of the British Westinghouse Electric Manufacturing Co. nearing completion in 1901. The three sheds from left to right are: the iron foundry, the brass and malleable iron foundry, and the forge and steel foundry; the large block in the distance is the machine shop.

111 Battersea Power Station as finally completed in 1955; when opened in 1934 it had just two chimneys.

roof to provide space for the manufacture of the biggest electrical equipment such as generators, gas engines and tramcars. 'The whole works', it was observed in 1902, 'are arranged on the most logical method of progression, for the raw materials from their arrival are passed gradually forward from process to process until they leave the machine shop in their finished state.'[45] Parallel to the machine shop were four smaller sheds which comprised the various foundries, forges, pattern shops and stores. The six-storey offices, which fronted the works and faced West-inghouse Road, were a virtual replica of those in Pittsburg. Heathcote, the architect, could not therefore have played a leading role in the development, though they did provide him with an enduring precedent – one that he drew upon at Dagenham.

Externally, with the exception of the gabled offices, there was no attempt at architectural ornament. The steel frame of the sheds had simply been surrounded by plain walls of brick. However, the ironwork of the water tower (210 ft), to provide pressure for the hydraulic lifts and sprinklers, was crowned with a copper-covered dome surmounted by a hand grasping forked lightning. Like a smaller version of Blackpool tower, it stood as a local landmark. The works when fully equipped cost well over £1,250,000, and existed as an example of bold factory planning.

Battersea Power Station, with its massive blocks of brick and column-like chimneys was influenced by the expressionist movement. The first half had been built in 1929–34 by S.L. Pearce, the engineer, and James T. Halliday (1882–1932) of the Manchester partnership of architects, Halliday and Agate,[46] in conjunction with Sir Giles Gilbert Scott (1880–1960),[47] the remainder being completed in 1955.[48] Ornament was reduced to a bare minimum, and as at Bankside Power Station, also by Scott, a monumental effect was achieved by the confident massing of large areas of brick accentuated by pilasters and simple indentations.[49]

112 The Thames elevation to Hays Wharf (1928–32), Tooley Street, Southwark.

Difficult to categorize but falling within the realm of the Continental modern style, Hays Wharf, an office and store on the Thames, completed between 1928 and 1932, was an individual design with original elevations to Tooley Street and the river.[50] The clever fenestration, arranged to catch as much light as possible, was permitted by the use of a steel frame. H.S. Goodhart-Rendel (1887–1959), the architect, expressed the windows of the directors' board and common rooms prominently within a black granite frame ornamented by panels of gilded faience.[51] The panels, which represented the various activities taking place at the wharf, had been modelled by the sculptor Frank Dobson (1886–1963).

Reference has already been made to a number of industrial buildings erected during the inter-war years whose allegiance to established styles made it appropriate to include them within earlier periods. Fort Dunlop New Store, Sir John Holden's Mill in Bolton and Elk Mill in Royton, all completed in the 1920s, fell in this category. Not for them, or many other lesser works of architecture, the appeal of expressionism, as their designers or patrons held to traditional interpretations. In fact, Britain never wholeheartedly entered the modern movement in the twenties and thirties, the impetus for change in industry, as in other areas of building, remaining principally in Germany and America.

Art Deco industry

While not exhibiting the expressionist features of

Williams' factory for Boots at Beeston, a number of Art Deco industrial buildings were erected along the main arterial roads leaving London where they could serve the extra purpose of advertisements for their companies. With their sleek lines, smart gardens, and imaginative entrances (not so dissimilar to those facing contemporary cinemas), they formed a procession of light-industrial showpieces.[52] Among the finest were the Firestone Factory (1928) and the Hoover Factory (1931–5) both by Wallis, Gilbert & Partners. The practice had been founded by Thomas Wallis (1872–1953),[53] who in 1914 was approached by Kahncrete, the American engineering company that specialized in reinforced-concrete structures for industry and had developed its interests in the UK through a subsidiary, the Trussed Concrete Steel Co.[54] Wallis was to have worked with Kahncrete in partnership with an American architect, Gilbert, and set up a firm styled Wallis, Gilbert & Partners – the latter being Frank Cox and, later, Wallis' son, Douglas. The name was retained despite the fact that Gilbert never came to Britain to join the practice.

Adopting a monumental style, leavened by neo-classical detailing, the firm proceeded to undertake a series of industrial and commercial commissions which included that for the bus and lorry manufacturers Tilling-Stevens, at Maidstone (1917); the Caribonum Co.'s offices (1918); Napier & Son's motorworks, Acton (1920) and the Albion carworks, Glasgow (1927);[55] together with H.G. Saunders' tube-factory, Southall; the Commer Cars' new motorworks at Luton; and a cocoa factory for Nestlés at Hayes. Using reinforced concrete for the monumental staircase tower and 450-ft extension to the Witton Engineering Works (1920), near Birmingham, Wallis also adopted simplified classical elements for the street entrance.[56] Having thus established his architectural credentials, in 1926 Wallis designed, in just four days, the Wrigley factory, Wembley, his first commission for an American company. It was one of the buildings in Britain to rely on a structure of reinforced-concrete mushroom columns (predating Williams' Beeston plant) to support the

curtain walling.[57] Adjacent to the LMS main line, it was observed daily by thousands of commuters and travellers destined for Euston.

It was, however, in the Art Deco style that Wallis' best-known commissions were executed. The Brentford factory for the Firestone Tyre & Rubber Co. established a formula that he was to exploit successfully elsewhere on the Great West Road, and for Hoover on Western Avenue. Long office blocks, punctuated by massive pseudo-Egyptian columns, adorned with coloured tiles and entered through splendid doorways, fronted the factory sheds behind. The Firestone example was all the more remarkable when it is considered that the works had been designed in twenty-one days and a mere eighteen weeks had elapsed between the start of construction and the manufacture of the first tyre.[58] The two-storey administration building and the four-storey warehouse were of reinforced concrete (the general contractors being Sir Robert McAlpine & Sons and the reinforced steel supplied by the Trussed Concrete Steel Co., while the single-storey factory situated between them was steel framed.[59] The layout, arranged to accommodate the flow of mass-production processes, the growing emphasis on the workforce's welfare and the building's dramatic appearance led *The Architect* to comment that:

both in design and planning, British factories are noticeably improving. In design the improvement is due to the increasing realization that nothing made for human use is unworthy of the attention of the designer; and in planning to the pressure of competition necessitating efficiency both in lay-out and in detail.[60]

Whilst these points contained much truth, the fact could not be ignored that Wallis responded to a certain hierarchy of decorum. For the greatest architectural thought and finest detailing had been almost exclusively concentrated upon the office buildings which concealed the plant behind. The factory and warehouse possessed a stark simplicity that contrasted sharply with the glamorous administrative façades which served as architectural billboards to passing motorists. In this respect both the Firestone and Hoover buildings, like the Tilling-Stevens Works, offered comparison with the Wrigley factory or the East Surrey Waterworks pump house (1925) at Purley where no such distinction had been made.

The Hoover Factory, opened in 1932,[61] advanced the Firestone composition further by the addition of two futuristic staircase towers. The Egyptian columns, false pediment and ornate entrance were all present but more vigorously interpreted. In 1935, to raise the plant's manufacturing capacity, a four-storey extension was added by the architects. This steel-framed building (rendered in white cement) was designed to 'provide clear floor space for machinery, any necessary planning being carried out by means of movable glazed steel partitioning'.[62] The canteen, erected in 1938, featured generous areas of externally hung glass, some of the windows curving around to form the striking entrance.

Another showpiece of light industry, the Gillette Factory (1936), on the Great West Road, by Sir Banister Fletcher (1866-1953)[63] could be discerned from a distance by its lofty clock tower of Bedford grey brick.[64] The three-storey block below (containing the offices, dining and recreation rooms), with its central entrance and columns of metal-framed windows, had a more conventional appearance. Referring to the nearby Coty Factory (1933), by Wallis, Gilbert & Partners, and the Berlei Factory (1937) at Slough by Sir John Brown & Henson, Martin Briggs concluded:

> whether you like them or not, the new factories built on the north and west of London ... during the last few years are cheerful and bright ... Manufacture goes on in spacious sheds behind with roof lighting ... Modern construction in reinforced concrete has permitted an enormous increase in the window area of multi-storey factories ... and trusses

113 On the Western Avenue, the entrance to the Hoover factory (1931–2), a showpiece for the new motoring public.

114 (*opposite*) Thomas Wallis's factory for Coty (1933) on the Great West Road at Heston.

formed of steel lattice-work allow roofs with huge unsupported spans ... Canteen and rest rooms are normal adjuncts of every large modern factory, and usually playing fields are provided. Whatever the product, the buildings are always planned to allow an orderly sequence from the reception of raw materials at one end through the various processes of manufacture, to the final stage where packing and storage precedes loading for despatch.[65]

The tower recurred as a feature of Art Deco architecture, not least when Albert W. Moore (1876-1953)[66] was commissioned in 1928 by Oxo Ltd to remodel their River Plate Wharf on the Thames at Blackfriars.[67] He designed a 202 ft tower of reinforced concrete (supplied by the Trussed Concrete Steel Co.), in profile like a skyscraper, whose windows were arranged vertically to form the word 'OXO' and could be illuminated at night, unashamedly serving as an advertisement. Topped by a simplified pineapple finial, it drew much contemporary comment. Art Deco generally did not find adherents in heavy industry or in the traditional manufacturing districts, but was favoured in the south-east, where new businesses flourished and buildings were overtly used to publicize products.

Summary

The thirties, though not witnessing the wholesale import of expressionistic principles into British industrial architecture, did exhibit the widespread adoption of reinforced-concrete and steel construction methods. These, in turn, affected the outward form of many factories and warehouses. Greater thought was given to the arrangement of plant, both to facilitate manufacturing processes and to meet the social, educational and health needs of the workforce. Economic growth in the period – concentrated in motor vehicles, chemicals and electricity – also made for change by providing factory commissions, often in areas such as the Midlands and South-east where the traditional industries had no established hold. Estates of light, modern factories (showpieces in themselves) were erected in the suburbs of London and in such towns as Coventry, Leicester and Birmingham, creating

opportunities for firms such as Wallis, Gilbert & Partners to erect exciting and innovative designs. Depression and decline evident in textiles, steel and shipbuilding meant that few comparable developments took place in Lancashire, the North-east, Scotland and Wales.

Notes

1 Alan Windsor, *Peter Behrens, Architect and Designer*, London (1981), pp. 77-105.
2 Gustav Adolf Platz, *Die Baukunst der Neuesten Zeit*, Berlin (1927), pp. 547-8; Gerd Hatje (Editor), *Encyclopaedia of Modern Architecture*, London (1963), p. 48; Hitchcock, *Nineteenth and Twentieth Centuries, op. cit.*, pp. 454, 458-9; N. Pevsner, *The Sources of Modern Architecture and Design*, London (1968), p. 147.
3 Windsor, *op. cit.*, pp. 87-91.
4 Walter Müller-Wulckow, *Bauten der Arbeit und des Verkehrs*, Königstein (1925), p. 24; Platz, *op. cit.*, p. 262.
5 *Ibid.*, p. 27; Platz, *op. cit.*, p. 260; Windsor, *op. cit.*, pp. 94-9.
6 *Ibid.*, p. 21; Platz, *op. cit.*, pp. 556-7, 302-3; Hitchcock, *op. cit.*, p. 491; Pevsner, *Sources, op. cit.*, p. 176.
7 Hitchcock, *op. cit.*
8 *B*, Vol. CCXVI, No. 6576, 30 May 1969, Obituary, p. 61; *Who was Who 1961-1970*, Vol. VI, London (1972), p. 1206.
9 *MPICE*, Vol. 44, Sept.-Dec. 1969, Obituary, p. 303.
10 Information from Birds Eye Walls, Ltd.
11 RIBA Biography File, Sir Owen Williams.
12 J.M. Richards, *An Introduction to Modern Architecture*, Harmondsworth (1940), p. 130; Pevsner, *BoE, Nottinghamshire, op. cit.*, p. 70; Brockman, *op. cit.*, pp. 168-9.
13 McGrath and Frost, *op. cit.*, p. 164.
14 *The Architects' Journal*, Vol. 76, 3 August 1932, p. 673.
15 *The Architects' Journal*, Vol. 149, 4 June 1969, Obituary, p. 1490.
16 *The Architects' Journal*, Vol. 81, 10 January 1935, pp. 49-53; Brockman, *op. cit.*, pp. 153, 155.

17 R. Blomfield, *Modernismus*, London (1934), pp. v–vi.

18 *The Listener*, Vol. X, No. 237, 26 July 1933, Wells Coates, 'Is Modern Architecture on the Right Track?', p. 132.

19 Grant Hildebrand, *Designing for Industry, The The Architecture of Albert Kahn*, MIT (1974), pp. 6–8.

20 *Ibid.*, pp. 28–31.

21 *Ibid.*, pp. 45–54.

22 *Ibid.*, p. 99.

23 Michael E. Ware, *Making of the Motor Car 1895–1930*, Hartington, Buxton (1976), plate 12.

24 Roy Church, *Herbert Austin, The British Motor Car Industry to 1941*, London (1979), p. 21.

25 *Ibid.*, plate 14.

26 *B*, Vol. CXXXVIII, No. 4558, 13 June 1930, Obituary, p. 1147; RIBA Biography File.

27 *The Post Office London Directory for 1902*, Finsbury Square, No. 4, William T.M. Walker, Architect, p. 406.

28 Information from Kensington Central Library, Local History Department: Application for Planning Permission for a *porte cochère*, 877, 1903–04; Ware, *op. cit.*, plate 55.

29 Candidate's statement for admission as Fellow of the RIBA, 12 October 1906.

30 *B*, No. 4558, *op. cit.*, p. 1147; Candidate's statement.

31 Nixon, *Derbyshire, op. cit.*, p. 171.

32 *DBB*, Vol. 3, London (1985), Andrew Handyside.

33 *B*, Vol. CVIII, No. 3733, 21 August 1914, pp. 197–8.

34 *Ibid.*, p. 198.

35 Charles Heathcote, FRIBA, had been articled to Charles Hansom, a church architect of Clifton and was employed for a year in the offices of Lockwood & Mawson before commencing his own practice in 1872 at Manchester. He was also responsible for a number of bank and insurance buildings there, including the Commercial Union and Alliance Assurance offices. *MG*, 29 January 1938.

36 *B*, Vol. CLIV, No. 4957, 4 February 1938, Obituary, p. 263; *Who's Who in Architecture* (1926), p. 143.

37 Burnett Tracey, *op. cit.*, p. 211.

38 RIBA Biography File: Ernest Grigg Heathcote.

39 RIBA Biography File: Edgar Horace Heathcote; *RIBA Journal* November 1972, Obituary, p. 498; *Building*, Vol. CXXIII, 14 July 1972, Obituary, p. 95.

40 *B*, Vol. CXXXVIII, No. 4549, 11 April 1930, pp. 707, 710.

41 Edward D. Mills, *The Modern Factory*, London (1959), p. 204.

42 Burnett Tracey, *op. cit.*, p. 211.

43 John Dummelow, *1899–1948*, Manchester, Metropolitan-Vickers Electrical Co. Ltd (1949), p. 4.

44 *Ibid.*, p. 7.

45 *The Journal of the Manchester Geographical Society*, Vol. XVIII (1902), 'Notes of a Visit to the British Westinghouse … Works', p. 178.

46 *B*, Vol. CXLIII, No. 4686, 25 November 1932, Obituary, p. 892.

47 *The Architects' Journal*, Vol. 78 (1933), p. 563.

48 Alastair Forsyth, *Buildings for the Age, New Building Types 1900–1939*, RCHM, HMSO London (1982), plates 42, 43.

49 N. Pevsner, *London Volume Two*, Harmondsworth (1952), p. 403; *The Compact DNB*, Vol. II, Oxford (1975), p. 2878.

50 *AR*, Vol. CXXI, February 1932, pp. 49–53; *Building*, Vol. 7 (1932), p. 129.

51 *Ibid.*, p. 50.

52 Bevis Hillier, *Art Deco of the 20s and 30s*, London (1968), p. 13.

53 *B*, Vol. CLXXXIV, No. 5752, 15 May 1953, Obituary, p. 744; *Who's Who in Architecture* (1926), p. 304.

54 *AR*, Vol. CLVI, No. 929, July 1974, J.J. Snowdon and R.W. Platts, 'The Work of Wallis, Gilbert & Partners', p. 21.

55 *Ibid.*, p. 22; C.G. Powell, *An Economic History of the British Building Industry 1815–1979*, London (1980), pp. 96, 116.

56 Brockman, *op. cit.*, p. 114–15; *The British Builder*, Vol. 8 (1923), p. 14.

57 *The Architects' Journal*, Vol. 67, 1928, p. 351; Brockman, *op. cit.*, pp. 136, 138–9.

58 *B*, Vol. CXXXVII, No. 4509, 5 July 1929, p. 27.

59 *Ibid.; The Architect and Building News*, Vol. CXXI, No. 3133, 4 January 1929, p. 30.

60 *The Architect, op. cit.*, p. 29.

61 *B*, Vol. CXLII, No. 4647, 26 February 1932, pp. 386, 396, plates 389-91; Hillier, *Art Deco, op. cit.*, pp. 40, 50.

62 *The Architects' Journal*, Vol. 81, 28 February 1935, pp. 342-3.

63 *B*, Vol. CLXXXV, No. 5767, 28 August 1953, Obituary, p. 310.

64 *B*, Vol. CLI, No. 4889, 16 October 1936, pp. 728, 729-32a.

65 Martin S. Briggs, *Building Today*, Oxford (1948), p. 95.

66 *B*, Vol. CCIX, No. 6386, 8 October 1965, p. 768.

67 *B*, Vol. CXXXV, No. 4480, 14 December 1928, pp. 972, 980-1.

TEN

Epilogue

Simply to say that British industrial buildings have been unjustifiably neglected in architectural histories is not to describe the situation properly, though as a general comment it contains much truth, for this study has been the story of the factory's growing acceptance in the circle of architectural respectability. From being an outsider in the early days of the Industrial Revolution during the 1760s and 1770s, manufacturing enterprise slowly won recognition as a subject fit for the architect's attention in the manner in which entrepreneurs themselves, often of humble origins, gained wealth and secured a leading place in British society. Masters and the buildings that they commissioned worked their way towards the centre of the social and architectural stages and, whilst they may never have consistently occupied the topmost ranks of its hierarchy, their advance was sufficient to afford them a major place in both. In this fashion, a Lancashire cotton magnate in partnership with friends or relatives during the 1780s, giving scant consideration to the architectural features of his mill, would probably have employed a local builder to erect a simple structure, whose diluted detailing had been borrowed from Palladian pattern books. By 1880, when Oldham was in the throes of becoming the mightiest cotton-producing town the world has ever known, the directors of what would have been a limited liability company automatically sought the services of a qualified architect to design their mill – a man who by now probably specialized in such buildings. To retain the confidence of the shareholders and because they were appreciative of the value of impressing their clients and the local community, the boards of these textile companies increasingly wanted smart mills distinguished by decorative towers of coloured brick and stone, and a fashionable appearance.

What, then, were the forces responsible for this transformation? First, the Industrial Revolution had worked a fundamental change in the way in which society earned its living. No longer was the country's wealth based primarily upon agriculture and commerce. The growth of industry through its ironworks, factories and coalmines had created a new industrial workforce which came to dominate those engaged in farming, finance and trade. Mills, therefore, from being unusual structures whose value was perceived in local terms and which were often situated in areas remote from established centres of population, had become, by virtue of their number and the growth in the very size of plant, buildings upon which the fortunes of the nation now relied. Their migration to the towns, or the formation of great terraced settlements around their factory gates (a movement consequent upon the application of steam power in place of the waterwheel) brought factories more and more into the public's eye. The prosperity of the economy now rested on these manufacturing conglomerations. Industrial buildings, along with the office block and the railway station, were the latest arrivals at the architectural gathering of Victorian Britain.

As well as these practical considerations, there were, of course, major changes in attitudes. The philosophy of architecture had experienced a dramatic transformation in the hundred years from 1780. At the outset of industrialization a rigid hierarchy of decorum ruled that only those buildings believed most worthy should receive the attention of the best architects and most elevated treatment. Factories and warehouses should be built merely to perform a task, interpreted with restraint, following the general principles of symmetry and order, but without excessive adornment. Yet as the hierarchy concept weakened and Gothic architecture replaced a classical adherence, notions of 'fittedness' came to the fore. Commentators such as Ruskin argued, that buildings should reflect in their exterior design the purpose for which they were constructed, and that the achievement of an effective and vigorous appearance was of far greater importance than the observance of ranking niceties. For Ruskin no building performed a function so humble that its execution should be neglected. Nevertheless, in practice many Victorian architects continued to believe that the richest ornament and finest materials should be reserved for churches, palaces and buildings of state. In theory no substantial objection existed by 1900 to prevent factories and warehouses from being treated as conscientiously or grandly as a cathedral or royal residence, but the fact that this was commonly not the case fell to other factors.

Why, then, were so many industrial buildings of the late nineteenth and early twentieth centuries constructed of drab and repetitive materials in an unimaginative and sometimes unsightly fashion? First, at a time when fierce competition from America and Germany forced British manufacturers to reduce prices, expenditure on new plant had to be trimmed of anything that smacked of luxury. A works' appearance, if advertising and public image ranked low in an owner's considerations, could be sacrificed in favour of more expensive machinery or greater space. Secondly, Britons did not value their entrepreneurs or managers highly in the Victorian period; the sons of successful businessmen commonly preferred to enter the forces or professions rather than soil their hands at the forge or mill. Insofar as an architect gained kudos from the person he served, there was little

to be earned at the industrialist's doorstep. To work for government or stately landowner carried a higher cachet, and attracted the senior or most talented members of the profession. Hence a considerable number of industrial buildings were executed by young architects, men just beginning in their careers, as yet unknown, inexperienced and less costly than their elders. Alfred Waterhouse, for instance, designed very few warehouses, and those in his youth; Voysey produced just a single factory in his career. The leading architects of the nineteenth and early twentieth centuries avoided industrial work. Sir Charles Barry, C.R. Cockerell, G.E. Street, William Butterfield, Sir George Scott and Sir Edwin Lutyens between them appear not to have designed a single warehouse or factory. Architects preferred on the whole to work on palaces, town halls, country houses and churches rather than mills. Sir John Vanbrugh presumably undertook the Woolwich Arsenal commission because of its military importance and royal patronage, not being given to the authorship of foundries and workshops. The standard of design for industrial structures suffered as a result. Talented young architects tended to congregate in London and follow the example of their leaders.

This situation persisted well into the twentieth century and, even in the 1930s when architects ranked high among the professions, it was considered undignified for a qualified man to leave private practice for industry. To surrender the chance of designing houses or churches for a salaried post in a manufacturing company, many able architects regarded as too high a price to pay. Although through government contracts the First World War had drawn the profession more closely into industry, it was not until the Second World War that a major change in attitudes came about. The dearth of domestic commissions and a rising demand for well-planned shadow factories during 1939–45 meant that architects had to employ their talents much more in an industrial context. By the end of hostilities many ingrained ideas had been loosened, and the need to rebuild parts of Britain after the Blitz raised the status of the industrial architect further.

However, many industrial buildings of merit had been erected during the nineteenth century. Because fashionable architects gravitated to the capital and focused their attentions on other types of commission, numerous talented practices grew up in the manufacturing towns, devoted to answering their particular architectural needs. They may be divided into two categories: those provincial firms (including civil engineers) whose widespread involvement in the community drew them naturally to factory work; and the specialist industrial designers. In the former category were Lockwood and Mawson in Bradford, Thomas Ambler and George Corson, both in Leeds, Bradshaw Gass & Hope in Bolton, John Gordon in Glasgow, Joseph Kaye in Huddersfield and Roger Ives in Halifax. Their intimate knowledge of manufacturers' needs and experience of local conditions meant that these architects could produce distinctive buildings fitted to their business purpose and in keeping with the vernacular tradition of the neighbourhood.

Less common, and more in evidence towards the end of the nineteenth century when the volume of major industrial projects multiplied, was the specialist. Edward Potts and the various Stott family partnerships that dominated Oldham fell into this category; so also did George Woodhouse in Bolton, W.J. Morley in Bradford and Charles Heathcote in Manchester. Though not exclusively concerned with factories and warehouses, they earned the bulk of their fees from this work and gained such a reputation that they attracted clients from all over Britain and occasionally overseas. In the twentieth century Sir Owen Williams, and Wallis, Gilbert & Partners followed in their footsteps.

The value of industrial buildings has so far only been properly assessed in terms of their contribution to civil engineering. And, indeed, their value there was undeniable. In the adoption of cast- and later wrought-iron beams for internal frameworks in the search for fireproof structures, the mills and warehouses of the late eighteenth century served as important proving grounds. Similarly, the substitution of rolled-steel girders and the use of reinforced concrete often occurred in industry before it was adopted in other

building types. In addition, new materials were among the very products of the Industrial Revolution (various metals, terracotta, special cements), while the mass-production methods that it generated made traditional products such as glass and brick cheaper and available in greater quantities and a wider variety of types, shapes and styles. The increasing use of blue engineering bricks in the latter part of the nineteenth century, for example, showed how industrialization both demanded new engineering solutions and at the same time threw up the means of solving these problems. The need for stronger, harder brick (for load-bearing structures and to resist the corrosive atmospheres of manufacturing regions) was created by the onward march of industrialization but, through the sinking of deep mines into these clays and the mechanization of brick production, the problem offered its own answer.

The contribution of industrial buildings to Britain's architectural heritage has, by comparison, not been fully appreciated. While American scholars have begun to reassess the importance of their nation's factories, mills and warehouses, the movement has been slow to gain momentum in this country, where the focus of research has remained primarily in the field of industrial archaeology.[1] Yet it has been asserted that recent functional architecture may be traced back through various antecedents in Britain's manufacturing areas to an earlier tradition in which a powerful emphasis on utility arose from the needs of the Industrial Revolution. The argument involved linking together warehouses, mills, breweries, sheds and bridges erected in the period 1760-1840, to suggest that functional building did not have its origins in the modern era, but was critically associated with industrialization. Writing in 1957, J.M. Richards argued:

> there exists, in fact, a tradition of functionalism ... running parallel with the evolution of successive styles and weaving its way, as it were, in and out of them. Sometimes it is dominant and sometimes recessive, and to bring into focus another earlier episode in our architectural history when functional values that we look up to now were dominant ...

may serve to put our own age into its proper perspective ...[2]

Whilst serving the desirable purpose of shifting the architectural spotlight on to these structures, the case had a serious methodological weakness, for it required that buildings be taken from their historical context and joined together in a chain of putative connection. When, in fact, these examples are set in relation to other contemporary buildings and the architectural thoughts of their time, a different picture emerges. No explicitly stated philosophy of 'functionalism' existed in Britain before the twentieth century, and even then it was slow to emerge, arriving not from the indigenous past but from a continental tradition, based primarily in Germany. The literature of the late eighteenth and nineteenth centuries made no reference to such ideas and when British architects were designing so-called functional buildings in this period their attitudes reflected contemporary architectural opinion, not the thoughts of Behrens or Gropius. It may be that modern architects drew inspiration from these earlier buildings but it was never the intention of their authors to break contemporary conventions and use industry as a proving ground for novel architectural theories.

If we place industrial buildings properly in the context of their age, rather than trying to trace their development backwards from some point in the present, then it becomes apparent that they mirrored in various degrees the thoughts and characteristics of their time. Darley Abbey Mills (1789-92) reflected Palladian principles, just as the Abbey Cloth Mills (1875) may be seen as an example of Victorian Romanticism, its medieval image and bold interpretation in keeping with contemporary fashion and attitudes towards industrial buildings. That the Shropshire Union Canal Co.'s Shrewsbury warehouse (1835) possessed a stuccoed Doric entrance was evidence not of the existence of a 'functional tradition' but of the fact that businesses tended to dress their premises in the clothes of the age, in this instance the popular Greek Revival.

What may be true, however, is that industrial buildings were among some of the finest expressions of the sublime, and gave considerable weight to those who advocated its use. The size of mills and warehouses, the common absence of unnecessary ornament, the repetition of deeply profiled features and the awesome aspect created by blackening pollution meant that their characteristics fitted the requirements of the sublime. The picturesque and the beauty of strict classical interpretation were less often seen in factories and were better represented by other types of building. In this respect some mills and a number of warehouses (constructed with the aim of preventing theft) offered close comparison with prisons. The latter, executed in the sublime to deter and subdue, needed to be fireproof and in this way also resembled industrial structures.

As with so many architectural studies, this book has not been based wholly on the typical, though where buildings had representational qualities it has been indicated. This study has drawn on the best in industry. Buildings such as Bonomi's Temple Mills in Leeds; Leiper's Templeton Carpet Factory, Glasgow; or the India Mill, Darwen, were atypical in the style or degree of ornament that they manifested. However, so many others, such as Frost's Mill, Macclesfield (1785); Rykneld Mills, Derby (c.1823); Dean Clough Mills, Halifax (c.1854-7); and Dee Mill, Shaw (1906), reproduced features of their time and may serve as characteristic examples. In certain areas (such as Burnley's Weavers Triangle, the Potteries, the warehouse districts of Manchester and Bradford and the environs of Oldham) a conformity of design and consistency in the use of materials arose, a feature reinforced by the growth of specialist architects' practices drawing their clients (who shied from employing expensive London names) almost exclusively from these districts. The plainly ugly, poorly planned factories executed in inferior materials have been omitted from this work. In Victorian Britain, when the economy grew at a rapid pace and enterprises rose and fell with astonishing frequency in an architectural environment largely unregulated by building acts, there was no shortage of these. Most have, of course, perished. It is only disturbing that so much good industrial architecture has been demolished, and much more is threatened with the same fate.

To conclude, George Orwell's judgement (the product of a tour through Lancashire and Yorkshire in the 1930s) may be recalled. 'I do not believe', he wrote,

> that there is anything inherently and unavoidably ugly about industrialization. A factory or even a gasworks is not obliged of its own nature to be ugly, any more than a palace or a dog-kennel or a cathedral. It all depends on the architectural tradition of the period.[3]

Notes

1 John Coolidge, *Mill and Mansion*, New York (1942); H.-R. Hitchcock, *Rhode Island Architecture*, Providence (1939); John B. Armstrong, *Factory under the Elms*, MIT (1969); Gilbert Herbert, *Pioneers of Prefabrication*, Baltimore (1978); Hildebrand, *Designing for Industry*, *op. cit.*

2 *AR*, Vol. 122, No. 726, July 1957, J.M. Richards, 'The Functional Tradition as shown in Early Industrial Buildings', p. 5.

3 George Orwell, *The Road to Wigan Pier*, London (1937), Harmondsworth (1962), p. 96.

Abbreviations used in notes

AR	*Architectural Review*	MCA	Merseyside County Archives, Liverpool
B	*The Builder*	MCL	Manchester Central Library, Local History Department
BA	Bolton Archives		
BCL	Bristol Central Library	*MG*	*Manchester Guardian*
BGH	Bradshaw Gass & Hope	*MPICE*	*Minutes of the Proceedings of the Institution of Civil Engineers*
BH	*Business History*		
BL	Bradford Central Library, Local Studies Department	*OC*	*Oldham Chronicle*
BN	*Building News*	OLIC	Oldham Local Interest Centre
BO	*Bradford Observer*	*PIME*	*Proceedings of the Institution of Mechanical Engineers*
BoE	*The Buildings of England* series by N. Pevsner		
		PRO	Public Record Office, Kew
BRL	Birmingham Reference Library	RCHM	Royal Commission on Historical Monuments
CCL,H	Calderdale Central Library, Halifax		
DBB	*Dictionary of Business Biography*	RIBA	Royal Institute of British Architects
DNB	*Dictionary of National Biography*	SYCRO	South Yorkshire Record Office, Sheffield
GLC	GLC Historic Buildings Division		
GMRO	Greater Manchester Record Office	*THAS*	*Transactions of the Halifax Antiquarian Society*
GRO	Glamorgan Record Office, Cardiff		
HAS	*Transactions of the Halifax Antiquarian Society*	*TLCAS*	*Transactions of the Lancashire and Cheshire Antiquarian Society*
		TM	*The Textile Manufacturer*
HC	*Huddersfield Chronicle*	*TNS*	*Transactions of the Newcomen Society*
HE	*Huddersfield Examiner*	*VCH*	*Victoria County History*
ICE	Institution of Civil Engineers	*E*	for *Essex*
JRL	John Rylands University Library of Manchester	*L*	for *Leicester*
		M	for *Middlesex*
KLH	Kirklees Central Library, Huddersfield	*S*	for *Stafford*
LivRO	Liverpool Record Office	WRO	Wigan Record Office, Leigh
LRO	Lancashire Record Office, Preston		

Sources

Manuscript sources

The notes to the individual chapters should be consulted for a detailed note of the original sources employed, though the following record offices or libraries were of particular value: Bradford Central Library, Local History Department; Bolton Metropolitan Borough Archives; Birmingham Reference Library; Calderdale Metropolitan Borough Archives Department and Reference Library, Halifax; Derbyshire Record Office; GLC Historic Buildings Division; Greater Manchester Record Office; Glamorgan Record Office; Institution of Civil Engineers; Institution of Mechanical Engineers; John Rylands University Library of Manchester; Kirklees Libraries and Museums Service, Huddersfield; Lancashire Record Office; Liverpool Record Office; Manchester Central Library, Local History and Archive Departments; Merseyside County Archives; Oldham Local Interest Centre; Public Record Office; Royal Commission on Historical Monuments; Royal Institute of British Architects, Library and Drawings Collection; South Yorkshire Record Office; and the Wigan Record Office. Further details are contained in *Record Repositories in Great Britain*, London HMSO (1982) compiled by the Royal Commission on Historical Manuscripts.

Journals

The Architect and Building News
The Architects' Journal
Architectural History
Architectural Review
The Builder
Building News
Derbyshire Archaeological Journal
Industrial Archaeology
Industrial Archaeology Review
Journal of the Royal Institute of British Architects
Textile History
The Textile Manufacturer
Transactions of the Lancashire and Cheshire Antiquarian Society
Transactions of the Newcomen Society

Articles

ARCHER, J.H.G., *TLCAS*, Vols 73 and 74, Manchester (1966), 'Edgar Wood: a Notable Manchester Architect'.

BANNISTER, Turpin C., *AR*, Vol. CVII, April 1950, 'The First Iron-Framed Building' *Journal of the Society of Architectural Historians*, Vol. XV (1956); 'Bogardus Revisited, Part One: The Iron Fronts'; 'Part Two', Vol. XVI (1957).

BRIGGS, Martin S., *AR*, Vol. XXI, April 1907, 'Iron and Steel in Modern Design'.

CANTRELL, J.A., *BH*, Vol. XXIII (1981), 'James Nasmyth and the Bridgewater Foundry: Partners and Partnerships'.

CLEGG, Herbert, *TLCAS*, Vol. LXV, Manchester (1956), 'The Third Duke of Bridgewater's canal works in Manchester'.

ETTLINGER, L., *AR*, Vol. XCVII, May 1945, 'A German Architect's Visit to England in 1826'.

HAMILTON, S.B., *Transactions of the Newcomen Society*, Vol. XXI (1940-1), 'The Use of Cast Iron in Building'.

HARRIS, John, *AR*, Vol. CXXX, July 1961, 'Cast Iron Columns 1706'.

HITCHCOCK, H.-R., *AR*, Vol. CI, May 1947, 'London Coal Exchange'
AR, Vol. CV, January 1949, 'Victorian Monuments of Commerce'
AR, Vol. CIX, February 1951, 'Early Cast Iron Façades'
AR, Vol. CXV, April 1954, 'Brunel and Paddington'.

HUGHES, J. Quentin, *Architectural History*, Vol. 4 (1961), Supplement II, 'Dock Warehouses at Liverpool'.

KESSELS, S.H., *AR*, Vol. CXVIII, September 1955, 'A Great Georgian Warehouse'.

MACKENZIE, M. H., *Derbyshire Archaeological Journal*, Vol. LXXXVIII (1968), 'Cressbrook and Litton Mills 1779-1835'
Derbyshire Archaeological Journal, Vol. XC (1970), 'Cressbrook Mill 1810-1835'.

MUSSON, A. E., *BH*, Vol. III (1960), 'An Early Engineering Firm: Peel, Williams & Co., of Manchester'.

MUTHESIUS, Stefan, *Architectural History*, Vol. 13 (1970), 'The "Iron Problem" in the 1850s'.

PACEY, A.J., *AR*, Vol. CXLV, February 1969, 'Earliest Cast Iron Beams'.

PEVSNER, Nikolaus and S. LANG, *AR*, Vol. CXIX, May 1956, 'The Egyptian Revival'.

RICHARDS, J.M., *AR*, Vol. CXXII, July 1957, 'The Functional Tradition in early Industrial Buildings'.

RIMMER, W.G., *Transactions of the Shropshire Archaeological Society*, Vol. LVI (1959), 'The Castle Foregate Flax Mill'.

SEALY, A.W. and D.W. WALTERS, *AR*, Vol. CXXXIII, March 1963, 'The First Iron Railway Bridge'.

SKEMPTON, A.W., *TNS*, Vol. XXXII (1959-60), 'The Boat Store, Sheerness (1858-60)'
Architectural History, Vol. 14 (1971), 'Samuel Wyatt and the Albion Mill'.

SKEMPTON, A.W. and H.R. JOHNSON, *AR*, Vol. CXXXI, March 1962, 'The First Iron Frames'.

SNOWDON, J.J. and R.W. PLATTS, *AR*, Vol. CLVI, July 1974, 'The Work of Wallis, Gilbert & Partners'.

SUTHERLAND, R.J.M., *AR*, Vol. CXIV, December 1953, 'Telford'.

STURGES, W. Knight, *AR*, Vol. CXIV, October 1953, 'Cast Iron in New York'.

TAYLOR, Jeremy, *AR*, Vol. CXXXV, March 1964, 'Charles Fowler: Master of Architects'.

TOMLINSON, V.I., *TLCAS*, Vol. 71, Manchester (1963), 'Early Warehouses on Manchester Waterways'.

TYSON, R.E., *TLCAS*, Vol. 80, Manchester (1980), 'William Marcroft (1822-94) and the Limited Liability Movement in Oldham'.

Theses

FARNIE, D.A., 'The English Cotton Industry 1850-1896' (Manchester University, MA, 1953).

FIDLER, D.M., 'Building for the Cotton Industry' (Manchester Polytechnic, School of Architecture MMSA Diploma, 1950).

JONES, Fred, 'The Cotton Spinning Industry in the Oldham District from 1896 to 1914' (Manchester University MA(Econ.), 1959).

NIXON, Malcolm Ian, 'The Emergence of the Factory System in the Staffordshire Pottery Industry' (Aston University, PhD, 1976).

ROBERTS, John Stewart, 'The Bradford Textile Warehouse 1770-1914, A study of the location, architecture and function of textile warehouses in a developing industrial community' (University of Bradford, MSc, 1976).

TYSON, R.E., 'The Sun Mill Company Ltd – A Study in Democratic Investment 1859-1959' (Manchester University, MA, 1962).

Select bibliography

Published works pre-1939

ABRAM, William Alexander, *A History of Blackburn, Town and Parish*, Blackburn (1877).

AITKIN, J., *A Description of the Country from Thirty to Forty Miles round Manchester*, London (1795).

ALLEN, Zachariah, *The Practical Tourist, or Sketches of the State of the Useful Arts, and of Society*, Providence (1832).

The Architect's, Engineer's, and Building-Trades' Directory, London (1868).

AXON, William E.A., *The Annals of Manchester*, Manchester (1886).

BAINES, Edward, *History, Directory & Gazetteer of the County of York*, Leeds (1822)
History, Directory and Gazetteer of the County Palatine of Lancaster, 2 Vols, Liverpool (1824–25)
History of the Cotton Manufacture in Great Britain, London (1835).

BANCROFT, Robert M. and Francis J. BANCROFT, *A Practical Treatise on the Construction of Tall Chimney Shafts*, Manchester (1885).

BANKS, *A Treatise on Mills*, London (1795).

BIRKMIRE, William H., *Architectural Iron and Steel*, New York (1892)
Skeletal Construction in Buildings, New York (1893)
The Planning and Construction of High Office-Buildings, New York (1898).

BLACKNER, John, *The History of Nottingham, embracing its Antiquities, Trade and Manufactures*, Nottingham (1815).

BRAY, William, *Sketch of a Tour into Derbyshire and Yorkshire*, London (1783).

BUCHANAN, Robertson, *An Essay on the Warming of Mills and other Buildings by Steam*, Glasgow (1807).

BURKE, Edmund, *A Philosophical Enquiry into the Origin of our Ideas of the Sublime and Beautiful*, London (1757).

BURNETT, Tracy W., *Manchester and Salford at the close of the Nineteenth Century*, [1899].

BUTTERWORTH, Edwin, *A Statistical Sketch of the County Palatine of Lancaster*, London (1841).

CHAMBERS, William, *A Treatise on Civil Architecture*, London (1759).

CHANDLER, Dean, *Outline History of Lighting by Gas*, London (1936).

CHATTERTON, Frederick (Editor), *Who's Who in Architecture*, London (1923); London (1926).

CLEGG, James, *Annals of Bolton*, Bolton (1888).

COOKE TAYLOR, W., *Notes of a Tour in the Manufacturing Districts of Lancashire*, London (1842).

COTTINGHAM, L.N., *The Smith and Founder's Directory*, London (1823).

CRABTREE, John, *A Concise History of Halifax*, Halifax (1836).

CRIPPS, F. Southwell, *The Guide framing of Gasholders*, London (1889).

CRUMP, W.B. and Gertrude GHORBAL, *History of the Huddersfield Woollen Industry*, Huddersfield (1935).

CUDWORTH, William, *Manningham, Heaton and Allerton*, Bradford (1896).

DAVIES, Revd D.P., *A New Historical and Descriptive View of Derbyshire*, Belper (1811).

DEFOE, Daniel, *A Tour through the whole Island of Great Britain*, London (1724–26).

DENT, R.K., *The Making of Birmingham*, Birmingham (1894).

DISRAELI, Benjamin, *Sybil; or, the Two Nations*, 3 Vols, London (1845).

DODD, George, *Days at Factories; or, the Manufacturing Industry of Great Britain Described*, London (1843).

EASTLAKE, Charles L., *A History of the Gothic Revival*, London (1872).

The Engineering and other Industries of Manchester reprinted from 'The Ironmonger', London (1887).

EVERETT, J., *Panorama of Manchester and Railway Companion*, Manchester (1834).

FAIRBAIRN, William, *Report of William Fairbairn, Esq. C.E., on the Construction of Fireproof Buildings*, Liverpool (1844)
On the Application of Cast and Wrought Iron to Building Purposes, London (1854)
Treatise on Mills and Millwork, 2 Vols, London (1861–5)
Iron its History, Properties and Processes of Manufacture, Edinburgh (1861).

FELKIN, William, *A History of Machine-Wrought Hosiery and Lace Manufacturers*, London (1867)
The Fine Cotton Spinners' & Doublers' Association Ltd, Manchester (1909).

FOX BOURNE, H.R., *English Merchants: Memoirs ... of the Progress of British Commerce*, 2 Vols, London (1866).

FREEMAN, Albert C. (Editor), *The Architects and Surveyors Directory and Referendum*, London (1910).

GUEST, Richard, *Compendious History of the Cotton-Manufacture*, Manchester (1823).

HALFPENNY, William, *Practical Architecture, or a sure guide to the true working according to the Rules of Science*, London (1730).

HANDYSIDE, Andrew & Co., *Works in Iron*, London (1868).

HODGKINSON, Eaton, *Memoirs of the Literary and Philosophical Society of Manchester*, Vol. V, London (1831), 'Theoretical and Experimental researches to ascertain the strength and best form of Iron Beams'.

HUMBER, William (Editor), *A Record of the Progress of Modern Engineering*, 2 Vols, London (1864–5).

HUTTON, W., *The History of Derby*, London (1817).

The Industries of Yorkshire, 2 Vols, London (1890).

JAGGARD, Walter R., *Brickwork and its Construction*, Oxford (1931).

JAGGARD, Walter R., and Francis E. DRURY, *Architectural Building Construction*, Cambridge (1927).

JAMES, John, *History of the Worsted Manufacture in England*, London (1857)
Continuation and Additions to the History of Bradford, London (1866).

KOHL, J.G., *Ireland, Scotland and England*, London (1844).

LEIGH, Evan, *The Science of Modern Cotton Spinning*, 2 Vols, Manchester (1873).

LOCKWOOD, Henry F. and Adolphus H. CATES, *The History and Antiquities of the Fortifications of the City of York*, London (1834).

LOMAX, Edward and Thomas GUNYON (Editors), *Encyclopaedia of Architecture*, 2 Vols, London (1852).

LOVEDAY, James Thomas, *Loveday's London Waterside Surveys*, London (1857).

Manchester of Today, An Epitome of Results, Business Men and Commercial Interests, Wealth and Growth, London (1888).

A Century of Fine Cotton Spinning 1790–1906, McConnel & Co Ltd, Manchester (1906).

MARCROFT, William, *Sun Mill Company Limited: Its Commercial and Social History from 1858 to 1877*, Oldham (1877).

MATHESON, Ewing, *Works in Iron, Bridge and Roof Structures*, London (1873).

MEADE, Alwyne, *Modern Gasworks Practice*, London (1921).

MIDDLETON, James, *Oldham, Past and Present*, Rochdale (1904).

MÜLLER-WULCKOW, Walter, *Bauten der Arbeit und des Verkehrs*, Königstein (1925).

NASMITH, Joseph, *The Students' Cotton Spinning*, Manchester (1896).

NASMITH, Joseph and Frank NASMITH, *Recent Cotton Mill Construction and Engineering*, Manchester [c.1895], third edition (1909).

PAPWORTH, Wyatt (Editor), *The Dictionary of Architecture*, 8 Vols, London (1852–92).

PIKE, W.T., *An Illustrated Account of Halifax, Brighouse and District*, Brighton (c.1890).

PLATZ, Gustav Adolf, *Die Baukunst der Neuesten Zeit*, Berlin (1927).

POLE, William (Editor), *The Life of Sir William Fairbairn, Partly Written by Himself*, London (1877).

PRICE, Uvedale, *An Essay on the Picturesque, as compared with the Sublime and the Beautiful*, London (1796).

PUGIN, A.W.N., *Contrasts: or, a Parallel between the Architecture of the Fifteenth and Nineteenth Centuries*, London (1836), revised 1841
The True Principles of Pointed or Christian Architecture, London (1841)
An Apology for the Revival of Christian Architecture in England, London (1843).

PYNE, W.H., *Lancashire Illustrated*, London (1831).

RAWLINSON, R., *Designs for Factory, Furnace and other Tall Chimney Shafts*, London (1859).

RHEAD, G.W. and Frederick A. RHEAD, *Staffordshire Pots and Potters*, London (1906).

RUSKIN, John, *The Seven Lamps of Architecture*, London (1849)
The Stones of Venice, London (1851-53).

SCHOLES, James Christopher, *History of Bolton*, Bolton (1892).

SCOTT, George Gilbert, *Remarks on the Secular and Domestic Architecture Present and Future*, London (1857).

SHAW, Revd Stebbing, *The History and Antiquities of Staffordshire*, 2 Vols, London (1798-1801).

SHAW, William Arthur, *Manchester Old and New*, 2 Vols, London [1894].

SHEPHERD, Thomas H., *Metropolitan Improvements; or London in the Nineteenth Century*, Vol. I, London (1828).

SINGTON, Theodore, *Cotton Mill Planning and Construction*, Manchester (1897).

SKINNER, Thomas, *Skinner's Cotton Trade Directory for 1923*, London (1923).

SMILES, Samuel, *Industrial Biography, Iron Workers and Tool Makers*, London (1863)
James Nasmyth, Engineer, An Autobiography, London (1883).

STREET, George Edmund, *Brick and Marble in the Middle Ages, Notes of Tours in the North of Italy*, London (1874).

SWINDELLS, T., *Manchester Streets and Manchester Men*, 2 Vols, Manchester (1906-07).

SYKES, D.F.E., *The History of Huddersfield and its Vicinity*, Huddersfield (1898).

THWAITE, B.H., *Our Factories, Workshops and Warehouses, Their Sanitary and Fire-resisting Arrangements*, London (1882).

TIMMINS, Samuel (Editor), *Birmingham and the Midland Hardware District*, London (1866).

TOMLINSON, Charles, *Cyclopaedia of Useful Arts, Mechanical and Chemical*, 2 Vols, London (1854).

TREDGOLD, Thomas, *Practical Essay on the Strength of Cast Iron and other Metals*, London (1842).

UNWIN, George, *Samuel Oldknow and the Arkwrights, The Industrial Revolution at Stockport and Marple*, Manchester (1924).

URE, Andrew, *The Cotton Manufacture of Great Britain*, 2 vols, London (1836)
The Philosophy of Manufactures, London (1861)
A Dictionary of Arts, Manufactures and Mines, London (1843).

WADSWORTH, Alfred P. and Julia DE LACY MANN, *The Cotton Trade and Industrial Lancashire 1600-1780*, Manchester (1931).

WHITE, George, *A Practical Treatise on Weaving, by Hand and Power Looms*, Glasgow (1846).

WILKINS, Charles, *The History of the Iron, Steel, Tinplate and Other Trades of Wales*, Merthyr Tydfil (1903).

WILSON, Robert, *Boiler and Factory Chimneys, Their Draught-Power and Stability*, London (1877).

WRIGHT, Revd G.N., *An Historical Guide to Ancient and Modern Dublin*, London (1821).

Published works post-1939

ALLSOPP, Bruce and Ursula CLARK, *Historic Architecture of Northumberland and Newcastle upon Tyne*, London (1977).

ALDERTON, David and John BOOKER, *The Batsford Guide to the Industrial Architecture of East Anglia*, London (1980).

ARMSTRONG, John Borden, *Factory under the Elms: A History of Harrisville, New Hampshire 1774-1969*, Cambridge Massachusetts (1969).

ASHMORE, Owen, *The Industrial Archaeology of Lancashire*, Newton Abbot (1969).

ATKINS, Philip, *Guide across Manchester*, Manchester (1976).

ATKINSON, Frank, *The Industrial Archaeology of North-East England*, 2 Vols, Newton Abbot (1974).

BARKER, T.C., *The Glassmakers, Pilkington: the Rise of an International Company 1826–1976*, London (1977).

BARRACLOUGH, K.C., *Sheffield Steel*, Sheffield (1976).

BENNETT, J.D., *Leicestershire Architects*, Leicester (1968).

BIDDLE, Gordon, *Victorian Stations, Railway Stations in England and Wales 1830–1923*, Newton Abbot (1973).

BIDDLE, Gordon and Jeoffrey SPENCE, *The British Railway Station*, Newton Abbot (1977).

BINNEY, Marcus (*et al.*), *Satanic Mills, Industrial Architecture in the Pennines*, London (1979).

BINNEY, Marcus and David PEARCE (Editors), *Railway Architecture*, London (1979).

BLYTHE, H.E., *Through the Eye of a Needle, The Story of the English Sewing Cotton Co.* [*c.*1947].

BOUCHER, Cyril T.G., *James Brindley, Engineer 1716–1772*, Norwich (1968).

BOYSON, Rhodes, *The Ashworth Cotton Enterprise*, Oxford (1970).

BRACEGIRDLE, Brian, *The Archaeology of the Industrial Revolution*, London (1973).

BRETTON, R., *Crossleys of Dean Clough*, Halifax (1954).

BRIGGS, Asa, *Iron Bridge to Crystal Palace*, London (1979)
The Power of Steam, London (1982).

BRIGGS, Martin S., *Building Today*, Oxford (1948).

BROCKMAN, H.A.N., *The British Architect in Industry 1841–1940*, London (1974).

BROOK, Fred, *The Industrial Archaeology of the British Isles, 1 The West Midlands*, London (1977).

BUCHANAN, R.A., *Industrial Archaeology in Britain*, Harmondsworth (1974).

BUCHANAN, R.A. and Neil COSSONS, *The Industrial Archaeology of the Bristol Region*, Newton Abbot (1969).

BURROUGH, T.H.B., *Bristol*, London (1970).

BURTON, Anthony and Clive COOTE, *Remains of a Revolution*, London (1975).

BUTT, John, *The Industrial Archaeology of Scotland*, Newton Abbot (1967).

CHADWICK, George F., *The Life and Works of Joseph Paxton 1803–1865*, London (1961).

CHAPMAN, S.D., *The Early Factory Masters*, Newton Abbot (1967)
The Cotton Industry in the Industrial Revolution, London (1972).

CHURCH, Roy A., *Economic and Social Change in a Midland Town, Victorian Nottingham 1815–1900*, London (1966).

CLARK, Kenneth, *The Gothic Revival*, London (1962).

CLOUGH, Robert T., *The Lead Smelting Mills of the Yorkshire Dales, Their Architectural Character, Construction and Place in the European Tradition*, Leeds (1962).

COLVIN, H.M., *Biographical Dictionary of English Architects 1660–1840*, London (1954).

COOLIDGE, John, *Mill and Mansion: A Study of Architecture and Society in Lowell, Massachusetts*, New York (1967).

COSSONS, Neil, *The BP Book of Industrial Architecture*, Newton Abbot (1975).

COWAN, Henry J., *Science and Building, Structural and Environmental Design in the Nineteenth and Twentieth Centuries*, New York (1978).

CRANKSHAW, W.P. and Alfred BLACKBURN, *A Century and a half of Cotton Spinning 1797–1949, The History of Knowles Limited of Bolton* [*c.*1947].

CUNNINGHAM, Colin, *Victorian and Edwardian Town Halls*, London (1981).

DERRY, T.K. and Trevor I. WILLIAMS, *A Short History of Technology*, Oxford (1960).

DIXON, Roger and Stefan MUTHESIUS, *Victorian Architecture*, London (1978).

DOAK, A.M. and Andrew McLAREN YOUNG (Editors), *Glasgow at a Glance*, London (1977).

DUMMELOW, John, *1899–1949*, Manchester, Metropolitan-Vickers Electrical Co. Ltd (1949).

DUNWELL, Steve, *The Run of the Mill, A Pictorial Narrative of the Expansion, Dominion ... of the New England Textile Industry*, Boston, Massachusetts (1978).

DYOS, H.J. and M. WOLFF (Editors), *Victorian City*, 2 Vols, London (1973).

ENGLISH, W., *The Textile Industry*, London (1969).

FALCONER, Keith, *Guide to England's Industrial Heritage*, London (1980).

FARNIE, D.A., *The English Cotton Industry and the World Market 1815-1896*, Oxford (1979)
Saddleworth Historical Bulletin, Vol. 12, No. 3 (1982), 'The Emergence of Victorian Oldham as the Centre of the Cotton Spinning Industry'.

FAWCETT, Jane (Editor), *Seven Victorian Architects*, London (1976).

FITTON, R.S. and A.P. WADSWORTH, *The Strutts and the Arkwrights 1758-1830*, Manchester (1958).

FITZGERALD, R.S., *Liverpool Road Station, Manchester, An Industrial and Architectural Survey*, Manchester (1980).

FRASER, Derek (Editor), *A History of Modern Leeds*, Manchester (1980).

FURNEAUX JORDAN, Robert, *Victorian Architecture*, Harmondsworth (1966).

GLOAG, John, *Victorian Taste, Some Social Aspects of Architecture and Industrial Designs from 1820 to 1900*, London (1962).

GLOAG, John and Derek BRIDGWATER, *A History of Cast Iron in Architecture*, London (1948).

GOMME, Andor, and David WALKER, *Architecture of Glasgow*, London (1968).

GOMME, Andor, and Michael JENNER and Bryan LITTLE, *Bristol, an Architectural History*, London (1979).

HADFIELD, Charles, and A.W. SKEMPTON, *William Jessop, Engineer*, Newton Abbot (1979).

HARRIS, Robert, *Canals and their Architecture*, London (1980).

HARTE, N.B., and K.G. PONTING (Editors), *Textile History and Economic History, Essays in Honour of Miss Julia de Lacy Mann*, Manchester (1973).

HASELFOOT, A.J., *The Batsford Guide to the Industrial Archaeology of South-East England*, London (1978).

HENRIQUES, David Q. & Co., *The Textile Industry of Lancashire*, Manchester (1952).

HERBERT, Gilbert, *Pioneers of Prefabrication, The British Contribution to the Nineteenth Century*, Baltimore (1978).

HILDEBRAND, Grant, *Designing for Industry, The Architecture of Albert Kahn*, MIT (1974).

HILLIER, Bevis, *Art Deco in the 20s and 30s*, London (1968).

HILLING, John B., *Cardiff and the Valleys*, London (1973)
The Historical Architecture of Wales, Cardiff (1975).

HILLS, Richard, *Power in the Industrial Revolution*, Manchester (1970)
Beyer, Peacock, Locomotive Builders of Gorton, Manchester, A Short History, Manchester (1982).

HITCHCOCK, Henry-Russell, *Rhode Island Architecture*, Providence (1939)
Early Victorian Architecture in Britain, 2 Vols, London (1954)
Architecture: The Nineteenth and Twentieth Centuries, Harmondsworth (1958).

HOBHOUSE, Hermione, *Thomas Cubitt, Master Builder*, London (1971).

HOGG, O.F.G., *The Royal Arsenal*, Vol. I, Oxford (1963).

The Story of Horrockses, Preston (1950).

HUDSON, Kenneth, *Building Materials*, London (1972).

HUGHES, J. Quentin, *Liverpool*, London (1969).

HULME, John R., *The Industrial Archaeology of Scotland: 1 The Lowlands and Borders*, London (1976); *2 The Highlands and Islands*, London (1977).

International Council of Monuments and Sites, *Eisen Architektur, Symposium on the Role of Iron in the Historic Architecture in the first half of the Nineteenth Century*, Mainz (1979), R.S. Fitzgerald, 'Technical Aspects of Early English Iron Architecture'.

JENKINS, D.T., *The West Riding Wool Textile Industry 1770-1835: A Story of Fixed Capital Formation*, Edington (1975).

JENKINS, D.T., and K.G. PONTING, *The British Wool Textile Industry 1770-1914*, London (1982).

JEREMY, David J., *Transatlantic Industrial Revolution: The Diffusion of Textile Technologies between Britain and America 1790-1830s*, Massachusetts (1981).

KAYE, Barrington, *The Development of the Architectural Profession in Britain, A Sociological Study*, London (1960).

KLINGENDER, Francis, *Art and the Industrial Revolution*, London (1968).

KNOWLES, C.C. and P.H. PITT, *The History of Building Regulation in London 1189-1972*, London (1972).

The Mills and Organization of the Lancashire Cotton Corporation 1929-1950, Manchester (1951).

LEE, C.H., *A Cotton Enterprise 1795-1840, A History of M'Connel & Kennedy, Fine Cotton Spinners*, Manchester (1972).

LINSTRUM, Derek, *Historic Architecture of Leeds*, Newcastle (1969)
West Yorkshire, Architects and Architecture, London (1978).

LLOYD, Humphrey, *The Quaker Lloyds in the Industrial Revolution*, London (1975).

MCGRATH, Raymond and A.C. FROST, *Glass in Architecture and Decoration*, London (1961).

MCFADZEAN, Ronald, *The Life and Work of Alexander Thomson*, London (1979).

MARSHALL, J.D., *Furness and the Industrial Revolution*, London (1958).

MARSHALL, J.D., and Michael DAVIES-SHIEL, *The Industrial Archaeology of the Lake Counties*, Newton Abbot (1969).

MARSHALL, John, *A Biographical Dictionary of the Railway Engineers*, Newton Abbot (1978).

MATHIAS, Peter, *The Brewing Industry in England 1700-1830*, Cambridge (1959)
The First Industrial Nation, London (1983).

MEEKS, Caroll L.V., *The Railroad Station, An Architectural History*, Yale (1956).

MILLS, Edward D., *The Modern Factory*, London (1959).

MORDAUNT CROOK, J., *The Greek Revival*, London (1972)
William Burges and the High Victorian Dream, London (1981).

MORGAN, Bryan, *Civil Engineering: The Railways*, London (1971).

MUSSON, A.E. and Eric ROBINSON, *Science and Technology in the Industrial Revolution*, Manchester (1969).

MUTHESIUS, Stefan, *The High Victorian Movement in Architecture 1850-1870*, London (1972)
The English Terraced House, Yale (1982).

MUTTER, W. Grant, *The Buildings of an Industrial Community, Coalbrookdale and Ironbridge*, London (1979).

NICOLSON, Benedict, *Joseph Wright of Derby, Painter of Light*, 2 Vols, London (1968).

NICOLSON, Nigel, *Lord of the Isles*, London (1960).

NIXON, Frank, *The Industrial Archaeology of Derbyshire*, Newton Abbot (1969).

NUSSEY, John, *Smithies Mill, Birstall*, Chester (1984).

OLSEN, Donald J., *The Growth of Victorian London*, London (1976)

The Cotton Mills of Oldham, Oldham and District Historical and Antiquarian Society (1979).

PANNELL, J.P.M., *Man the Builder, An Illustrated History of Engineering*, London (1964).

PEVSNER, Nikolaus, *Buildings of England Series*, Harmondsworth (1951 onwards)
The Sources of Modern Architecture and Design, London (1968)
A History of Building Types, London (1976).

PICKLES, Walter, *Our Grimy Heritage*, Fontwell (1971).

POWELL, C.G., *An Economic History of the British Building Industry 1815-1979*, London (1980).

PREST, John, *The Industrial Revolution in Coventry*, Oxford (1960).

RAISTRICK, Arthur, *Industrial Archaeology, A Historical Survey*, London (1973).

REES, D. Morgan, *Mines, Mills and Furnaces, An Introduction to Industrial Archaeology in Wales*, London HMSO (1969)
The Industrial Archaeology of Wales, Newton Abbot (1975)
Historic Industrial Scenes, Wales, Ashbourne [n.d.].

REYNOLDS, Jack, *Saltaire, An Introduction to the Village of Sir Titus Salt*, Bradford (1976).

RICHARDS, J.M., *The Functional Tradition in early Industrial Buildings*, London (1958)
An Introduction to Modern Architecture, Harmondsworth (1940).

RIMMER, W.G., *Marshalls of Leeds, Flax Spinners 1788-1886*, Cambridge (1960).

RITCHIE-NOAKES, Nancy, *Jesse Hartley, Dock Engineer to the Port of Liverpool 1824-60*, Liverpool (1980)
Liverpool's Historic Waterfront, London HMSO (1984).

ROBERTS, John S., *Little Germany*, Bradford (1977).

ROBINSON, John Martin, *The Wyatts, an Architectural Dynasty*, Oxford (1979).

ROSE, Mary B., *The Gregs of Styal*, Quarry Bank (1978).

SERVICE, Alistair, *Edwardian Architecture*, London (1971).

SHEPPARD, Richard, *Cast Iron in Building*, London (1945).

SHERLOCK, Robert, *The Industrial Archaeology of Staffordshire*, Newton Abbot (1976).

SIGSWORTH, Eric M., *Black Dyke Mills, A History*, Liverpool (1958).

SINGER, Charles (Editor) *et al.*, *A History of Technology, Vol. IV c.1750–c.1850*, Oxford (1958); *Vol. V The Late Nineteenth Century* (1958); *Vol. VI The Twentieth Century* (1978).

SMITH, David M., *The Industrial Archaeology of the East Midlands*, Newton Abbot (1965).

SPENCER, Hugh, *London's Canal, An Illustrated History of the Regent's Canal*, London (1976).

SUMMERSON, John, *Georgian London*, London (1945)
Architecture in Britain 1530–1830, Harmondsworth (1977).

STAMP, Gavin and Colin AMERY, *Victorian Buildings of London 1837–1887*, London (1980).

STANTON, Phoebe, *Pugin*, London (1971).

STEVENS CURL, James, *Victorian Architecture, Its Practical Aspects*, Newton Abbot (1973).

STEWART, E.G., *Historic Index of Gasworks ... in the area served by the North Thames Gas Board 1806–1957*, London [n.d.].

TANN Jennifer, *Industrial Archaeology, Gloucestershire Woollen Mills*, Newton Abbot (1967)
The Development of the Factory, London (1970).

TARN, J.N., *The Peak District National Park, Its Architecture*, Derby (1971).

TAYLOR, Nicholas, *Monuments of Commerce*, London (1968).

THOMAS, John, *The Rise of the Staffordshire Potteries* (reprinted with a preface by G.D.H. Cole), New York (1971).

[THORNE, Robert], *Liverpool Street Station*, London (1978).

VAUGHAN, A., *A Pictorial Record of Great Western Architecture*, Oxford (1977).

VIOLLET-LE-DUC, E.-E., *Discourses on Architecture*, 2 Vols (1889), translated by Benjamin Bucknall, London (1959).

VITRUVIUS, *The Ten Books on Architecture* (translated by M.H. Morgan), New York (1960).

WARE, Michael E., *Making of the Motor Car 1895–1930*, Huntington (1976).

WILLIAMS, D.R.H., *Textile Factory Organization and Management*, Manchester (1934).

WINDSOR, Alan, *Peter Behrens, Architect and Designer 1868–1940*, London (1981).

WINTER, John, *Industrial Architecture, A Survey of Factory Buildings*, London (1970).

ZIMILES, Martha and Murray, *Early American Mills*, New York (1973).

Index